The Poems of
Patrick Cary

The Poems of
Patrick Cary

EDITED BY
Sister Veronica Delany

WITH BIOGRAPHICAL AND
CRITICAL INTRODUCTION

Clarendon Press · Oxford
1978

Oxford University Press, Walton Street, Oxford OX2 6DP

OXFORD LONDON GLASGOW NEW YORK
TORONTO MELBOURNE WELLINGTON CAPE TOWN
IBADAN NAIROBI DAR ES SALAAM LUSAKA ADDIS ABABA
KUALA LUMPUR SINGAPORE JAKARTA HONG KONG TOKYO
DELHI BOMBAY CALCUTTA MADRAS KARACHI

© *Oxford University Press 1978*

All rights reserved. No part of this publication may be reproduced, stored in a retrieval system, or transmitted, in any form or by any means, electronic, mechanical, photocopying, recording or otherwise, without the prior permission of Oxford University Press

British Library Cataloguing in Publication Data

Cary, Patrick,
   The poems of Patrick Cary
   I. Delany, Veronica
   821'.4   PR3339.C43A17   77-30206
  ISBN 0-19-812566-6

Printed in Great Britain by
Cox & Wyman Ltd
London, Fakenham and Reading

Preface

ALTHOUGH Patrick Cary is only one of the common people of the skies of Caroline verse, those skies are so unusually brilliant that even their meaner beauties shine with an uncommon lustre. Up to the present he has received rather less than his due. With two early editions, one merely a selection, long out of print, his poems are now available only as included in Saintsbury's *Minor Poets of the Caroline Period*, in a version made without reference to the one extant manuscript. To my knowledge no single work now in print is devoted to him. To misuse a noble phrase of Sir Thomas Browne, he has contrived only to subsist in articles and to be extant in appendices.

I hope I have done a modest service in providing this edition from the original text, with a commentary, bringing together with a few fresh details all the known facts of Cary's varied career and assessing his poetic achievement. Of particular interest are the original emblematic drawings illustrating the unique manuscript; these I have reproduced, drawing attention, I believe for the first time, to Cary's link with the emblem tradition.

I owe a considerable debt of gratitude to the present owner of the manuscript, Mrs. Patricia Maxwell-Scott, who not only allowed me to examine and transcribe it amidst the delightful hospitality of Abbotsford, but also gave leave for it to be deposited in the National Library of Scotland for examination, and authorized the publication of this edition, including four pages of the manuscript in facsimile and reproductions of the original illustrations. My gratitude extends also to Dr. J. C. Corson, honorary librarian of Abbotsford, who patiently answered my many queries and supplied me with much valuable information.

For bibliographical help I gratefully acknowledge the assistance of Dr. William Beattie, Dr. T. Ian Rae, Mr. J. H. Loudon, and Dr. Robert Donaldson, all of the National Library of Scotland. I am particularly grateful to Dr. Rae, who corrected and supplemented my own study of the manuscript and its binding, providing a detailed description, which he has allowed me to quote, and by his expert knowledge helping to illuminate its probable history.

I must also offer sincere thanks to Professor Norman Davis, the late Mr. J. C. Maxwell, and Mr. David Foxon, for their criticism and suggestions; and to Miss Grace Guiney and Professor T. A. Birrell, who graciously gave me access to unpublished material of the late Miss Louise Imogen Guiney.

My thanks also go to R. P. Graham-Vivian Esq., Norroy and Ulster King of Arms, and to the present Viscount Falkland, for genealogical data; to Dame Veronica Wedgwood and Mrs. E. Duncan-Jones for biographical suggestions; to Dom Gregory Freeman, O.S.B. and Father Francis Edwards, S.J., for details of monastic and theological interest; to Dr. F. W. Sternfeld and Miss Margaret Crum, who kindly advised me about musical settings; to Mr. John Horden, Leeds University, for help with emblems, to Mr. C. P. Finlayson, Keeper of Manuscripts, Edinburgh University, for readings of the original manuscript, and to Mr. R. Alton, Oxford, for advice on transcription.

I am most grateful to the staffs of the Bodleian Library, the British Museum, and the library of Trinity College, Dublin, for their courteous assistance.

My last debt is immeasurably the greatest. I am very happy to have this chance to pay a tribute of admiration and gratitude to my Oxford supervisor, Dame Helen Gardner, who suggested that I should work on Patrick Cary, and at every stage, from my early investigations to the preparation of this book for publication, has encouraged and helped me with a breadth of scholarship that is matched only by the depth of her generosity.

Auckland, N.Z. S.V.D.

Contents

List of References and Abbreviations	xi

GENERAL INTRODUCTION

I. THE DISCOVERY OF PATRICK CARY	xiii
II. LIFE OF PATRICK CARY	
i. The Background	xv
ii. Ireland and England (1623–36)	xix
iii. France and Italy (1636–50)	xxxi
iv. England and Ireland (1650–7)	l
v. Epilogue	lxvi
A Note on Variant Spellings of 'Cary'	lxviii
III. PATRICK CARY'S POETIC ACHIEVEMENT	lxix

TEXTUAL INTRODUCTION

I. THE MANUSCRIPT	lxxxiii
II. THE EDITIONS	lxxxix
III. THE TEXT	xciii

TRIVIALL BALLADES

An Octave	5
To the tune *Once I lov'd a Mayden Fayre* &c.	5
('Fayre-One! if thus kind You bee')	
To the tune *I'le doe by Thee, as n'ere was donne*	6
('The Ermine is without all spott')	
To the tune *I would give twenty pound* &c.	7
('There's noe Woeman, but I'me caught')	
To the tune of *Bobbing Joane*	8
('I n'ere yett saw a lovely Creature')	
To the tune of *Troye-towne*	9
('Fayre Beautyes! if I doe confesse')	
To the tune *But I fancy lovely Nancy* &c.	10
('Surely now I'me out of danger')	

To the tune of *The Healths*	13
('Come (fayth) since I'me parting')	
To the tune *I'le tell thee Dicke that I have beene* &c.	15
('And can You thincke that this Translation')	
To the tune *That we may row with my P. over the Ferry*	18
('Good People of England! come heare mee relate')	
To the tune *Will and Tom* &c.	19
('*Jacke!* nay prithee come away')	
To the tune *But that n'ere troubles mee Boyes* &c.	22
('And now a Figge for th' lower House')	
The Country Life. To a French tune	23
('Fondlings! keepe to th' Citty')	
To the tune *And will you now to Peace encline* &c.	26
('The Parliament ('tis sayd) resolv'd')	
To a French tune	28
('Speake of somewhat else I pray;')	
To a French tune	29
('A greev'd Countesse, that e're long')	
To an Italian tune	30
('Poore Heart, retire!')	
To an Italian tune	31
('''Tis true. I am fetter'd')	
To a Spanish tune called *Folias*	32
('Cease t'exaggerate your Anguish')	
To an Italian tune called *Girometta*	33
('O, permitt that my Sadnesse')	
To the tune *To Parliament the Queene is gonne* &c.	34
('This Aprile last a gentle Swayne')	
To the tune *I'le have my Love, or I'le have none*	36
('Some prayse the Browne, and some the Fayre;')	
To the tune of *Phillida flouts mee*	37
('*Ned!* She that likes thee now')	
To the tune of *Francklin is fled away*	39
('Alasse! long since I knew')	

[DIVINE POEMS]

Triolets	43
O that I had wings like a Dove	44
('By Ambition raysed high')	
Servire Deo, Regnare est	45

The invisible things of him from the Creation of the world are cleerely seene ...	46
('Whilst I beheld the necke o' th' *Dove*')	
Crux VIA Cælorum	49
Crucifixus pro Nobis	52
Fallax, et Instabilis	55
Nulla Fides	57
[*Stulte, hac nocte animam tuam repetunt a te.*]	58
('What use has Hee made of his Soule')	
Dirige vias meas Domine!	60
Nobis natus in Pretium : nobis datus in Præmium	62
EXPRIMETVR	64
Dies Iræ, Dies illa	65
COMMENTARY	69
APPENDIX A: Patrick Cary's Use of Emblems	102
APPENDIX B: Musical Settings of Patrick Cary's Poems	115
Index of First Lines	127

ILLUSTRATIONS

Reproductions of pp. 4–7 of Cary MS.   following p. xcvi

References and Abbreviations

References to the text of Patrick Cary's poems:

Cary MS. — Carey's Poems, 1651, the unique holograph manuscript in Abbotsford library.

Poems, *1771* — *Poems from a Manuscript written in the Time of Oliver Cromwell*, 1771 (the first edition, editor unnamed, containing only nine poems, ascribed to 'one Carey').

Scott — *Trivial Poems and Triolets, written in obedience to Mrs. Tomkin's Commands, by Patrick Carey. 20th Aug. 1651*, edited by Walter Scott, 1819.

Saintsbury — *Minor Poets of the Caroline Period*, edited by George Saintsbury, 3 vols. (1906), reprinted 1968, vol. ii.

Other references:

A.V. — Authorized Version of the Bible.

Chappell — William Chappell, *The Ballad Literature and Popular Music of the Olden Time*, 2 vols. (1855–9; republished New York, 1965).

C.S.P. — *Calendar of State Papers.*

D.N.B. — *Dictionary of National Biography.*

Dobson — E. J. Dobson, *English Pronunciation, 1500–1700*, 2 vols. (Oxford, 1957; 2nd edn. 1968).

Guiney — Louise Imogen Guiney, unpublished Introduction, 'The Hon. Patrick Cary: 1623–1657'.

H & G — *Herald and Genealogist.*

Harrison — Fairfax Harrison, *The Devon Careys*, 2 vols. (New York, 1920).

Kökeritz — H. Kökeritz, *Shakespeare's Pronunciation* (New Haven, 1953).

MS. C.S.P. — Clarendon State Papers, manuscript collection in the Bodleian Library.

MS. Harleian	Manuscript letters in British Museum.
MS. Lansdowne	Manuscript letters in British Museum.
MS. Lille	'The Lady Faulkland her Life', manuscript in the Imperial Archives, Lille.
MS. Sloane	Manuscript letter of Patrick Cary in British Museum.
N & Q	*Notes and Queries.*
O.E.D.	*Oxford English Dictionary.*
Osborne	*The Letters of Dorothy Osborne*, edited by G. C. Moore Smith (Oxford, 1928; reprinted 1959).
S.A.C.	*Surrey Archaeological Collections.*
Scott, Letters	*The Letters of Sir Walter Scott*, edited by H. J. C. Grierson, 12 vols. (London, 1932–7).
Simpson	Claude Simpson, *The British Broadside Ballad and its Music* (New Brunswick, 1966).
Ulster Transcript	Transcript of records of College of Arms, supplied by the Norroy and Ulster King of Arms, R. P. Graham-Vivian Esq.
Weber	K. Weber, *Lucius Cary, Second Viscount Falkland* (Oxford, 1940), Appendix on Patrick Cary.
Wyld, Rhymes	H. C. Wyld, *Studies in English Rhymes from Surrey to Pope* (London, 1923).

Quotations from Scripture, including those occurring in English in the text of the poems, are from the Authorized Version. References to Shakespeare are to the edition by P. Alexander, 1951. Page and line references, unless otherwise stated, are to my edited text of Cary's poems, Introduction, Commentary, and Appendices. Poems which are designated in the text only by tune-titles or Scripture texts are referred to by their first lines.

General Introduction

I. THE DISCOVERY OF PATRICK CARY

'Ah, you do not know Pat Carey[1]—a younger brother of Lord Falkland's?' says the disguised Charles II in Scott's *Woodstock*.[2] Most of us would have to admit that we share Dr. Rochecliffe's ignorance of Patrick Cary, for today, over a hundred and fifty years after *Woodstock*, the case is not much better: even his name is scarcely known except to those who follow the remoter by-ways of literature. This may well be regretted, for Patrick Cary, both as man and as poet, proves to be a figure of considerable appeal and charm. His story has never been fully told, yet is worth telling; his verse has never attracted much attention, yet is worth reading. Even the discovery of his identity is a literary oddity that bears relating: chance, coincidence, and curiosity united to solve a puzzle going back almost two centuries.

In the latter part of 1651, in a small Hampshire village, some thirty poems were written in a clear, precise hand on the blank pages of a notebook bound in black leather, already somewhat worn. To them was prefaced a courtly dedication under which with a flourish the writer had signed his name: 'J. Patr: Carey'. After this there is no record of the book until, one hundred and twenty years later, it reappeared, bearing traces of much handling. This time it was in the possession of a Nottinghamshire clergyman, who in 1771 had nine of the poems printed; but the poet was given only a casual allusion as 'one Carey, a man whom we now know nothing of'. No trumpets sounded either for the poems or the author, and both fell back into virtual oblivion for another forty years.

Then by good fortune the notebook came into the hands of Walter Scott, who liked what he saw in it, and introduced it to the literary world, publishing an account of the poems with examples in the *Edinburgh Annual Register* for 1810.[3] At this time Scott was

---

[1] For a note on the spelling of the name, see p. lxviii.
[2] Scott, *Waverley Novels* (1832), xl, 261.
[3] *Edinburgh Annual Register* for 1810 (pub. 1812), Part II, pp. lxvii–lxxvi.

unaware both of the previous publication and of the poet's identity, and knew only his name and what could be deduced from the verses themselves: that the writer was a Royalist gentleman, a High-Churchman or a Catholic. There was only one other clue he noticed —a separate part of the book had its own title-page with a distinctive coat of arms, a motto, and an inscription with the date 1651. These particulars Scott included in his article in the hope that someone interested in antiquities might discover from them the poet's parentage. Soon after the appearance of this account, he was writing to Robert Surtees to the same effect and adding 'perhaps your knowledge of heraldry can help me to a probable guess at his family'.[1] However, in 1819 when Scott printed all the poems under the title *Trivial Poems and Triolets,* he admitted in his Introduction that his researches had given him no further information.

About the time Scott's edition was ready for publication, when Surtees was visiting Abbotsford with his friend James Raine, the subject was again raised in their conversation. This time the discussion bore fruit, as Raine describes:

The poems of Carey formed another subject of conversation.... Surtees' attention became again drawn to the history of the author, and he soon afterwards, with the assistance of a friend, discovered him to be Patrick Carey, a younger son of Henry, Viscount Falkland, Lord Deputy of Ireland, and the husband of Susan, daughter of Francis Uvedale of Bishop's Waltham Esq. and niece of William Uvedale of Wickham. The cross moline on the title is the bearing of Uvedale. A pedigree of the family was soon afterwards printed by Surtees, of a size to bind with the book as edited by Scott, and the mystery has disappeared.[2]

Some further details of this investigation are filled in by Saintsbury in his Introduction to the text of Patrick Cary's poems which he included in *Minor Poets of the Caroline Period.*[3] The friend who assisted Surtees in his search was Sir Cuthbert Sharpe, to whom Scott had sent a copy of his edition in September 1819. This copy of Sharpe's was in Saintsbury's hands as he prepared his text, and he is apparently relying on notes written by Sir Cuthbert when he explains the three clues that led to the solution of the puzzle: the coat of arms with the cross moline, the mention in the poems of Sir

---
[1] Scott, *Letters*, ii, 427.
[2] G. Taylor, *Memoir of Robert Surtees* (Surtees Society, 1852), i, 161.
[3] Saintsbury, pp. 447–9.

William and Wickham, and the name Victoria, unusual at that period. Research in the British Museum proved that Sir William Uvedale of Wickham had married Victoria Cary, daughter of the first Viscount Falkland, and that the poet was a brother to her and to Lucius Cary, the second Viscount, a leading figure in Civil War politics. Saintsbury adds that Sir Cuthbert compiled the family pedigrees and sent a copy to Sir Walter but 'got no reply as Sir W. was ill at the time, and it was perhaps laid aside and forgotten'. Sir Cuthbert seems to have been aggrieved over Scott's failure to thank him for his efforts; but it appears from Raine's letter that Scott regarded Surtees as the moving spirit in the matter, and there is no need to impute to him an uncharacteristic discourtesy.

However that may be, Scott made good use of the material a few years later, by placing a graceful tribute to this 'brother of the immortal Lord Falkland' on the lips of Charles II, sheltering incognito in the 'towers of sweet Woodstock', and added a note embodying the new information that had come to light about the poet he had edited earlier, although by a curious slip he confuses Lucius Cary with his father.[1]

Once the identification of the fluent, witty poet of the *Trivial Poems and Triolets* with the brother of the famous Lord Falkland had been established, further data gradually emerged. The main outlines of Patrick Cary's story were to be found in various official records, notably the Clarendon State Papers, and as time went on scholarly curiosity sketched in more strokes to his shadowy figure. A few lines from Evelyn's *Diary*, a reference in contemporary correspondence, an entry in the guest-book of the English College in Rome—from such trivia it became possible to build up a fairly complete portrait; even better, to let him speak for himself in the conversational ease of his letters as well as in the varying moods of his poetry; and finally to trace in some detail the outlines of his changeful and restless life.

II. LIFE OF PATRICK CARY

i. *The Background*

If it were still fashionable for biographers to begin with the most distant and most elevated ancestors of their subject, I could trace Patrick Cary's royal descent from Edward I through his second

[1] Scott, *Waverley Novels*, xl, 261–2, 275.

son, Edmund Plantagenet of Woodstock—appropriately enough, considering the connection with Scott—and Edmund's daughter Joan, the Fair Maid of Kent.¹ However, I do not think this would help to pluck out the heart of his mystery. The keys to his character and career are to be found much closer to his own time. It will be sufficient to start with his father, Henry Cary, first Viscount Falkland, founder of the fortunes and misfortunes of Patrick's branch of a family long seated in Devon and Somerset and 'remarkable for iterated loyalty to lost causes'.²

Henry Cary,³ born in about 1575, was the eldest son of Sir Edward Cary, knight of Berkhamsted and Aldenham, Hertfordshire, who enjoyed several offices of trust at the court of Queen Elizabeth. After acquiring at Oxford the literary tastes and accomplishments that he preserved throughout a full and stormy public life, young Henry was introduced to court, where he rose to favour with Elizabeth and later James I, and held various posts of honour with, on the whole, more diligence than distinction. A picturesque interlude was his participation in the War of Independence in the Low Countries, which brought him the humiliation of being captured and held to ransom in Spain, and the tribute of an epigram from Ben Jonson:

> That neither fame, nor love might wanting be
> To greatness, Cary, I sing that, and thee.
> Whose house, if it no other honor had,
> In onely thee, might be both great, and glad.
> Who, to upbraid the sloth of this our time,
> Durst valour make, almost, but not a crime.⁴

This propensity for being gallantly but often wrong-headedly on the losing side was to characterize Henry Cary throughout his career. It was all very well for Jonson to urge him 'Love thy great losse, which a renowne hath wonne'. In fact this unlucky capture was the beginning of the financial difficulties that dogged, and sometimes influenced, his steps, as payment of the ransom made crippling inroads into his patrimony.

¹ Transcript of records of College of Arms, kindly supplied by R. P. Graham-Vivian Esq., Norroy and Ulster King of Arms (called hereafter Ulster Transcript).
² Harrison, I, xiii.
³ For Sir Henry Cary's career, see *D.N.B.* iii, 1149–51; Harrison, ii, 405–19.
⁴ *Poems*, ed. Newdigate (1936), p. 21.

LIFE OF PATRICK CARY

It was, it seems, mainly from financial considerations that in about 1600 he had married Elizabeth Tanfield, only child and heiress of Sir Lawrence Tanfield, magistrate, of Burford Priory in Oxfordshire. The main primary source of information on the life of this remarkable woman, Patrick Cary's mother, is a manuscript biography, 'The Lady Faulkland her Life',[1] written by one of her daughters, which happily survived its share of wars and revolutions and is preserved in the Imperial Archives at Lille. From this loving but clear-eyed view of the strange life and character of Elizabeth Cary, described from so intimate a standpoint, we learn that her husband

. . . married her only for being an heire, for he had no acquaintance with her (she scarce ever having spoke to him) and she was nothing handsome though then very faire.[2]

Elizabeth Tanfield, born in 1585 or 1586, though an only child was far from being spoiled and pampered, and had led a strange, solitary childhood, in which she showed unusual precocity in reading and mastery of languages. We may feel credulity a little strained by her daughter's proud assertion that she learned French in five weeks at the age of four or five, and soon afterwards mastered Spanish, Italian, and Latin by herself, and Hebrew with very little teaching; as well as Transylvanian—'she then learnt allso of a transilvanian, his language, but never finding any use of it, forgott it intirely'.[3] However, there is no reason to doubt that the future Lady Cary was a highly intelligent girl who acquired a reading knowledge of these languages during the long nights when she read in secret by the light of candles sold to her by the servants at an exorbitant price, since her mother had forbidden her to have any. Nor was her command of languages limited to reading. In the dedication of one of his *English Heroicall Epistles* Drayton addresses her, at twelve, as his 'deere and modest Mistresse', adding

Sweete is the French tongue, more sweet the Italian, but most sweet are they both if spoken by your admired self.[3]

---

[1] Referred to as MS. Lille to distinguish it from the printed version, *The Lady Falkland: her Life*, ed. R. Simpson (1861).
[2] MS. Lille, f. 3ᵛ. In all quotations from this and contemporary documents, I have modernized spelling of i/j, u/v, and expanded contractions such as yᵉ. The spelling of the Lille manuscript is highly eccentric, but, as the continual intrusion of *sic* would be distracting, I have not drawn attention to its vagaries.
[3] MS. Lille, f. 2ᵛ. [4] Drayton, *Poems* (1608), p. 59.

xviii GENERAL INTRODUCTION

Dedications, it is true, are not evidence, but they are usually at least indications.

After her marriage at the age of fifteen she saw very little of her husband, who spent his time at court or abroad, while she remained for a year or so with her parents and communicated with him only by letters which she was not allowed to write herself. Then, probably during his Spanish imprisonment, he arranged for her to live with his mother. This, however, was far from making life more bearable for her. Her mother-in-law, 'being one that loved much to be humored and finding her not to apply herself to it',[1] thought to punish her by confinement to her room. This was Elizabeth Cary's natural habitat, and the restriction pleased rather than distressed her: books were all the company she needed. The dowager, frustrated in her purpose, then removed the books, at which the resourceful Elizabeth took to writing poetry. From this predicament she was rescued by her husband who, returning from Spain, made effective acquaintance with her for the first time, recognized her intellectual gifts and her much-tried virtues, and began somewhat tardily to make their marriage a reality. So it came about that 'she was married seven yeare without any child, after, had eleven borne alive'.[2] The second of these and the eldest son was Lucius Cary, later the second Viscount, the famous Lord Falkland, in the shadow of whose reputation his younger brother Patrick was so long to be eclipsed.

Lady Cary, in the intervals of caring devotedly for her household and her children, continued to read deeply, turning to the study of religion, and in particular of the Catholic Church:

> She continued to read much, and when she was about twenty yeare old, through reading, she grew into much doubt of her religion; the first occasion of it, was reading a protestant booke much esteemed, called Hookers Eclesiasticall Politie, it seemed to her, he left her hanging in the aire, for having brought her so farre (which she thought he did very reasonably) she saw not how, nor att what, she could stop, till she returned to the church from whence they were come.[3]

For the moment her doubts were set at rest by the Bishop of Durham and other divines, but they were to recur for many years and finally to erupt into explosive action, with far-reaching consequences for her family.

[1] MS. Lille, f. 4.   [2] MS. Lille, f. 5ᵛ.   [1] MS. Lille, f. 4ᵛ.

In the meantime Sir Henry Cary, that 'most accomplished gentleman and complete courtier',[1] continued his career in the King's service under the aegis of the rising favourite, Buckingham, becoming in turn comptroller of the royal household, master of the jewel house, and privy councillor. In 1602 he was created Viscount Falkland in the county of Fife in the Scottish peerage, by one of those happy transactions of James I that ennobled the subject and enriched the sovereign. Falkland himself seems to have been a master of financial ineptitude; he was constantly in difficulties and, as Clarendon observes, 'instead of enriching himself by his great places, wasted a full fortune at court in those offices and employments by which other men use to obtain a greater'.[2] In 1622 he was in such need of money that he persuaded his wife to mortgage her jointure—an act which so enraged her father that he disinherited her and settled his estates on her eldest son. But the Viscount's prospects seemed bright enough: he had just been appointed Lord Deputy of Ireland. It was at this point in the Falkland fortunes that the scene was being set for the appearance of one of the most gifted members of the family—our poet, Patrick Cary.

ii. *Ireland and England* (1623–36)

To Ireland then in September 1622 Lord Falkland removed his wife and seven of their children—the eldest girl, Catherine, had just gone to live in Scotland as the bride of the young Earl of Home;[3] the third son, Edward, had died six years before.[4] Accompanying their parents to Ireland were the two elder sons, Lucius and Lorenzo, and five daughters, ranging from eight-year-old Anne through Elizabeth, Lucy, and Victoria to Mary, who was almost two. Strange contrasts of turbulence and peace would mark the destinies of these boys and girls: Lucius, heir to his father's title and his grandfather's estates, would become famous as scholar and statesman, and meet an untimely death amidst the conflicting loyalties of the Civil War; Lorenzo would be drawn into the same struggle, knighted for gallantry and killed in the field a year before his brother; Victoria would be three times wooed and twice won, a gracious lady of the manor in rural England; Anne, Elizabeth, Lucy, and Mary would all die in France, after serene lives in a

---

[1] *Fuller's Worthies*, ed. Nuttall (1840), ii, 46.
[2] Clarendon, *History of Rebellion*, ed. Macray (1888), Bk. VIII, vol. iii, p. 181.
[3] MS. Lille, f. 6ᵛ.   [4] *H & G* (1866), iii, 39 *et seq.*

Benedictine cloister.[1] Soon to complete the family there would be two young brothers, Patrick and Henry, whose fortunes would be more chequered still.

Lord Falkland embarked on his new duties with his usual blend of conscientiousness and imprudence. Scarcely had he been four months in the country when he issued a proclamation banishing all priests from Ireland. This could scarcely have been worse timed, coming as it did in the midst of delicate negotiations for the Spanish marriage of Prince Charles, and Falkland was hastily directed to modify his policy. In the meantime Lady Falkland, with the passionate absorption she displayed in all the causes she adopted, devoted herself to bettering the condition of the Irish peasants (pausing, as we might expect, long enough in her exertions to learn, with her linguistic compulsion, 'to read Irish in an Irish bible').[2] In a grandiose industrial project she imported raw materials and skilled workers—weavers, dyers, lace-makers, and others—swept in a great number of poor children ('8 score prentices, refusing none above seven yeare old'), and started training schemes of impractical magnitude, which eventually broke down, owing partly to natural disasters but more to her own mismanagement; as her daughter wryly remarks, 'she was better att contriving then executing'.[3]

In spite of all this Lady Falkland was no Mrs. Jellyby, neglecting her own family in welfare schemes for some Irish Borrioboola-Gha. She continued to devote herself to them, for 'she always thought it a most misbecoming thinge in a mother to make herself more her busynes then her children';[4] and in the intervals of these well-meant but ill-managed works of philanthropy she gave birth to two more sons. At this stage in the Falkland story we meet Patrick Cary himself, complete with his birthplace, his distinctive name, and his position as fourth son and elder of the two youngest boys—a status which incidentally is still denied to him by both Burke and Debrett:[5]

The eldest of tow sonnes she had there (being her last children) in devotion, to the great patron of the country, she called by his name, who she did beleive did take them both into his protection, assisting them with his prayers, she living to see them both catholiks. Soone after she

---

[1] Harrison, ii, 419–21. [2] MS. Lille, f. 8ᵛ.
[3] MS. Lille, f. 9. [4] MS. Lille, f. 6ᵛ.
[5] *Burke's Peerage* (1967), p. 922; *Debrett* (1968), p. 438.

was churched of the younger of them, she came out of Ireland, having bene there three yeare.¹

No official record of Patrick's birth or baptism has been found: it does not appear in any of the printed Dublin church registers covering the period. No registers are available for the Chapel Royal, and those of St. Werburgh's Church (in which parish the castle is) do not begin till 1704. All the information we have is contained in his sister's statements quoted above. Since Lady Falkland, reaching Ireland in September 1622, left it in 1625, shortly after her youngest son was born, Patrick's birth must have occurred in 1623 or 1624; and this on the present evidence is as close as we can get. As for his name, his usual signature in later life was 'J. Patricke Carey'—on one occasion he expands 'J' to 'John';² but it is clear from references in letters and other documents that he was always known as 'Patrick'. This Christian name, not common among Englishmen at this time, shows his mother's continuing interest in the faith held by the Irish people, and no doubt was not unacceptable to his father as signifying goodwill on the part of the Lord Deputy towards those he governed. The youngest boy, as we learn from other sources,³ was called Henry, receiving the privilege of the paternal name, more often given to the eldest son. If this was a sign of increased happiness and understanding between his parents, it indicated a state that had not much longer to last. A certain amount of confusion has surrounded Henry's name. He was to become a Benedictine, known as (Dom) Placid, and under this name he often figures in the earliest biographical records.

Soon after Henry's birth Lady Falkland left Ireland with her three youngest children and the second daughter, Anne, to help mind them. One gathers the impression that Lord Falkland was not sorry to be relieved of his wife's presence and the embarrassment her activities must often have caused him. After a stormy and adventurous trip—at one stage the baby Henry was nearly washed out of his mother's arms into the Irish Sea—they reached England, and soon were in the security of Burford's quiet fields and warm Cotswold stone.⁴ This interlude of peace, however, was to be very brief. A storm far more turbulent than bad weather on the Irish Sea was about to disrupt the entire family.

¹ MS. Lille, f. 11.   ² MS. Sloane 3299, f. 177.
³ Birt, *Obit Book of English Benedictines* (1913), p. 33.
⁴ MS. Lille, f. 11.

In the following year, 1626, Lady Falkland, determined to delay no longer in embracing Catholicism, to which she had been strongly attracted since girlhood, was received into the Church in London by Father Dunstan Pettinger, a Benedictine monk, thus being introduced to the Order which was to afford such kindly protection to her youngest sons not many years later.[1] This act, carried out and avowed with characteristic impetuosity at a most inauspicious time —when a Catholic Queen meant that even the tolerant Charles must tread warily—brought on her head storms of protest from both her husband and the Privy Council. Everyone tried to persuade her to withdraw, but, says her daughter with an emphatic triple negative, she was 'not moved nether by persawsions—nor displeasurs'.[2] In thus following her passionate convictions, Elizabeth Cary had given no thought to the effects of her action on her younger children, who were still with her. Estranged from her husband, who was furiously angry, reduced to penury by the cutting-off of her allowance and the harsh removal of even modest means of subsistence, she was

... in a little while brought to some extreamity, being constrained to send her children ... and those that waited on them abroad to thier frinds to dinners and suppers, not being willing to part with them alltogether, till they should be taken from her.[3]

Certainly the dominant feature of Patrick Cary's childhood was insecurity. Here he is, at the age of two or three, with his little brother and sister, being shuttled precariously around among his mother's friends and relatives for meals which must often have been unsuitable and disturbing. It was an intolerable situation, and the Viscount put an end to it by taking the children from her and recalling them to Ireland, where he did his well-intentioned best to be both father and mother. But life for them must still have been perplexed and unsettling in the extreme:

The bewildered childhood that Patrick and Henry must have endured as a result of their mother's apostasy, could not have brought them to expect a stable future as their due. Fearful impressions of an exasperated father, incomprehension of their mother's distraught behaviour, so many new faces, such sudden changes, unsettled ways and frequent deprivations and departures—how could the two children not be frightened by all this topsy-turvydom?[4]

[1] MS. Lille, f. 13ᵛ.   [2] MS. Lille, f. 13ᵛ.   [3] MS. Lille, f. 14.
[4] Weber, p. 302.

Nor were things going smoothly for their father. His financial affairs were in their usual tangle, and his rash and short-sighted administrative policy brought upon him the hostility of his political rivals, the distrust of his superiors, and finally a recall to England. So in May 1630 the children once again left Ireland.[1]

Lady Falkland, in spite of her husband's displeasure, had been making valiant if unsuccessful efforts at court on his behalf, and thanks to these and to the good offices of the Queen, some measure of harmony was at last restored between them:

> At length by the interposition of the power of her most Excellent Majesty (who was pleased to make herself the mediatrix of their reconciliation, and who both before and after by her Royall charity releived her, and many other ways afforded her Gracious assistance to her and hers) they were reconciled.[2]

For a brief St. Martin's summer of reciprocal affection they lived together and planned a permanent home for the children, who were still scattered. But the Viscount had not yet drained the cup of his misfortunes. Towards the end of the summer of 1633 he fell and broke his leg while in attendance on the King, who was shooting in the park at Theobalds; and when Charles, full of concern, came across to speak to him, the punctilious courtier struggled to his feet, thereby multiplying the fracture. It was badly set, gangrene developed, and the surgeons decided on amputation.[3]

So the next time we meet Patrick Cary in his sister's narrative he, a lad of nine or ten, has the unnerving experience of unexpectedly being summoned with Henry from school to wait outside the door of a lodge at Theobalds while his father is stoically undergoing this grim operation. It is pleasant to read that the Viscount, immediately after his agonizing ordeal, sent for the children to reassure them:

> ... and as soone as ever it was done and he layd in his bed he sent for them in, smiling on them, spoke cheerfully seeking to comfort them, then giving them his last blessing, sent them home.[4]

This was the last time Patrick saw his father. The loving attention of Lady Falkland, who refused to leave him night or day, could not counteract the shocking neglect and bungling of the surgeons, and the Viscount, with perfect courage and unshaken courtesy, died

---
[1] *The Lady Falkland, her Life*, p. 173.   [2] MS. Lille, f. 19ᵛ.
[3] MS. Lille, f. 21.   [4] MS. Lille, f. 21.

within a week. So young Patrick Cary lost his father, a man 'more distinguished by his rectitude than abilities'.¹ The boy's chances of security were now further off than ever.

For a short while after their father's death the younger children lived with their mother, who also supported four of her daughters, Anne, Elizabeth, Lucy, and Mary, in the modest establishment which was all she could afford. Typically the Viscount had died intestate, leaving a vast array of debts which his eldest son tried to discharge by selling Burford Priory, which he had by then inherited. The purchaser, incidentally, was William Lenthall,² whose name will recur in these pages. Although Lady Falkland was careful not to press her religion on her children, by example and atmosphere she led their interest towards it, and in time they came to share something of her enthusiasm for Catholicism. This began with the elder daughters, who were now maids of honour to the Queen, and within a year of their father's death all four girls became Catholics.³ There is no mention of their sister Victoria in this connection—she was also a maid of honour, and was probably living with one of her mother's friends at this time—and it does not seem that she ever changed her religion. The eldest daughter, Catherine, had died in childbirth in 1625.⁴

A frequent visitor to Lady Falkland's house was William Chillingworth, the apostle of tolerance, who, although he had returned to Anglicanism after a brief flirtation with Rome, was esteemed by her for his pious conversation, and trusted to discuss religion with her daughters until she became convinced his influence was harmful and forbade him the house.⁵ Meanwhile several things had happened. Lady Falkland's resources had dwindled to such an extent that she was practically penniless:

Having now continued for tow yeares since her Lords death, and having used all meanes possible for the maintaining of her family, she was brought to the last extreamity, not being able to find any way to hold out longer; having so conceald this from her children, that they were the last that knew it; and having disfurnished her owne chamber wholy (even of her very bed, being faine to sleepe in a chaire) she kept the doore of it locked, that they (who yet were not disaccomdated in any thinge) might not perceave it.⁶

---

¹ Leland, *History of Ireland* (1773), iii, 3. ² Weber, p. 79.
³ MS. Lille, f. 25ᵛ.   ⁴ MS. Lille, f. 11ᵛ.   ⁵ MS. Lille, ff. 27ᵛ–32ᵛ.
⁶ MS. Lille, f. 35.

The two younger boys had already been sent to live with their eldest brother, now the second Viscount, on his estate at Great Tew in Oxfordshire. At last she had no option but to ask him to receive his sisters also. So another change took place in Patrick's family circle —if indeed that can properly be called a circle which is constantly in the process of breaking up.

The quiet village of Great Tew is very little changed, although no trace beyond brick garden walls now remains of the manor into which Lucius and his militantly virtuous wife Lettice welcomed their brothers and sisters. However, though secluded, it was far from being unfrequented. Falkland kept open house for his scholarly friends:

All men of eminent parts and faculties in Oxford ... found their lodgings there, as ready as in the Colleges; nor did the lord of the house know of their coming, or going, or who were in his house, till he came to dinner, or supper, where all still met; otherwise, there was no troublesome ceremony, or constraint to forbid men to come to the house, or to make them weary of staying there; so that many came thither to study in a better air, finding all they could desire in his library, and all the persons together, whose company they could wish, and not find in any other society.

The wits and the poets from London found their way there too, and then, enlivened by their society, Lucius Cary

... looked upon no book ... and truly his whole conversation was one continued Convivium Philosophicum, or Convivium Theologicum, enlightened and refreshed with all the facetiousness of wit and good humour and pleasantness of discourse.[1]

Accomplished poets like Suckling and Carew, and lesser lights like Sidney Godolphin, affectionately styled 'little Cid'; philosophers like Thomas Hobbes and John Earle; diplomats like Edward Hyde, Kenelm Digby, and Walter Montagu: such were the guests who sat long over Falkland's table, and walked, deep in conversation, in the high-walled gardens.[2]

It would be a gross exaggeration to imply that Patrick Cary, at the age of eleven or so, was deeply affected by this climate of ideas, this exhilarating atmosphere of talk and opinion; but he was intelligent and quick-witted, accustomed to adjusting himself to places

[1] Clarendon, *Life*, ed. Oxford (1759), p. 22.
[2] Weber, pp. 77–82.

and people. The poems he would later write hint that snatches of their lively discourse and witty verses had lingered in his memory. At the very least, his wits would be sharpened, his intellectual curiosity aroused.

But there was the obverse of the coin. One of his brother's most trusted friends was Chillingworth, who now became the little boys' tutor and urged on them and their sisters a sceptical attitude to religious authority. Patrick and Henry, encouraged and instructed by the girls, were still anxious to embrace their mother's religion, and already tried in their limited way to practise it. Their mother was soon

... informed by her daughters of the extraordinary desire her little sonnes had to see themselves catholiks, and how they were desirous to refuse to goe to church, though they should be never so much whipped for it, if it would not make them to be taken away from their sisters, and from having ever meanes to be so; and of what diligence and art they used to observe fasting dayes without being perceaved, induring for it (especially one of them) extreamity of hunger, they not being lett to eate most fasting meates as unwholsome for children.[1]

Lord Falkland felt it his duty to combat these tendencies vigorously. He himself, arguing gravely and courteously with young Patrick,

... did use to the elder of them to shew his writings against Catholicks (he then writing much in the matter, but privatly, and allways as pretending to be rather an inquirer than an absolute defender of any thing ...) and did treate with that brother as capable of the matter then though so young.[2]

Meanwhile Mr. Chillingworth 'did not faile to deale with the younger, giving him for a first principle that there was not any certainty in matter of religion'.[3]

Their mother, becoming alarmed at this threat to the boys' religious belief, begged Lucius to send them away to school; otherwise she threatened to 'steal them away'. The Viscount did not take her seriously, but to be on the safe side proposed to send his little brothers to be educated amongst Puritans. Finding it necessary to act at once, Lady Falkland went ahead with her extraordinary scheme of kidnapping the boys. This exploit, surprisingly enough, she contrived to bring off with the connivance of her daughters, two of whom, Anne and Mary, were still living at Great Tew. This

[1] MS. Lille, f. 36ᵛ. [2] MS. Lille, f. 34. [3] MS. Lille, ff. 34–34ᵛ.

occurred at some time about the beginning of May 1636, according to the records of the Privy Council,[1] whose concern it soon became.

There is first-hand authority for the kidnapping episode in 'The Lady Faulkland her Life', where it is told with a wealth of graphic detail. This manuscript biography was written by one of the four daughters who became Benedictine nuns in Cambrai; it is impossible to be certain which, but the probabilities favour Anne, afterwards Dame Clementia, the eldest living daughter, and the one most in her mother's confidence; the one, moreover, who took up her pen later on to write long and earnest letters in favour of her brother Patrick. The style of the manuscript—loose, disjointed, and rambling, with sentences as long and involved as boa constrictors (to borrow a simile from Belloc's *Milton*)—closely resembles that of Dame Clementia's letters. The handwriting in the Lille manuscript is not, I think, that of the letters; but it gives on the whole the impression of having been carefully copied out, and there is no reason why more than one copy should not have been written. An interesting feature is the corrections that have been made to the text. Some passages have been roughly deleted, presumably of details considered inept or superfluous—fortunately most of the deletions are still legible; and marginal comments have been inserted, mainly supplying names for people referred to anonymously. Some of these interpolations are in Patrick Cary's writing, others in a different hand, which may be Henry's—it would be natural for the sisters to show the completed manuscript to both their brothers. The important point for my purpose is that here we have a narrative of which the accuracy is vouched for by at least one of the persons most intimately concerned. This account of the kidnapping—to return to it—is surely one of the most complete records of a single incident in the youth of a seventeenth-century English poet.[2]

Lady Falkland scraped together enough money to hire two men, of dubious appearance, and a couple of horses, and devised an elaborate plan which she sent to her eldest daughter, fortunately in an unfamiliar writing, as Mr. Chillingworth—always cast as the villain of the piece—was peering curiously at it when it arrived:

---

[1] *Privy Council Register of Charles I*, xii, p. 194 (quoted in *The Lady Falkland: her Life*, pp. 182–3).

[2] For the kidnapping episode, see MS. Lille, ff. 39–43; *The Lady Falkland*, pp. 94–106.

'for Mr Chillingworth (who allwayes pried very narrowly) was just behind her that had the letter, and looked over her shoulder when she opened it'.[1] It was impossible to follow Lady Falkland's complicated strategy, as her daughter says with amused exasperation:

... the most she could do was to lay such a plott, that if every body in the house would stand still in the place she supposed them, till all was done, it might succeed, the uttermost she could reach to, being to contrive a possibility, without all maner of apparence of any probability.[2]

With commendable dispatch Anne and Mary took matters into their own hands. They went out walking with their little brothers, and showed them their mother's messengers, 'that were intirely strangers to them, whose persons were no way promising'.[3] They persuaded the men to wait a day or two longer, paying them with some money that, providentially delayed, had just come into their hands. Then, knowing that their sister-in-law was going by coach to London on a certain day, they asked to be taken with her—Anne had court business as a pretext—and begged a holiday for the boys for that day, so that their activities would be less under scrutiny.

The night before, the girls guilelessly expressed a wish to rise very early, and their brothers undertook to wake them—a counsel of audacity, as Patrick and Henry shared a room with Mr. Chillingworth, who had a reputation for wakefulness. On the next morning the two boys

... rising att 3, with as much noise as they could, went to call their sisters; and having runne about the house an hower and shewed themselves to all that were up, they were by one of their sisters carryed downe, and seene safe out of all the courts of the house, without being discryd by any.[4]

With something of their father's courage, they ran a mile through the breathless darkness before dawn to join their mother's agents, hiding behind bushes near the village when dogs began to bark and sleepy householders peered out to investigate. When they reached the men, they still felt far from safe and insisted on riding off the road into cover every time they heard a coach or a rider approaching. With all these alarms and excursions it was well on in the morning by the time they reached Oxford. Here the boys dismounted, gave the horses to their guides to lead, and, their hearts

---

[1] MS. Lille, f. 40. [2] MS. Lille, f. 39. [3] MS. Lille, f. 40ᵛ.
[4] MS. Lille, ff. 40–40ᵛ.

thudding with excitement and apprehension, and their hats and coats off to look like lads of the town, made their way through St. Giles and the Cornmarket, past the busy inn-yard of the Golden Cross and the unfinished but majestic buildings of Christ Church, to the comparative safety of Abingdon and the river.

The excitement mounts, even through the complicated, sometimes clumsy periods of their sister as she records the progress of their adventure. By noon they were in Abingdon, where a young man, a friend of their mother's, waited with 'a pair of oars' to get them to London by water. Unfortunately, the oars had beguiled the time by drinking themselves into such a state that there was nothing for it but to stay until they were sober; and in the meantime a quarrel broke out between the two sets of escorts, in whose angry brawling the facts of the escape became public property. The constable arrived to take them into custody, and was only with difficulty persuaded that no laws were being infringed. To delay longer would have been dangerous:

... but having so scaped they durst not venture to stay till next day, least some noise of an inquiry coming to this towne (one that resorted much to their brothers house living neere it) might renew the suspicion, but were faine to take watter att ten a clock, att darke night, with water men not only not able to row, but ready every minute to over turne the boat with reeling and nodding.[1]

The reader of this graphic account in the Lille manuscript—where the entire incident runs to nine closely written pages—shares the relief Lady Falkland must have felt when they eventually reached London, and she 'did receave them safe, and most joyedly'.[2] (The writer began to say 'gladly', and decided it was not expressive enough.)

But all was not yet over. If the boys were to be brought up as Catholics she must get them—illegally—out of the country. Pursuit was hot from Great Tew; and if the law in Abingdon could be placated it was a very different matter to hoodwink the authorities in London. In a cloak-and-dagger atmosphere the indomitable woman had them switched from house to house in London for three weeks, each host ignorant of the identity of the next; while she herself, summoned before the Privy Council, argued with her examiners like the magistrate's daughter she was, and disconcerted

[1] MS. Lille, f. 40^v. [2] MS. Lille, f. 41.

them so effectively at every turn that it seems they were glad in the end to let the matter lapse. Thus the Lord Chief Justice began by threatening to send her to the Tower, and ended by sending her home in his own coach. Her main anxiety now was to get the boys out of England, and this she finally achieved when a generous Jesuit was found to finance their trip and an obliging Benedictine to escort them to France. After one last flare of excitement, when they were threatened with kidnapping or robbery in a French inn, they arrived without mishap at Rouen, and thence made their way to Paris, where they were kindly received by the Benedictine Fathers at St. Edmund's Priory.[1]

With all the intensity of her passionate nature Lady Falkland had made a supreme effort to ensure the temporal and spiritual welfare of her younger sons. For her

... the little drama was her last defiance of the practical world she lived in, the last proof of her unconquerable zeal. However petty its character, it was a fitting last appearance for her in the strong light of court and state.[2]

Now her figure—small, dumpy, unattractive, clad in rusty black, yet strangely magnetic—disappears from their story, although it is clear that it was her decisions that a few years later determined their divergent careers. She withdrew from London to a quiet village, and busied herself with the literary work which was her constant solace, brushing up her Latin and Hebrew, translating Blosius, as earlier she had translated Cardinal Perone. It was a time reminiscent of the early days of her marriage, when she wrote her verse life of Tamburlaine,[3] now lost, and perhaps *The Tragedie of Mariam*, which there is a good case for attributing to her.[4] All priests were welcome in her home, but a special warmth of cordiality was reserved for the Benedictines: amongst the latter who enjoyed her hospitality was the famous Father Augustine Baker.[5]

By 1639 her surviving sons and daughters were all established, Lucius at Great Tew and in the councils of state, Lorenzo with his regiment in Ireland, Victoria under the Queen's protection at court, the other four girls Benedictine nuns in Cambrai,[6] the

[1] MS. Lille, f. 43.
[2] K. B. Murdock, *The Sun at Noon* (New York, 1939), p. 33.
[3] MS. Lille, f. 4ᵛ. [4] Harrison, ii, 408–10.
[5] *Ampleforth and Its Origins*, ed. McCann and Cary-Elwes (London, 1952), p. 177.
[6] Harrison, ii, 419–21.

younger boys safe in the care of the Benedictine Fathers. She could, and did, sing her *Nunc dimittis*, dying in October of that year, characteristically enough from the effects of a cough which she had persistently neglected. She was buried in the Queen's Chapel at Westminster,[1] but her memory lingers most vividly in the memorial chapel built in Burford church to the parents who had not, on the whole, greatly cherished her. Her whole life is summed up as she kneels there in effigy at their tomb, in an intense attitude of filial, wifely, maternal, and spiritual dedication.

iii. *France and Italy* (1636–50)

Meanwhile, across the Channel, Patrick and Henry had been preparing for their future; and by the time the news of their mother's death reached them, they were already many miles apart. After their Benedictine guide got them safely to Paris, they were accepted into the monastic school of St. Edmund's, which had been established as a centre for the English Benedictine Congregation about twenty years before.[2] An entry in the Council Book of St. Edmund's records the facts:

1636 Nov. 2: He [the Prior] likewise proposed that my Lady Faulkland had sent hither 2 of her sons hear to be made Catholiques and brought up amongst us in learning and vertue and for their maintenance she would allow 56 pounds English money yearly, of which money Fa. Bennet Jones and Fa. Cuthbert [Fursdon] now living with the said Ladie did promise to see duly paid, and upon the said consideration it was thought fit that they should be received to live amongst [us] here in our Convent and that in these times of War between France and Spain we would not but with great difficulty have recourse to our V. Rev. Fa. President for his leave for the said two young gentlemen, according to the obligations we have to our Laws and Constitutions, and the danger that the letter might miscarry by the way of England, and for the young men bee discovered to [indecipherable] who are by the order of their friends to live very privately ...[3]

This payment guaranteed by Lady Falkland came from the Queen herself, who continued throughout all the reverses of her own fortunes to supply these funds for the support of her friend's children:

For the maintenance of her sonnes where they were, she did allotte somethinge which she receaved from the Charity of her most Excellent

---

[1] MS. Lille, f. 49. [2] *Ampleforth and Its Origins,* p. 93.
[3] 'Council Book of St. Edmunds', Paris.

Majesty, who was graciously pleased to continue it to them after her death, till the extreamity of these times.[1]

At St. Edmund's they pursued their studies 'in learning and vertue' under the most settled conditions they had known for many years; and there some three years later Henry at his own request was clothed as a novice, receiving the name of Brother Placid. The Council Book records under the date of 28 December 1639 that consent was asked

... for the admission of Mr Harry Carye to the habite of our holy fa. St Bennet, and in consideration of the long and earnest perseverance he had made in his petitions ... it was granted he should be received into the holy habit.[2]

By this time Patrick had embarked on another journey and, by the express arrangement of his mother, had gone to seek his fortune in Rome. The Lille manuscript relates Lady Falkland's plans for the career

... of her elder sonne att Rome; whom she had sent thither, being recommended to Cardinall Barbarin, by the Queenes most Excellent Majesty; whose Eminency incited by so powerfull a recommendation, and his owne charity, shewed him much favour. And in this occasion she was very highly obliged to m^r Mountague,[3] both for the persawding her to the sending him thither ... and for his most free and willing offering himself to be imployed by the Queene to make the recommendations.[4]

Only a phrase or two in his sister's narrative marks his departure from Paris, and of the actual journey we have merely a passing reference, in a letter he wrote much later, to an incident which was not without influence on his future. On the way to Rome the party turned aside for a devout visit to some place of pilgrimage, and there the more fervent members of the group made pledges of devotion. Not to be outdone, the fifteen-year-old Patrick followed their example:

When I went into Italy (a very Boy) in the journey, being where many of the company made vowes, I then made mine allsoe; and itt was to enter a Religious life under S. Bennetts habitt.[5]

In this spirit of boyish piety Patrick Cary came to Rome. He himself says this was three years after arriving in France, but in this he is

---

[1] MS. Lille, f. 43.   [2] 'Council Book of St. Edmund's'.
[3] Walter Montagu: see p. 81.   [4] MS. Lille, f. 45.
[5] MS. C.S.P. 40, f. 169^v.

speaking in round numbers, as he certainly reached Paris in 1636, and we can date his arrival in Italy quite accurately as 1638 from an entry in the Pilgrim Book of the English College in Rome. The English College, directed by the Jesuits, was a natural meeting-place for expatriate Englishmen and travellers from England. It was bound by its statutes to provide hospitality for all Englishmen visiting Rome 'out of devotion', an elastic phrase, which the Jesuits interpreted generously.[1] Each year on 29 December, the feast of St. Thomas of Canterbury, the College entertained at dinner all English residents and visitors, sometimes to the number of more than a hundred. Here throughout his stay in Rome, Patrick Cary would have kept in touch with events and people at home. The Pilgrim Book of the College records the names of all who stayed or dined there on various occasions; and for 30 October 1638 the entry reads: 'The Hon. Mr Cary, brother of Lord Falkland, an English gentleman, dined'.[2] This brief statement is tinged with significance when we read the next name—John Milton; a tantalizing glimpse of Patrick Cary at fifteen in the company of the thirty-year-old poet who had just written *Lycidas*. It was the first of several such literary encounters.

In Rome Patrick lived under the generous protection of Father John Wilfrid, Procurator of the English Benedictines there. Also known by his own name, Richard Wilfrid Selby, and sometimes by the alias 'Reade', and even its Latin equivalent 'Rubens'[3]—for these were times when letters might miscarry to a man's cost, and pseudonyms were a reasonable precaution—Father John Wilfrid remained for twelve years young Cary's mentor and beneficent guardian. On a number of occasions he lent him money, and did not seek repayment even when he himself was in need. To do the young man justice, in the midst of the dire financial necessities that later overtook him, he remained warmly grateful and honourably tried to repay. But for the time being Cary was in a pleasant, even an enviable, position, as he describes in a letter written to his brother's friend, Edward Hyde, some twelve years later:

Whilst the Queen had the wherewithall, I had a smale but sufficient pension under hand from her Majestye. Afterwards I was better provided by

---

[1] *Records of English Province S.J.*, ed. Foley (1880), vi, 548.
[2] *Records S.J.* vi, 617.
[3] Bennet Weldon, 'Memorials of the English Benedictine Congregation' (MS. dated 1707, 2 vols., in archives of Douai Abbey, Woolhampton), i, 322.

the last Pope; who uppon her Majestyes recommendation conferr'd uppon mee an Abbey and a priory *in commendum* [*sic*]; and besides, some pensions or other benefices: wherewith I subsisted well, and from the pitty became the wish of many English travaylours as one that was disingaged from those tumults, and had a being, besides better hopes.[1]

Thus favoured by the humanist Pope Urban VIII and his powerful nephew, Cardinal Francesco Barberini, Cary continued his studies under the guidance of the Benedictines. His lineage opened to him the fashionable circles of the English colony, and his patronage the cultured ecclesiastical society of Rome.

In 1644, an accomplished young man of twenty-one, he met another eminent visitor from England, John Evelyn, who recorded the occasion in his *Diary*:

I came to ROME on the 4th of November 1644. . . . The very next morning (for resolv'd I was to spend no moment idly here) I got acquaintance with several persons that had long lived in Rome; being especialy reccommended to Father John a Benedictine Monke . . . also to Mr Patric Cary, an Abbot and brother to our Learned Lord Falkland, a pretty witty young priest; but one that afterwards came over to our Church.[2]

Evelyn's reference to Cary's eventual defection to the Anglican Church shows that the entry was revised in the light of later events. He is wrong in one particular: Patrick Cary was never a priest, or even in minor orders, and only nominally an abbot. Evelyn was not likely to be well versed in the niceties of Roman ecclesiastical terminology, or to realize that the young man's abbacy and priorship were technically *in commendam*—that is, he held the advowson of these offices, and derived from them financial rather than spiritual profit.

One last notable encounter is recorded in the Pilgrim Book. On 27 December 1646 Cary dined in the vineyard of the English College in company with Crashaw,[3] who had been staying there for several weeks previously, soon after his arrival in Rome. As expatriates, converts and fellow protégés of Henrietta Maria, they would have had more in common than an interest in poetry.

But Patrick Cary's years of pleasant humanistic ease, spent in this setting of historic splendour, were almost over; and even as he sat

---

[1] MS. C.S.P. 39, ff. 92ᵛ–3.
[2] *Diary*, ed. de Beer (London and New York, 1955), ii, 213.
[3] *Records S.J.* vi, 634.

with Crashaw in the cool of the Jesuit vineyard he could look back over the past two years and see the clouds massing on his bright horizon. Pope Urban VIII had endowed him with benefices; Cardinal Francesco Barberini had made him an allowance and promised him 'more efficacious favour'. Unfortunately for Cary's hopes of the influential Barbarini, the Cardinal, together with his brothers, Don Taddeo and Cardinal Antonio, had become so involved in war with Parma that, as Patrick writes later, 'in time of vacanceyes I was forgott, and military officers kindred remembred onely'. The Pope had died in 1644, and his successor, Innocent X, 'seeking to bee contrary to him in all things beganne to show an aversion from strangers'. Besides this disinclination to lavish papal favours on foreigners, the new Pope instituted a severe, not unwarranted, inquisition into the financial affairs of Urban's nephews. The first effect of this on Patrick Cary was that he lost the pension the Cardinal had allowed him. It is to his credit that he did not seek compensation from Barberini 'who was then in persequution, and I thought itt unworthy to exact ought from him who had given mee all'.[1]

Rome soon became too uncomfortable for the Barberini. Cardinal Antonio fled in October 1645,[2] and on a stormy night in the following January he was followed by his brothers. We have first-hand evidence of this latter episode in part of a letter written by Cary, which is preserved in the British Museum.[3] This manuscript, the only document of his written from Rome that has survived, appears from the opening words to be a long postscript:

Since this letter ther has happened an accident which my desire of satisfying your curiositye lett's not mee passe in silence.

The name of his correspondent does not appear, but it is obviously an Englishman well versed in the intricacies of the contemporary Roman scene. As Cary addresses him as 'Noble deare S^r', and signs himself 'Yours most really, most affectionately, John Patricke Carey', one would conjecture it is someone like his aristocratic kinsman and benefactor, Walter Montagu. The letter does not throw any fresh light on the poet's character or career, but it does convey in lively fashion the atmosphere of palace politics in which

---

[1] All quotations in this paragraph are from MS. C.S.P. 39, f. 93.
[2] Leopold Ranke, *The History of the Popes* (1856), ii, 323.
[3] MS. Sloane 3299, f. 177.

he obviously moved. Although it is undated, it is evident from the contents that it is concerned with the crisis which the Barberini had reached early in 1646. Cary writes almost as vividly as an eyewitness of the disappearance of Cardinal Francesco, Don Taddeo, and the latter's family:

... they departed about 8 i'th'night all afoot and disguis'd in poore men's habits till they were gott out of towne where they mett wth coaches and men to guard them, att seaside they were taken up, but wth much difficulty by reason of the stormy weather, by a genouese fishing boate and soe conducted safe some twenty miles unto the sea were 6 tall shippes, to witt 4 french and two genoueses received them, and this is what wee know of them yett.

He goes on to recount the 'gallant closenesse' with which the whole affair was managed. Don Taddeo and his family contrived to have it thought that they were staying at a resort outside Rome. The Cardinal feigned to be indisposed:

... his Phisitian visited him duely, made candles and phisicke bee brought in his chamber, his meat, as use was, served upp, his antecamera open.

His friends visited his empty bedroom assiduously, spending hours there as if entertaining him during his illness. And yet, Cary comments:

... fortune had like to have spoiled all, for had not the aforementioned cockeboate fortunately adventured to carry them a shipboard the wheather was soe rough that they had been forc't to have returned.

Adroitly weighing the situation, he shrewdly guesses that, although the flight seemed voluntary, the Pope and his officials indirectly inspired it as the subtlest means of ridding themselves of the Barberini encumbrance; and in a few graphic lines he evokes the tense, uneasy atmosphere then surrounding the papal court:

This action has left us in a world of suspence every one curious to know the past, and politicke to prognosticate the future, forseing the events of this and relating the manner of what has allready succeeded, variously; and as 'tis ordinary, according to their inclinations or desires, blame and applaud ...

This fall from power of the late Pope's nephews meant the seizure of their palaces and properties, and incidentally the loss of whatever benefits Cary had enjoyed from them. However, he still drew revenues from his abbey and his priory, and several other sources—he could still subsist well; but not for long. Misfortunes now came upon him, 'not single spies, but in battalions'. A combination of natural disasters and human contrivance lost him his priory and his revenue from France. Then in July 1647, in Naples a fanatical fish-hawker named Masaniello led a riot against a tax on fruit,[1] which developed into a violent revolt against Spanish rule, and wrought destruction in the surrounding districts in which Patrick Cary's abbey did not escape. To use his own words:

... then an inundation in Sicily spoyl'd my Priory soe, that as fruitlesse I made itt away. Then a Cannon dyed in Cambray who pay'd mee a pension of 25 pounds yearely, and since that time ... I have receaved nothing, and now am att law with his successour in great likelyhood of loosing my suite. Lastly the warres broke out in Naples and such havocke was made of my Abbey that in a great dispayre I renounced itt, where 300 bandittos had made their nest not onely in the troubles but allmost ever since.[2]

Innocent X was not hostile to Cary, but neither was he helpful. 'From this Pope all the while, I had extraordinary fayre words';[3] but it was clear that he meant to do no more than talk, and Patrick was in no condition, any more than Hamlet, to 'eat the air promise-crammed'. There was nothing more he could do with Rome but leave it as soon as possible. Still, not for nothing was he the son of that punctilious courtier, Henry Cary. He was in Rome by the Queen's behest, and he would not quit it without her sanction:

I writt to Court to crave leave to come away; for having been placed there by Her Majestye I held it my duety not to quitt the place without her licence.[4]

The Queen sent word by letter and by personal message through Sir Kenelm Digby for him to stay: the Pope was not immortal; if times improved he would find her gracious; however, when he could subsist there no longer, he had leave to go. It was not long before this point was reached: 'In complyance to this order I ranne out both in purse and creditt.'[5] The only course open to him was to

---
[1] David Ogg, *Europe in the Seventeenth Century* (1943), pp. 385-8.
[2] MS. C.S.P. 39, ff. 93-93ᵛ.   [3] MS. C.S.P. 39, f. 93ᵛ.
[4] Ibid.   [5] Ibid.

return in the first instance to France. He had been in Italy for twelve years, and it was now 1650.

For the first time in his life Patrick Cary turned his wits to the business of sheer survival; and at this stage we are fortunate in being able to trace his plans and his movements in a most interesting series of letters preserved in the Clarendon State Papers in the Bodleian Library. The first of these,[1] dated 4 March 1650, 'from the English Cloyster in Cambray', is written by Patrick's eldest sister Anne, now Dame Clementia, to Edward Hyde at the court of Madrid. It is a moving appeal to Hyde for the sake of her dead brother, his friend, on behalf of her living brother, whom she had helped to escape from England fourteen years before. In this long, elaborately written letter Anne first spends about three hundred words in courtly expressions of deference and esteem, then decides Polonius-like to come to the point; makes her request with a touching blend of dignity and affection; and finally rounds off her appeal with an even lengthier assurance of submission and gratitude. Apparently her training in court etiquette had taught her the right approach, for her letter bears in Hyde's own hand the approving endorsement: 'A very modest application in behalf of her Brother, for some Employm^t either from the K. of Gr. B. or Spain. She was Sister to Ld Falkland.'

From Anne Cary's letter we learn that Patrick had gone from Rome to Paris, and at the time of her writing was in Brussels, 'where he lives only upon hopes, having very little else in this world'.[2] He is a loyal subject to the King, says his sister proudly, and had occasion offered would have given his life in the royal cause as his two elder brothers gave theirs. Thus he is anxious for some post in the King's service, in England—if there is any opening for Catholics there—or abroad. Failing that, perhaps there is some office for him in Madrid: the fact that he is a devout Catholic, which has made him an exile from his own country ever since he was a child, should recommend him to the Court of Spain. For herself she asks only that Hyde will let her know speedily what hope he can offer. It is perhaps worth noting that the summary of this letter in the *Calendar of the Clarendon State Papers*[3] records that Anne Cary is writing on behalf of her 'sole surviving brother Patrick'. A manuscript note by Miss L. I. Guiney, inserted in the Bodleian Library

[1] MS. C.S.P. 39, ff. 75–6^v. [2] MS. C.S.P. 39, f. 75.
[3] *Calendar of the Clarendon State Papers*, ed. Macray (1869), ii, 44.

copy, points out that what Dame Clementia actually says is 'hee beeing the onely Brother wee have now allive that hath any [word omitted] to the things of this world'. Her other brother, Henry Cary, as a Benedictine monk, would need no recommendation for secular employment.

Anne Cary was not the first person to seek Hyde's help on Patrick's behalf; for on 18 March 1650 the Ambassador himself was writing to Sir Toby Mathew to report that he had pursued with all 'the mettle and spiritt of friendship' the latter's request in favour of the 'Canon'[1]—not a very accurate description of Patrick Cary, who had some years before lost the revenues of the canonry to which he held nominal title. He will commend Cary to the patronage of Archduke Leopold through the Count of Schwarzenburg, and is hopeful that some office can be found for him with 'noe more rubbs or delayes'—an ironic phrase, as the months dragged on for Patrick without result.

By a coincidence, on this same date in Brussels, Patrick Cary himself was writing to Edward Hyde in his clear, graceful hand a long and detailed letter, in which the strain and uncertainty he is enduring are not slow to break through the mesh of elegantly phrased compliments, as he begs to be either

... quickly favoured, or suddaynely denyed: two things my Lord, that equally would oblidge mee; I beeing now in a state to preferre allmost a dispatching noe before a lingering grant. I have beene brought upp in a tedious court, and inured to patience; 'tis not therefore out of want of itt that I am soe hasty but (were I never soe willing) I cannot attend my fortune more then some three or at most fower months. All temporall good lucke after that time will come too late to be enjoyed by mee.[2]

He goes on with a wealth of detail to a description of his fortunes, beginning with his boyhood flight out of England. For this, he says, his brother, Lord Falkland, never forgave him, never communicated with him, kept even his 'very nothing of portion' in his own hands. Then follows a graphic account of events in Rome, from which I have already quoted the salient passages. After his decision to leave Italy, his thoughts turned to Ireland, where some promise of office had been given him in his father's governorship; but by the time he reached Paris news of Ormond's defeat at the hands of Cromwell was before him, and put his Irish plans out of question.

[1] MS. C.S.P. 39, f. 102.   [2] MS. C.S.P. 39, ff. 92-2ᵛ.

He then crossed to England to collect some slender funds owing to him there, and without delay moved on to Brussels, from which he was writing:

There I receaved the remnant of my little dew, and fearefull of the least charge I might bring on my friends, one hower after they had dispatched mee I left London, and came hither. Here I desired to take some employment, whereby to make a subsistance of my stocke; though in a way of life extreamly new to mee, who had been bredd uppe in the schooles, and in a long robe.[1]

Rapidly he reviews his future projects. He thought of joining the household of the Archduke Leopold; but he has learned that those who serve there receive no pay. The royal service is even further beyond his means—'employment from the King is to bee had not att his but ones owne expences'. A friend in Rome—probably the loyal Father John Wilfrid—is chasing for him yet another elusive canonry, whereby, he says, 'I might live, and yett not be oblidged to take orders (a thing I am lesse willing to doe since my poor Nephew Falklands death).'[2] Slipped into this last sentence is a mention of his final resort, holy orders; towards this, however, his natural reluctance is increased since the death of his nephew Lucius, inheritor of the Falkland title, leaves only the latter's young brother Henry between Patrick and the headship of the family. If his brother's friend can help him, he begs it may be done 'very earnest and suddaynely': otherwise it will be too late.

It is impossible not to admire Hyde's reaction to these letters. He himself was in a difficult position, having been sent to Madrid partly to win support for Charles from Spain, partly to get him out of the way, while the King dallied with proposals from Scotland.[3] In Madrid he was reduced almost to penury, his allowance often unpaid, his presence eventually unwelcome. Yet his letters are full of real concern and kindness, and make it clear that he used every means in his limited power to help the family of the friend he had so deeply loved. This is admirably expressed in a later letter by Patrick Cary himself:

Few men now a dayes mayntayne constant friendshippe to the Living; but to retayne soe fresh a memorye of the dead, would have been a wonder even in those ages when most Vertue flourish'd. This is your

---

[1] MS. C.S.P. 39, ff. 93^v–94.   [2] MS. C.S.P. 39, f. 94.
[3] See e.g. Osmund Airy, *Charles II* (1904), pp. 65–8.

case, my Lord, who have transmitted your favours unto mee as it were by Inheritance; and have made mee your Posthume servant.[1]

Replying now to Cary's first letter in an answer dated 25 April, he shows genuine pleasure and sincerity:

You may very justly beleive me when I tell you that since the unspeakable losse of your excellent Brother, I have rarely felt soe great a pleasure as the first sight of your Name to a Letter gave me.[2]

He regrets not having seen the young man in Cambrai when visiting the Cary sisters—he could have given some useful advice about Patrick's financial prospects in England. Then, as if he can wait no longer, he launches into a loyal and handsome defence of Lord Falkland, now seven years dead. It is unthinkable, he says, that Falkland,

... a Person of incomparable Virtue, who would not have done an unjust thing to have procured the Peace of his Country, which he desired with the greatest passion imaginable, would have proved an unkinde Brother. I know his purposes were very contrary, and though he had been much afflicted with your leaving him (which yet he imputed to others, not to your owne Inclination at the time) yet he was comforted in your being still in a condition capable of his care, and if he had liv'd you had heard from him very effectually.[3]

Turning to Patrick's immediate prospects, Hyde regretfully informs him that there is no hope of employment at the Court of Madrid, where pensions are unpaid and petitioners unsatisfied. But will he not wait a little longer before submitting to 'that irreparable doom' of taking orders? Since Falkland's eldest son is dead, 'there is now only Harry left'; in case he should not survive, surely Patrick has some obligation in the matter of preserving 'a great Name and the memory of a Noble Family'. As to immediate plans, Hyde can offer only one practical suggestion: if Patrick will stay a little longer at the Court of Rome, there may be employment for him in the King's service there; and if so Hyde will do his best to finance him. But he may have some other proposal to offer when next he writes; and, for all the delays to the Spanish mails ('this Court taking lesse care to maintain quick correspondence with the other parts of the World then I think any other place doth . . .'),[4] he promises another letter soon.

[1] MS. C.S.P. 40, f. 169. [2] MS. C.S.P. 39, f. 160.
[3] Ibid. [4] Ibid.

The same day, 25 April, Hyde wrote very kindly to Anne Cary, assuring her with more than mere polite compliments that to help anyone to whom Lord Falkland's memory is precious 'will be a designe I shall be allwayes passionately exercised in'. He explains there is no hope of advancement for Patrick in Madrid, since 'pensyons are gotten heare with wounderfull difficulty and after tedious attendance, and very ill-payd afterwards'. Her brother needs no recommendation to King Charles because of Lord Falkland's memory and his own very good character; but he has written to Mr. Secretary Nicholas to seek his good offices at court. He has asked Patrick not to take any irreversible step yet—will not Dame Clementia join her persuasions to his, especially in view of her nephew's death? Something can surely be found for Patrick if he will wait for a brief time. 'All I aske', concludes the Ambassador with evident sincerity, 'is a little patience.'[1]

The promised letter to Nicholas left Madrid the next day, commending Patrick Cary to the Secretary and to the King. It would be the greatest comfort, writes Hyde, if any good turn might be done him, as he is a person of excellent parts, and able to do good service.[2] As for his own promise to write again, Edward Hyde was as good as his word, but when less than a month later, on 22 May, he addresses Cary once more, he can only reiterate his hopes that Patrick has done nothing rash, and his offer of a position at the Court of Rome. A new Cardinal, Don Antonio de Aragon, has just been created in Madrid and is on his way to Italy. His patronage would be an asset in the papal entourage—shall it be sought for Cary?[3]

Less than a fortnight after Hyde's letter left Madrid, on 5 June Anne Cary in Cambrai was again acting as her brother's secretary.[4] In her usual elaborate preamble she seems to be seeking the most tactful way of breaking news which she knows will be unwelcome; finally she comes to the point: she is writing on Patrick's behalf as he cannot write himself—he has just 'to his great contentment and all ours' become a Benedictine novice at Douai. She regrets, she adds with gentle dignity, she could not follow Hyde's advice to dissuade her brother from this step—in any case, his letter did not arrive until after it had been taken; but neither did she persuade him. She adds that what Patrick has done is not irrevocable: he has a year of

[1] MS. C.S.P. 39, f. 162. [2] MS. C.S.P. 39, f. 163^v.
[3] MS. C.S.P. 39, f. 200. [4] MS. C.S.P. 40, ff. 13–13^v.

probation, and if the life does not suit him he will be free to go. This she feels sure will not happen unless his health gives way.

Hyde's answer, written on 14 September, is typically generous. He assures her he would not be so ill-natured as to repine at anything which gave her so much joy as the news she has given him; but for himself he can only be sincerely sorry to be deprived of the chance to be useful to one he so much desired to serve; and he cannot help regretting that gifts such as her brother has are now so restricted in their employment for 'let the World be as vayne and as bad as it can be, good Men will be able to doe some good in it'. He himself promises still to keep in touch by letter and also by visit, if he returns from Spain, as he expects soon to do. It is to be hoped that Patrick will weigh soberly during his time of probation the gravity of his final choice; but he does not really expect a change of heart:

I know your Family too well, their steadynesse and constancy to what they once undertake, how uneasy soever they find it, to look that the severity of this yeare will fright him from proceeding further in the course he hath proposed.[1]

This last paragraph reads more than a little ironically in the light of the next letter, which I have delayed out of its chronological sequence: Patrick Cary wrote it to Hyde from Douai on 30 August 1650.[2] After three and a half months as a Benedictine novice he has been unable to endure the rigours of monastic life; he is leaving Douai immediately, and now intends to seek his fortune in England. This long letter is in a sense his apologia, and is so vividly stamped with the impress of his personality that I shall let him speak for himself as far as possible. Telling, as he says, his case *ab ovo*, he recalls the vow of devotion which he made as a lad of fifteen on his way to Rome, when he solemnly engaged himself to become a Benedictine monk at some unspecified time in the future. As the years went on and life in Rome absorbed all his energies, this flash of fervour subsided; occasionally, however, the memory returned to trouble his conscience. After a time he sought formal release from his obligation:

The exeqution of this I differred allwayes, and onely by fitts recovered any propension thereunto: which being seene by some (the aforesayde

[1] MS. C.S.P. 40, f. 188.   [2] MS. C.S.P. 40, ff. 169–70ᵛ.

Fa. John for one) not ignorant how I stood engaged; to free me from the torment of an unquiett mind, They sought for a Dispensation which was by Sundry Accidents still differred; and att last, by this Pope, absolutely denyed.[1]

Then came the series of disasters which he had described in his previous letter, and his journey to England to collect his 'little portion', of which, he adds ruefully, he spent a third in getting it, sent a third to Father John in Rome, and returned to Flanders with the rest. He was poor in money, but rich in plans—none of which, however, came to anything:

My Stocke was small ... but I had many very faire hopes of settling unto my selfe a Fortune. And really I thincke, none other than my selfe but would have succeeded in some one of twentye plausible probabilityes. But I mett with such contrary chances, such extravagant miscariages of Letters and Papers of necessary buisnesse ... that all my endeavours (though I may say, noe diligence was wanting) became frustrate. Amongst other things, His Majestye had been pleased in an extraordinarily earnest manner to desire the Archduke to accept of mee into his service: but the letter was so poorely reguarded that not to injure my Master, I resolved not to make a secound instance in that pretension; but rather to shew a carelessnesse of itt's beeing graunted. Many such particulars should I relate which would make anyone beleeve that I were the Unfortunate Spanyard translated into English; and indeed by that name I used to stile my selfe.[2]

At this stage in his misfortunes the thought of his youthful vow, unfulfilled and undissolved, returned to plague him: was it possible that all he was now suffering was a divine retribution—or, at least, a divine reminder? With something of his mother's impulsiveness, once this thought had crystallized, he swept into action upon it:

All these Crosses, and retirednesse from all company, which followed uppon them, gave mee a willingness and leasure to reflect upon *What might bee the occasion of soe much ill lucke*; and after due consideration I assured my selfe 'twas for nothing else but in punishment for my neglect of complyance with my Vowe: and thereuppon I resolved to bee clothed

---

[1] MS. C.S.P. 40, f. 169ᵛ.
[2] Ibid. Weber (p. 307, n. 17) suggests the 'Spanyard' refers to *Vida de Lazarillo de Tormes* (1554). However, Mrs. E. Duncan-Jones kindly pointed out to me that the reference is surely to a romance by Céspedes de Mendoza which had been translated into English by Leonard Digges in 1622 under the title *Gerardo or the Unfortunate Spaniard*.

without any further delay: and having obtayned admission, soone after putt that thought into exeqution.¹

The calm flow of life within the Benedictine cloister of St. Gregory's Priory at Douai was in welcome contrast to the turbulence and uncertainty he had lately been enduring; but if his mind was at peace, his body was not, and in the end physical weakness was too strong for him:

The Quiett of this life is beyond measure simpathizing with my humour; but the fare (for the first yeare onely fish) in some three monthes and an halfe has cast mee downe into such a weaknesse that I am forc't backe into England, least the winter should soe quite finish to decay my crazed health that I should ever after prove a tedious burden and noe way serviceable unto the communitye: And this the more, since that my long stay in Italy makes mee lesse fitt to beare with sharper weather where there is soe small allowance or commodity for firing. I am therefore now uppon my returne, repining att my weakenesse, as the hinderance of such felicitye prepared for mee in soe quiett a Life.²

This matter of Patrick Cary's vow and his brief inglorious effort at its fulfilment raise questions so vital to his sincerity that his biographer must pause and try to answer them. Was this vow—a private engagement of a boy of fifteen—really binding? Does the fact that, after ignoring it through twelve years of affluence, he suddenly decided to act upon it when his resources were exhausted, hint at a counsel of expediency rather than one of perfection? Do the shortness of his trial and the reasons given for his departure argue shallowness and superficiality in his whole approach to religion? The answers to these questions are crucial to his integrity as a person and as a poet. For if a man enters a monastery because he has no money and leaves it after three months because he detests fish, his words ring rather hollow when he writes verses ending 'On *God* I'le fix my Heart'.³

To begin with the vow itself, there is no doubt that it would be regarded by the Church at that period as binding. The classic teaching on the subject, which would obtain in the seventeenth century, is found in St. Thomas Aquinas, *Summa Theologica*.⁴ Without entering into a complex technical discussion, I shall briefly summarize

---

[1] MS. C.S.P. 40, f. 169ᵛ.   [2] MS. C.S.P. 40, ff. 169ᵛ–70.   [3] p. 56.
[4] *Summa Theological*, IIᵃ IIᵃᵉ Q.CLXXXIX: Art. V. What follows is based on the Leonine edition (1899), X, 545.

St. Thomas's ruling. The vow of religion, he says, is twofold, simple and solemn. A solemn vow is a promise gravely binding, and far-reaching in its implications and effects. A simple vow, a bare promise made to God, takes its efficacy from the deliberation of the mind, whereby one intends to take upon oneself an obligation. There are two ways in which this obligation can have no force: first, if it is taken by those with defect of reason; second, if the maker of the vow is subject to another's power. These two circumstances normally concur in children before the age of puberty; hence if a boy before puberty makes a simple vow before having the full use of reason, the vow does not bind. If, however, he has the use of reason before puberty, he is obliged as far as he is able (*quantum in se est*), but the vow can be annulled by his parents. If he is past the age of puberty, the vow must be regarded as binding: and the age St. Thomas associates with puberty is fourteen. Hence it is clear that Patrick Cary's simple vow to enter the Benedictine Order, taken at the age of fifteen, would be considered binding. It should be pointed out, however, that his vow would oblige him only to try his vocation, and if he proved unsuitable and left, he would be under no further obligation:[1] which is precisely what happened:

My Vow (which otherwise could not bee dispenced withall) is, by the tryall of my forces, in all Casuists opinions satisfyed even in all rigour; and my Conscience, in that reguard, most safe.

The conclusion from this is that Patrick Cary's youthful vow was binding, and that he honourably, if belatedly, discharged it.

The second question that arises is that of his motives for acting when he did—was it through pure expediency, as offering his only hope of maintenance? I think he can be cleared of this charge. Although he had frankly admitted his reluctance to embrace religious life, he spoke of it with respect and appreciation; before entering the monastery at Douai he wrote: 'I have a last refuge (perchance the happyest)';[3] after leaving it he regretted the loss of 'such felicitye prepared for mee'.[4] Far from waiting until he was destitute to fulfil his vow, he actually began his novitiate in the middle of May, when only two of the three or four months he had set as his limit had passed, and without waiting to receive Hyde's answer to his carefully composed appeal for preferment. Hyde's

---

[1] I owe this explanation to the kindness of Father Francis Edwards, S.J.
[2] MS. C.S.P. 40, f. 170.   [3] MS. C.S.P. 39, f. 94.   C.[4] MS.S.P. 40, f. 170.

first letter arrived after his entrance, and the second only shortly before his departure. His sister thought of his resolution to enter religion as

> ... purely the worke of god, as I truly thinke it was in him, he having had many humane respects to move him to deferre a little longer his good resolution, which I thinke hee would have done if hee had not been so forcibly drawne by god speedily to follow his vocation.[1]

I think we must accept his entire sincerity when in the passage I have already quoted he explains his reasons for deciding, in the terms of his boyish vow, to 'enter a Religious life under S. Bennett's habitt'.

So much for his reasons for embarking on this life when he did: what of those he gives for quitting it? Again I feel we must accept his simple word that the austerities of the Benedictine rule were physically too severe for him to bear. There is reason to believe his health was impaired by long residence in Italy. Elsewhere in this lengthy letter he speaks of Rome—'the Heats there exhaust my health'.[2] Before adopting his plan to seek entrance at Douai he had hesitated for this reason: 'I dare not recurr unto itt till I have tryed all other wayes, for I distrust my owne forces'.[3] His sister, proud and loving as she was, had shared this presentiment, and recurred to it several times in the letter by which she broke the news of his decision to Hyde:

> I verily belleeve nothing will have the power to make him change it but the finding it absolutely insupportable to him ... yet if his tender complexion make him find the austerityes of Relligion above his abillity to beare, hee will be forced againe to venture himselfe in those dangers of the world from which he is now happily retired.[4]

Patrick Cary became a monk—or rather, a novice—not from an ardent longing to consecrate his life to God, but on the honourable compulsion of his conscience. He is not likely to have been sustained for long by the spirit of fervent enthusiasm which carries the eager aspirant gaily through the early trials of monastic life, although I believe he caught enough of its flame to guarantee the sincerity of his religious verse. Add to this the miseries of an unvaried diet for a digestion affected by Italian food, the miseries of unrelieved cold for a constitution impaired by Italian heat; and it is

---

[1] MS. C.S.P. 40, f. 13. [2] MS. C.S.P. 40, f. 169.
[3] MS. C.S.P. 39, f. 94ᵛ. [4] MS. C.S.P. 40, ff. 13–13ᵛ.

not difficult to believe that the young man's superiors soon concurred with him that his way of life lay elsewhere.

Thus with goodwill on both sides he prepared to leave, with his respect for religious life undiminished. The phrase 'threw it [the habit] off', uncritically repeated in this connection by biographers[1] who copied it from Hyde's own endorsement on Patrick Cary's letter, suggests an attitude of impatient contempt for which there is, in fact, no evidence. It is perhaps worth repeating that he did not repudiate the priesthood, never having possessed it, nor did he at this time reject the Catholic faith. Anne Cary had the first word in recounting Patrick's trial of monastic life. It is appropriate to let her close the incident. Finding it, she says,

> ... absolutely insupportable to him ... hee will have cause to think that god called him to this much (for that hee can never doubt of) but intended hee should goe no further.[2]

Nothing had been lost by his brief time in the monastery, and much had been gained, for it was then, as I shall try later to show, that he wrote his strikingly individual religious poems.

What were his plans and prospects now? In the same letter which covers the events just related he gracefully refuses Hyde's offer of a post at the Court of Rome. Besides the effect of the climate on his health, and the loathing for Rome which has now replaced his youthful affection, he is *persona non grata* with many there, and could serve the King no further than with a 'fayre intelligence and correspondence', which would hardly justify the expenses. As for the recommendation to the new Spanish Cardinal which Hyde offered him, he asks with touching gratitude that it may be transferred to Fr. John:

> My obligations unto Him (amongst others) are, that for 12 yeares together I lived under his care; and in that time on severall occasions receaved in loane soe much money of him that (although when in England I endeavoured to quitt as much o'th'score as my possibilitye would bee stretched unto, yett) noe less than 400[11] sterling remayne on the Tally; and (what is more oblidging) unsought for, though excessively wanted. This Person lives in Rome, and perchance could make good use of that Cardinall's favour and protection whom you mention. Wherefor if for him Your Lordsh. would bee pleased to procure itt ... my Gratitude

---

[1] Harrison, ii, 467; Weber, p. 309.   [2] MS. C.S.P. 40, f. 13.

would esteeme herselfe most extraordinarily assisted by your goodnesse.[1]

Whether or not Fr. John received the favour his old pupil so warmly wished, he continued to live in Rome, engaged in works of charity, serving when he could the English cause, until he 'died in great esteem and reputation at Rome in 1657 swept away by the Pestilence which then raged there'.[2]

Patrick himself had other plans. He now hopes, he says, to gain an allowance from the estate of his nephew Henry, the young fourth Viscount, to tide him over his present difficulties, and asks Hyde for letters of commendation to young Falkland's executors:

... I must entreate your L. to write (since you are most particularly informed of my Nephewes estate) unto Dr Shelden, Dr Hammond, Mr Palmer, Hinton, my Nephew himselfe, or any one else whom you know to bee of power, and with whom you have most confidence, a letter to this effect. That itt would redound to my Nephewes greate shame if an onely Unckle should bee reduced to streights by Necessitye, when as soe small an Annuitye as that of 50 or 60[11] would save his credit, my life. This my Lord must bee press'd very urgently, and with all arguments; and I begge you to lett itt come as from your selfe; for I confesse that itt would breake into peices my very soule, to have any one aske in my name for mee and bee denyed. Others, not soe nearely allyed, have such pensions; and the addition of this (since my summe is soe little) would not much burden the estate. Nature perchance obligdes him to give mee aliments; nay Justice too. . . . Since then that hitherto I have never beene chargeable unto my Nephew or his father for one single token, Methinckes that I might now att last bee the sooner considered.[3]

The revealing phrase 'itt would breake into peices my very soule' shows what it cost Patrick Cary to come thus cap in hand to others; and a little later in the same passage he hints darkly that, were it not for his Christian beliefs, he might yet yield to a final temptation to suicide:

And indeed, rather then bee burdensome unto my Nephew or Any (if my Nature were not strongly curb'd in by my obedience to God's law) I should perchance not demurre for long uppon the casting of my selfe away. Having by your (and perchance my sisters) mediation, made this tryall, I shall thincke then to have donne all in my part, and afterward

---

[1] MS. C.S.P. 40, ff. 169–9ᵛ.
[2] Bennet Weldon, 'Memorials of the English Benedictine Congregation', i, 322.
[3] MS. C.S.P. 40, f. 170.

more confidently turne my selfe elsewhere to labour for a settlement in fortune or a grave.²

He goes on to give directions so minute for the dispatch of Hyde's reply that we realize the delays and hazards to which correspondence in those days was subject, and incidentally the good fortune by which the series of letters I have been quoting has been happily preserved:

What answer you are pleased to make (and I humbly entreate you to make mee one) pray, my Lord, send immediatelye to London to S Edward Bannister's house in the long acre over against (as I take itt) the red Lyon Taverne; thence to bee conveighed into Hampshire, to Sr William Uvedale's house called Wickeham. I am thus very precise because I have learn't to bee cautelous of my disaster in the many pregiudiciall miscarriages of my letters: and therefore I must begge of your L. allsoe to send by severall wayes *duplicates*, least your letters (on which my Welfare soe totally depends) should to my ruine bee lost.²

Earlier in this letter Cary had said: 'For this winter I shall dwell (if the Parliament will give mee the leave . . .) with my Sister Uvedale.' Mention now of 'Sr William Uvedale's house called Wickeham' indicates the next stage, in many ways the happiest, of his changing fortunes; and for this the scene shifts once again to England.

iv. *England and Ireland* (1650–7)

If Patrick Cary had for most of his life been deprived of the care and affection of his parents, he had always found loving and understanding support from his sisters. Up till now it had been his Benedictine sisters who were the refuge of his bewildered childhood and the champions of his adult cause. Now he turned to his remaining sister, in many ways the most interesting of the Cary daughters, of whom we have so far heard little. This was Victoria, whose name, it may be remembered, in her brother's verse was one of the clues that led to his identification. Before continuing Patrick's story, it will be useful to linger a little over Victoria's.³

She is not mentioned by name in her sister's memoir of their mother, nor does she find a place in the article on Lady Falkland in the *Dictionary of National Biography*. In the most informative of the

---

[1] MS. C.S.P. 40, f. 170. [2] MS. C.S.P. 40, ff. 170–70^v.
[3] See *N & Q* (1955), cc, 404–7, for a full account of Victoria Cary by Mrs. E. Duncan-Jones, to which I am much indebted.

Falkland pedigrees[1] she is referred to as the second daughter. In point of fact, she was the fifth, born in 1620 between Lucy and Mary, and was therefore only a few years older than her younger brothers. Baptized at Aldenham on 16 September 1620, she was given the unusual name of Victoria, which was spelt in the church register in its Italian form, Vittoria; and in contemporary references she sometimes appears as Victory. At the age of two she accompanied her parents to Ireland, and, after Lady Falkland returned to England in 1625, was one of those children who remained in Dublin with their father. When her mother became a Catholic, Victoria alone of the daughters seems to have been unaffected. She was apparently living with Lady Falkland at this period, according to a letter from the Viscountess to her close friend, Susan, Countess of Denbigh: 'I desire to know whether Victoria may wait upon you or no for she grieves so here.'[2]

After Lady Falkland's conversion to Catholicism in 1625, when the family was widely scattered, Victoria may have lived with Lady Denbigh. Like her elder sisters, she was a maid of honour at court, and (as 'Mrs Victoria Carew') appeared with Henrietta Maria and her ladies in the cast of Walter Montagu's pastoral marathon, *The Shepheard's Paradise*,[3] in which thirteen-year-old Victoria in the part of the gloomy poet Martyro had to declaim long speeches of platonic love to the Queen. Not long after, on 10 February 1634/5, she again took part in court theatricals in Davenant's masque, *The Temple of Love*; and in 1639 her dramatic talents were once more employed in his *Salamacida Spolia*.[4] After her father's death in 1633, two grants of £200 each made to her by the Crown show she was the special object of royal protection.[5]

Some time before 1638 Victoria was affianced to young William Uvedale, son and heir of Sir William Uvedale, Treasurer of the Chamber, who had soldiered with her father in the Netherlands.[6] The young man was involved in a scandal, and his father sent him abroad till it blew over, on a voyage from which he never returned. On 3 July 1638 a newsletter to Strafford told the story:

We have lately sad news of young William Uvedale's death at Venice, his Father's only son, who he had bred up with great Care and Cost...

[1] *H & G* iii, 39 *et seq.*   [2] *C.S.P. (Addenda)* (1625–49), p. 89.
[3] W. Montagu, *The Shepheard's Paradise* (1659), Sig. A 4ᵛ.
[4] Davenant, *Works*, ed. Maidment and Logan (1872), i, 309; ii, 327.
[5] *C.S.P. (Dom.)* (1635), p. 565; (1636–7), p. 442.
[6] Note by Patrick Cary in MS. Lille, f. 4.

on the way homeward he died of a burning Fever: he should have married Victoria Carey, a Sister of my Lord Falkland's who lives at Court: the King was a Wellwisher of the match, her Portion was 4000 L, and his Majesty gave him the Reversion of his Father's Office to make them better fortunes.[1]

Victoria was not left long lamenting. Adding grist to the mill of the court gossips, after a decent interval, in February 1639/40, she married Sir William the elder. For the fact we have a letter of 20 February 1639/40 from Robert Read to Thomas Windebank: 'Sir William Uvedale... either has married or is to marry her that should have been his daughter-in-law.'[2] For a feminine comment spiced with a little acerbity there is Dorothy Osborne's letter to Sir William Temple, recalling the affair at a later date:

Sr William Udall and his sonn were Rivalls and (which was stranger) shee pleased them both, the son thought himself sure of her as longe as hee lived, and the Father knew hee might have her when his son was dead.[3]

Sir William, a favourite of Somerset, was a man of striking good looks, courtly bearing, and chivalrous character. 'I could say absolutely', says a contemporary, 'he is one of the finest courtiers for figure and personage in the whole Court.'[4] An epigram of Jonson's salutes his gifts of body and spirit:

Who sees a soule in such a body set
Might love the treasure for the cabinet.
But I, no child, no foole, respect the kinde,
The full, the flowing graces there enshrined.[5]

Victoria Carey was twenty at the time of her marriage, her husband in his fifties, with two daughters considerably older than his bride. But that it was a happy marriage is indicated by Sir William's will, settling all his goods and personal estate on his 'entirely beloved wife the Lady Victoria Uvedale'.[6]

The manor of Wickham in Hampshire, at one time called Place House, was unfortunately demolished in about 1780,[7] and there is now no trace of the mansion to which in the September of 1650 Victoria welcomed her brother Patrick. At thirty, with ten years of married life behind her, a young son and two daughters at her side, she would still retain much of the beauty for which she had been

---

[1] *Letters and Dispatches of Strafford* (1740), ii, 180.
[2] See N & Q cc, 406. [3] Osborne, p. 78. [4] *S.A.C.* (1865), iii, 125.
[5] *Poems*, ed. Newdigate, p. 48. [6] *S.A.C.* iii, 179–80.
[7] *S.A.C.* iii, 133.

famous, as Dorothy Osborne admits: 'She was handsom Enough once, or Else some Pictur's that I have seen of her flattered her very much.'[1] At Wickham Cary found a household of cordial warmth and domestic felicity, a refreshing contrast to the formality of Roman court and college and the austerity of the Benedictine cloister. He could say of his sister's home, as Carew said of Saxham:

>...thou within thy gate,
> Art of thyself so delicate;
> So full of native sweets, that blesse
> Thy roofe with inward happinesse;
> As neither from, nor to thy store
> Winter takes ought, or Spring addes more.[2]

In fact, for Patrick Cary it was autumn, and the calm landscapes that now stretched about him, orderly, English, and beautiful, with their 'universal tinge of sober gold', symbolized the new climate of ease and freedom which he had entered. He need have no fear of saying what he thought politically, for his brother-in-law shared his Royalist loyalties; and although seven years before Sir William had held the post of Parliamentary Commissioner for collection of fines on papists, the appointment was never renewed.[3] It is not difficult to guess where his sympathies lay: his Catholic relatives—and Patrick was still a Catholic—need not fear to speak their mind.

One result of this was that a varied flow of verse now came from the young man's pen. Political satires pelted Cromwell with high-spirited abuse; pastoral poems reflected the pleasure of the exile returned; love poetry paid debonair tribute to the ladies of the Uvedale circle, an appreciative audience, while witty occasional verse captured the atmosphere of Wickham and the friendly mansions in the neighbourhood.

One of these occasional poems, 'Come (fayth) since I'me parting' (p. 13), brings to life the prosperous household over which Victoria Uvedale presided with indulgent grace. Cary is leaving on a journey and, not the first poet to feel he should sing for his supper, takes farewell of the assembled family, fitting his lines to the prancing rhythm and pleasant tune of an old drinking song. From stanza

[1] Osborne, p. 78.   [2] *Poems*, ed. Dunlap (1949), p. 27.
[3] B. Woodward, T. Wilks, and C. Lockhart, *A General History of Hampshire* (1869), iii, 146, n. 3.

to stanza the ray of witty teasing and compliment is trained in turn on each member, beginning with the urbane host, Sir William: 'More brave Entertaynements none e're gave then Hee'. The poet's sister gets her meed of praise as Sir William's 'chast Lady, who loves him alife', generous and charitable to the poor; and there is a good-humoured hint that house-keeping is not her strong point. This is not surprising as Victoria had never known a real home until her husband brought her to Wickham. The children are singled out: 'young *Will*, the Heyre', flushing with pleasure at his uncle's approval; his two little sisters, 'well-grac'd *Victoria*', who shares her mother's name, beauty, and virtue, and will have little difficulty in excelling her in domestic arts; and Elizabeth, the younger, who has little to distinguish her at the moment but her attractive dimples. The rest of the household pass in gay review: the chaplain comes in for his share of good-natured raillery; the steward, the butler, the footmen, even the ruddy-faced groom, are not mere nonentities in this manor. Patrick Cary (whose genial familiarity with the servants suggests, as Scott says, that he 'had not disdained a cup of sack in the buttery any more than in the oken parlour'[1]), knows their names, and knows that his host will be pleased for them to enjoy their flash of recognition.

The women in the company are gallantly coaxed to drink their share: the guests, Mistress Cary and Mistress Sculler, the housekeeper, Dame Nell (a seventeenth-century version of the dignified Mrs. Rouncewell of *Bleak House*), and the women around her—with airy banter the poet can name no fewer than seven. But there are more servants still, whose names he does not know.

Such was the happy intimate atmosphere in which Patrick Cary passed several months in the autumn of 1650. But the Uvedale circle extended beyond Wickham. Sir William had two married daughters, Lady Frances Griffin and Mrs. Lucy Tomkins, and two brothers, Sir Richard and Francis Uvedale,[2] whose estates were not far away. From all these families there was a large group of ladies, mostly young, to whom Patrick paid light-hearted attention and for whom he wrote love poems in a style of careless audacity. These 'fayre Beautyes' are celebrated in a witty poem, 'Surely now I'me out of danger';[3] in the Commentary (pp. 73–7) I have suggested identities for some of them.

Amongst these were two who in different ways had a special

[1] Scott, Note 1, p. 65. [2] *S.A.C.* iii, fol. p. 183. [3] p. 10.

significance in the poet's life. They were Lucy Tomkins, who persuaded him to write out his verses, and Susan Uvedale, whom he married. Mistress Lucy Tomkins was Sir William's daughter by his first wife, Anne Carey, and so the step-daughter of Cary's sister Victoria. By a previous marriage to Thomas Neale of Warnford, she must have inherited his estate, since it was there she induced Cary to write out his poems, which are dated 'Warneford 1651'. The dedication makes it clear that the incitement came from Lucy Tomkins: 'I blush, but must obay. You'l have itt soe . . .';[1] we can be grateful to her for the insistence which led to the preservation of the poems.

Of Susan Uvedale we know very little. She was the youngest of six daughters of Sir William's brother, Francis Uvedale, of Bishop's Waltham. The only mention of her in her husband's verse is a teasing reference: '*Susan's* head is full of rattles';[2] but the poem in which this occurs is not an apt vehicle for emotion. Perhaps a truer view of Cary's feeling for his wife appears in some lines from 'The Country Life':

> Yett our Girles love surely,
> And have purely
> Cheekes unpainted, Soules most cleare.[3]

It is not likely that Susan, the youngest daughter of a country gentleman, would have a large dowry; probably she fulfilled the condition her lover whimsically laid down for the lady of his choice:

> Thus, I have mine owne fancy too;
> And vow, None but the *Poore* to woe:
> My Love shall come (when e're I wed)
> As naked to the *Church*, as *Bed*.[4]

Nothing in the few details we can gather of their short married life suggests that they ever had much to live on.

It is not possible to establish the exact date of this marriage, the evidence for which rests on a Visitation of Dorset in 1677.[5] All that we can be sure of is that it took place before October 1654 when their first son was born. Kurt Weber in the Appendix on Patrick Cary in his life of Lucius, the second Viscount,[6] dates it November

---

[1] p. 5.   [2] p. 13.   [3] p. 24.   [4] p. 36.
[5] Ulster Transcript.   [6] Weber, p. 316, n. 32.

1650 on the slender evidence of a letter dated only 'Nov. 9' written by Henry Hammond to Gilbert Sheldon. They were friends of the second Viscount and trustees for his son. Hammond writes:

Of Pa: Carey I since heare that he hath marryed Sir W. Udals brothers daughter, having 300 l., is alow'd by his broth^r H[enry] 25 l. by the L^d 25 l. for his and wives life, leaves that to her and goes recommended by the Speakers lett^{rs} to all in power in Ireland for some place there. That of the Nunnes one is dead, a 2^d came over by pass from the Parl: to London to take Physick, but must return again.[1]

The nun who is dead is Patrick's sister, Dame Lucy Magdalena Cary, who died on 1 November 1650;[2] and Weber, invoking the Gregorian calendar, shows that this could have been 21 October by English reckoning. Even so it would require remarkably fast work on the part of both Patrick and Hammond. I do not think this letter was written in 1650. Dame Magdalena's death would have only incidental interest for Hammond and Sheldon, and the news may well have reached them some time after it occurred. It may be noted that Hammond writes 'is dead', not 'has died'.

In fact the best evidence that Patrick Cary was not married in November 1650 is his own letter to Hyde, dated 10 November 1650, with which the correspondence in the Clarendon State Papers now resumes. Hyde has not yet answered his request for letters of commendation to young Lord Falkland: Cary now bids him not bother:

. . . I find things in such a posture here that . . . I aprehend much that They [the letters] will not worcke the desired effect with Those Who (had they a will) have power.[3]

As it happened, the executors of the Great Tew estate were too anxious over young Harry Falkland's insubordinate behaviour on his Grand Tour to pay much attention to his uncle.[4] Since this source of income seems to have failed him Patrick is casting around for another, and has almost made up his mind to join the army in Spain:

Despayring therfore of This, I am a hammering unto some forme another Designe, in which I begge your Counsell. Perchance I shal bee able e're Spring to imburse some three hundred pounds, which must bee the foundation of my fortune. Having beethought my selfe where I might live

---
[1] MS. Harleian 6942, No. 73.
[2] Birt, *Obit Book of English Benedictines*, p. 215.
[3] MS. C.S.P. 41, f. 51. [4] MS. Harleian 6942, No. 13.

uppon soe small a stocke, I am inclined towards Spayne, as hoping by your meanes to bee recommended to the Generall of the Army either on the Catalonian, or Portughese side (the first I have a greater propension to, as the clearer Cause)....[1]

If Cary had been married before this date he would surely have mentioned it to Hyde as an added motive for obtaining an employment; and just as surely he would not have proposed to go from his new bride to seek his fortune so violently and precariously. It is also obvious that the £300 mentioned by Hammond as acquired by Cary is still a thing of the future.

The few facts we have tell quite a different story. Hyde did not get this letter till near the end of January 1651—in fact, all these last letters in the correspondence suffered lengthy delays. The long letter Patrick had written so laboriously from Douai in August did not reach Spain till November; and there is no record that the replies (obediently sent in duplicate as requested) found their way to Cary at all. Now writing on 9 February 1651, Hyde begs the young man to give up his Spanish design. The army is badly paid, with many English officers leaving it daily 'for pure want and inability to live'. He regrets to be so often 'under the reproach of a Negative Councellor', but can only advise that Cary with whatever funds he has should 'sitt still in some convenient place for security and observation'.[2]

Patrick Cary did not wait to receive Hyde's negative counsel. He had obviously changed his plans; and, just as the Clarendon letters run out, we fortunately strike another lode of information in the letters of Hammond to Sheldon, one of which has already been quoted. None is dated as to the year, but from them, and a few other sources, we can plausibly reconstruct the course of Cary's life after 1650. On 7 January (1651?) Hammond writes that Patrick is staying at Great Tew, and has obtained some funds from the executors of his brother Henry's property:

Well, but heer is a long letter for you to read from Mr P.C. who having an assignment of his broth^r Harryes portion hath by a composition made with him by the Exec: by the Speak^{rs} advise 100 l. p. ann: alowd him for his life and now is planted at Tew, & I suppose by the Gr^{dm} [Grandmother] incited to write this letter.[3]

[1] MS. C.S.P. 41, f. 51. [2] MS. C.S.P. 41, ff. 179-9^v.
[3] MS. Harleian 6942, No. 116.

The Speaker is Sir William Lenthall, who had bought Burford Priory from Lucius Cary,[1] and now showed himself as Patrick's advocate. The grandmother, Lady Morison, mother of Lucius's wife Lettice, who had stayed on at Great Tew after her daughter's death, was presumably well disposed towards Patrick Cary, having befriended his mother in her last illness.[2] Patrick was beginning to take an interest in his nephew's affairs, and perhaps saw himself as manager of the Great Tew estate. By 6 May Hammond was writing about the young Viscount: 'When he comes home he may sojourn with his grandmother & by his uncles help looke into his estate.'[3]

Lettice's chaplain, John Duncon, who was still in residence, took occasion to sound their guest out about his religious views, and on 4 March (1651?) Hammond wrote the good news that Cary had 'turned from Popery' and that he himself was 'very earnestly desired to come to Tew & settle him'.[4] The rejoicing over Cary's return to the Anglican fold was a little premature. About a month later, on 1 April, we read:

Mr Pa: Caryes conversion as yet is rather from the Romish then to the Prot: rel:, a seeker he saith he is & unravells & questions all, that he may build infallibly. A letter I had from him somewhat on this subject.[5]

One would give a lot to read this letter, but in fact Patrick's voice now falls silent in the few remaining letters and documents concerning him.

However, by the beginning of 1651 he had certainly made a formal profession of Protestantism, for without this he could not have been admitted to Lincoln's Inn as he was on 10 February 1651/2, on the sponsorship of Lenthall. The plain facts of the matter seem to me to be that he was by this time married or engaged to marry, and had no hope as a Catholic of making a living for his future family. I believe him to have been a sincere Christian, but in matters of dogma he seems to have had no very profound convictions, and to have been content to adapt himself to the theological climate surrounding him. As a boy he had wanted to embrace the religion of his sisters, and had been ready to conform to the Catholic atmosphere of the Benedictine monastery in Paris. As he wrote to Hyde:

---

[1] Weber, p. 79. [2] MS. Lille, f. 46ᵛ. [3] MS. Harleian 6942, No. 13.
[4] MS. Harleian 6942, No. 95. [5] MS. Harleian 6942, No. 4.
[6] *Records of Lincoln's Inn* (1896), i, 264.

Being made in secrett, of my mothers religion (for I knew not other distinction then betweene the Catholicke and Protestante one but that my mother was of that, my father of this); that I might continue in itt, and bee taught what itt was I was stolen into France.[1]

His boyish vow had been the result of pious enthusiasm, following the example of fervent companions. In Rome and in Douai he had drifted with the doctrinal tide. Now in England the currents ran another way. Who is to blame him if in the business of survival he went with them?

At all events he was moving purposefully towards a useful career. He cannot have spent more than a year at Lincoln's Inn, but the legal training he received, added to his own excellent education, would have sufficed to qualify him for an administrative post. In November 1652 friends were still trying to find him employment, for on 27 November John Ashburnham wrote to an unnamed lady of title:

What you finde in Mr Harvey his letter concerning Mr Patrick Carey (the late Lord Falkland's brother) is (at the least) but the just character that is due to him. . . .[2]

Whether by their efforts or his own, he found a position at last, in Ireland. His thought had often turned to the country of his birth. Several years before he had written to Hyde:

In my fathers time the office of secretary to the Crowne in Ireland had been given mee; the Queene had promist to reccomend mee earnestly to my Lord of Ormond; and Catholicks were now by the articles of peace made capable of bearing offices in that kingdom.[3]

The peace Cary refers to is no doubt that concluded between Charles and the Irish rebels in 1643 known as the 'Cessation', which was extended several times.[4] These terms of limited toleration had evaporated long before Ormond's defeat in 1650, and with them Cary's immediate hopes. By 1653, however, he had no need to look for religious tolerance, and had secured employment. No published work concerning him has so far had any light to throw on his activities in Ireland. I am able to supply some fresh details which

---

[1] MS. C.S.P. 39, f. 92ᵛ.
[2] Thurloe's Papers, ii, MS. Rawlinson A2, f. 503.
[3] MS. C.S.P. 39, f. 93ᵛ.
[4] See S. R. Gardiner, *History of the Civil War* (1893), i, 225; iii, 156.

the late Miss Louise Imogen Guiney had discovered and intended to use in the second volume of her *Recusant Poets*. This has not yet appeared, but through the generosity of Miss Guiney's literary executors I have had access to her material. The destruction of most of the Irish Public Records with the burning of the Four Courts in Dublin in 1922 makes it impossible to check a number of these references, which she collected before 1920. I have, however, verified several, and feel justified in relying on the accuracy of the rest. Cary's earliest appointment in Ireland was in 1653 when he became Commissioner of Revenue, Transportation, etc. for the precincts of Drogheda and Trim;[1] and on 12 October the following year a similar post was gazetted for him in Co. Louth.[2]

This same month was memorable for him for another reason. It would seem that he had brought Susan to stay at Great Tew, the scene of his boyish escape, while he was establishing himself in Ireland, for their first son John was born there on 30 October 1654 and baptized three days later at the chalice-shaped font in the old parish church of St. Michael adjoining the Falkland manor.[3] It would be full of memories for Patrick Cary. His elder brother Lucius lay near by in a grave of which today there is no trace; also buried there were his brother's wife Lettice and their three eldest sons. But Great Tew, and indeed England, had no further part to play in his life. Some time after John's baptism he brought Susan and the baby to the home he had secured in Ireland.

His public career was proceeding honourably. In 1655 he became Justice of the Peace for Co. Meath,[4] and in the same year, by letters patent of 6 December, he was appointed Clerk of the Pells, a responsible office in the Exchequer.[5] His private life was not unnoticed: we find several revealing comments on his change of religion—this time from the Catholic side. Percy Church, a firm supporter of the Queen and a purveyor of news to the Stuart Government in exile, wrote from Paris on 8 October 1655 to Sir Edward Nicholas of the conversion of Queen Christina of Sweden, trusting

... she will proove more regular than the two pillars your Honour mentions, though not more firme in principle and loyallty, which is a thing

---

[1] Guiney, p. 4.
[2] *An Assessment of Ireland for three months,* Dublin, 1654 (in Archbishop Marsh's Library, Dublin).
[3] MS. Rawlinson, B 400ᵉ (transcript of parish register of Great Tew).
[4] Guiney, p. 4.
[5] *Liber Munerum Publicorum Hiberniae* (printed 1824), Part II, p. 63.

alltogether forgotten by two other brothers, now pillars of the Protestant Church and famous for their undertakings since they reverted.¹

As the reference perplexed Nicholas, on 26 October Church elucidated his allusion:

> I perceave by your Honours not knowing whoe I ment by the two Protestant pillars that Mʳ Chancellor read not my letter, for then hee could have told you they were two Benidicten moncks and brothers to the Ld. Faulkland, Secretarie of State, the elder of them goeing as Secretary to Penn or Venables, in which voyage its sayed he dyed, and the other brother, as I heare, lives but an unhansome rambling life, sometimes in Ireland and sometimes in England. This, I am confident, will satisfie your honour both of theire persons and quallityes. . . .²

Henry Cary too, once Dom Placid, had, it appears, left the Benedictines and followed his brother to England and to civil employment —a puzzling move for which nothing in his monastic record suggests a motive. Whatever the reason, he entered Lincoln's Inn in 1654, following his brother, and, as Mrs. Duncan-Jones has shown in a full account of his career,³ in December of that year joined the expedition of Penn and Venables to the West Indies, on which, like so many other members, he died of fever. Church has one inaccuracy—he assigns this undertaking to the elder brother, Patrick; and in this error he is followed by the *Dictionary of National Biography*,⁴ although the supplementary index in the Bodleian Library corrects the slip. From Church there is one more reference to Patrick and Henry, in which he suggests a rather odd reason for their defection—'He thinks too much. Such men are dangerous':

> Your Honour tells me that the behaviour of the two brothers was no marvell in regard of theire witt; it's true I have not seene in my tyme, the witts to thrive. Nevertheless, Mr Chancellor Hyde and Mr Earles esteemed them as no small pillars when they forsooke their frock.⁵

This is the last mention of Hyde in documents relating to Cary. Although because of his own great difficulties he was unable to better Patrick's fortunes, the story of their relationship does honour to his enduring devotion to Lucius Cary, for whom his

> Friendship indeed was written, not in words,
> And with the heart, not pen.⁶

---

¹ *Nicholas Papers*, Camden Society (1897), iii, 71–2.
² *Nicholas Papers*, iii, 99.   ³ *N & Q* cc, 469 *et seq.*   ⁴ *D.N.B.* iii, 1160.
⁵ *Nicholas Papers*, iii, 129–30.   ⁶ Jonson, *Poems*, ed. Newdigate, p. 182.

I find one final reference to Patrick Cary in the voluminous correspondence of his contemporaries—a generous appraisal by Sir William Temple. Writing from Brussels on 16 February 1666 to Patrick's sister, Dame Elizabeth Augustina Cary, Temple says:

I cannot but tell you it was unkindly done to refresh the Memory of your Brother Da. Cary's Loss, which was not a more general one to Mankind, than it was particular to me. But if I can succeed in your Ladyship's Service, as well as I had the Honour once to do in his Friendship, I shall think I have lived to good Purpose here.[1]

This published version is based on transcripts of Temple's letters in the records of his secretary, Thomas Downton, and 'Da.' is an obvious mistake in transcription for 'Pa:', the capitals being easily confused. The reference certainly cannot be to any other of Elizabeth Cary's brothers—Lucius, Lorenzo, Edward, and Henry. The Temple and Falkland families would have known one another in Ireland in Patrick's childhood, between 1622 and 1630, when his father, the first Viscount, was Lord Deputy, and William's father, Sir John, was Master of the Rolls; and the two young men may have met during Temple's travels and Patrick's long residence abroad. A letter from Dorothy Osborne, dated 27 October 1653,[2] shows that both she and Temple were well acquainted with the Cary–Uvedale circle. There would be opportunity to renew the acquaintance in 1655 when Temple brought Dorothy to Ireland as his bride, and Patrick was establishing Susan and their little son in their home in Dublin.[3] This must have been before the early part of 1656, for the register of St. John's Church, Dublin, records the birth of another son thus: 'Edward Carie, sonne to Mr Patrick Cary, bapt. 25 April 1656.'[4] To his first child he had given his own first name; the second was named after Sir Edward Hyde, and perhaps also after the dead brother he had never known.

The picture we now get of Patrick Cary is very different from that suggested by the disapproving Church in the phrase 'his unhansome rambling life',[5] which has been seized on by some of his biographers. Instead we see the industrious and responsible public official, admired friend of a man of standing like Temple, hard-

---

[1] *Works of Sir William Temple* (1720), ii, 12.
[2] Osborne, pp. 77–8.
[3] I owe this reference to Cary and Temple to the kindness of Mrs. E. Duncan-Jones.
[4] Ulster Transcript.   [5] *Nicholas Papers*, iii, 99.

working provider for a wife and two sons. This makes it all the sadder that the next record we find of him is a sombre one.

Seven years before, leaving, as he thought, the world behind him for the cloister, he had written:

> Worldly Designes, Feares, Hopes, farwell!
> Farwell, all earthly Joyes and Cares![1]

Now he was to repeat those words in a different and final sense: all earthly joys and cares ended for Patrick Cary early in March 1657. In the Irish Funeral Certificates (Records of Ulster Office) there is an unusually sketchy entry, showing a rough drawing of the arms of Cary impaling those of Udall, and beneath it 'buried 15 March 1656'.[2] No name is given, but as it impales Udall (one of the many recognized forms of Uvedale) it may be accepted as referring to Patrick Cary. The date must indeed be March 1656/7, as their only daughter was baptized on 2 April 1657, at St. John's, Dublin. That she was the last pledge of their mutual love is hinted by the fact that she was christened Susanna Patricia, thus combining the names of both her parents.[3] The assertion that Patrick and Susan were living in the castle of Marivaux in France in 1660 (C. Almond, *History of Ampleforth Abbey* (1903), p. 118, and *Douai Magazine*, i, No. 2, 1920) is obviously unsound.

There is no indication of the cause of Cary's untimely death—he was thirty-four—but the Cary men of his generation were all short-lived. Earlier he had spoken of his fears for the effect of monastic austerities on his constitution: 'I am forc't backe into England, least the winter should quite finish to decay my crazed health . . .', and at the end of the same letter he complained of a violent headache: ' . . . allready I am oppressed by itt's rigorous payne'.[4] His work would have imposed much travelling and exposure to the weather on a state of health far from robust; and in the end it was probably the Irish climate, not the French, that cut short the career he had embarked on so hopefully. His death must have been comparatively sudden, for there is no record of a will, although there is evidence that his wife later made one. The expenses of finding a home and of maintaining his family seem to have

---

[1] p. 43.   [2] Ulster Transcript.
[3] Ulster Transcript. The double Christian name seems responsible for the incorrect record of two daughters. See Burke's *Peerage* (1967), p. 92.
[4] MS. C.S.P. 40, 169^v, 170^v.

exhausted most of his capital, and there had been little time for him to save. Moreover, I cannot believe he would have failed to restore to his brother Henry some of the latter's patrimony, when he too returned to secular life. Susan with three small children now found life precarious indeed. Fortunately she did not lack advocates. On 14 April 1657 Charles Fleetwood wrote to his brother-in-law, Henry Cromwell (who, as a former suitor of Dorothy Osborne, may have known her acquaintances, the Carys and the Uvedales):

I heare Mr Patricke Caryes widdow is left with a sadde condicion. I have bine moved by My Lord Broghill to wright that y[o]u would please to let hir have a lease of lands at a small rent. Surly, hir condicion is sadde and calls for charity.[1]

We do not know if this request met with success, but her husband's friends, Dr. Loftus and Mr. Petty, obtained an order on 16 May from the Treasury for her relief, and on 3 July another authorizing payment of his last quarter's salary.[2]

How she managed after this is not known, but in any case it was not for long, for she survived her husband by little more than a year, dying on 25 July 1658.[3] She left a will, dictated in her last moments, and now destroyed, of which Miss Guiney noted that it was a curious document, confirming Patrick's teasing remark in a Wickham poem: '*Susan's* head is full of rattles'. In it she named Dr. Dudley Loftus, mentioned above, as her executor, and tried to make provision for two of her children, John and Susanna.[4] That she did not mention Edward suggests that her relatives or Patrick's were already providing for him. He did, in fact, turn out to be the surviving hope of the whole family.

So closed the life of Patrick Cary, his circle (geographically speaking, at least) made just, ending in Ireland where he had begun; and yet not altogether ending. As Mr. W. H. was urged and promised, he had two defences against time—'breed to brave him', and verse to live on, however modestly. Before turning to these I may be permitted to pause and consider what manner of man he was. The biographer who has spent many months in close touch with all the surviving traces of a figure from the past may be pardoned for wishing to see him 'in his habit as he lived'. Unfortunately, few

[1] MS. Lansdowne, 822, f. 41. I owe this reference to Mr. T. C. Barnard.
[2] Guiney, p. 5.   [3] Burke's *Peerage*, p. 921.   [4] Guiney, p. 5.

artists are interested in painting impecunious younger sons, and there is no pictorial record of Patrick Cary. The only clue we have to his appearance is a sentence in one of his sister's letters to Edward Hyde:

To recommend him more to yr Lordshipes favour (since I knowe nothing can doe it so efficaciously) I will assure you hee is very like my Brother Falkland.[1]

I assume Dame Clementia speaks here of physical likeness, for she obviously goes on to refer to abstract endowments: '... & in my opinion & in that of all those that knowe him, hee is equall to him in all kinds'. As to the latter assertion, Hyde himself evidently caught in Patrick's style of writing echoes of his brother's voice:

You will not wonder that many parts of it [Patrick's letter] ... presented to the life that conversation to me I was once more blessed with then most.[2]

If Patrick indeed resembled his brother physically he would have been small of stature, like their mother. Lucius Cary used to jest that only when he was with little Sidney Godolphin, who was even shorter, could he feel himself a 'proper man'. Judging from the portraits of the second Viscount reproduced by Harrison[3] and Weber,[4] Patrick would have been dark, not over-handsome, with a broad face recalling their mother's rather than the narrow aristocratic features we see in their father as painted by Van Somer.[5] He would, however, from Evelyn's description of him as a 'pretty witty young priest', and from the evidence of his own gay verse, have been livelier of expression, with greater charm of manner than his celebrated brother, who was grave of bearing.

In character, his life, as I have recorded it, reveals him as intelligent, honourable, somewhat mercurial in temperament, somewhat pliable in outlook, generous, and with a saving grace of gratitude; while the study of his verse will reveal other and finer qualities. If he appears another Zimri, 'everything by starts and nothing long', this is due not to natural instability but to circumstance; as he said himself in another connection:

... a sinne ascribed perchance to mee, but committed by my Povertye; for whose Faults I have very often been held Guilty.[6]

[1] MS. C.S.P. 39, f. 75. [2] MS. C.S.P. 40, f. 160.
[3] Harrison, ii, frontispiece. [4] Weber, frontispiece.
[5] Harrison, ii, facing p. 404. [6] MS. C.S.P. 40, f. 169.

If he was by no means of the stuff of which heroes or saints are made, he was very attractively human. If he could not claim to have fulfilled in his life the lofty Falkland motto, *In utroque fidelis*, he could plead to have been impelled by that of Cary, *Comme je trouve*, and to have achieved the humbler Uvedale device, *Tant que je puis*.

v. *Epilogue*

In isolating the pattern of one life from those interwoven with it, one is bound to leave a number of loose threads. Let me briefly catch up those I have left untwined in the lives of Patrick Cary's immediate family. His elder brothers, Lucius and Lorenzo, had lost their lives in the Civil War; the third son, Edward, had never reached manhood.[1] Henry, the youngest, had left the Benedictine Order (the records of the English Congregation give his death as occurring on 17 February 1653,[2] but this is obviously his 'death' to the Order) and had died in the West Indies before 15 July 1655. The Cary women were mostly longer lived than their brothers. The eldest, Catherine, had met a tragic death at Burford in 1625,[3] and Lucy, Dame Magdalena, had died in Cambrai on 1 November 1650;[4] but the other Benedictine sisters enjoyed their cloistered peace for many years. In 1652 Anne, Dame Clementia, led a group of nuns from Cambrai, including her sister, Dame Mary, to found a convent in Paris, under the patronage of Queen Henrietta Maria and Abbot Walter Montagu; appointed as their ecclesiastical superior was Dom Hugh Serenus Cressy, who before his conversion to Catholicism had been chaplain to the second Lord Falkland. Out of humility Dame Clementia refused to accept the office of superioress, but remained a simple member of the Paris community until her death there on 26 April 1673. Mary eventually returned to Cambrai, where she died on 22 September 1693; her sister Elizabeth, Dame Augustina, Temple's correspondent, lived in the Cambrai monastery till her death on 17 November 1682.[5]

Victoria Uvedale outlived all her brothers and sisters. Her husband, Sir William, died at the end of 1652, being buried at Wickham on 3 December.[6] His 'entirely beloved wife' felt she was doing no outrage to his memory by a rather speedy remarriage with an old

---

[1] Harrison, ii, 419–20. [2] Birt, *Obit Book*, p. 33.
[3] MS. Lille, f. 11ᵛ. [4] Birt, *Obit Book*, p. 215.
[5] Birt, *Obit Book*, pp. 217, 219, 221. [6] *S.A.C.* iii, p. 127.

friend and faithful admirer. Dorothy Osborne is again our informant, as she writes to Temple on 27 August 1653:

I heard a good while agon that my Lady Udall was resolved to marry a blinde man that lived in the house with her, and mee thought twas an od story then, but since you tell mee hee has bin in love with her seventeen year, it appear's stranger to mee a great deal for if she did not love him what could perswade her to marry him, and if she did, in my opinion she made him but an ill requitall for seventeen year's service to marry him when she had spent all her youth & beauty with another.[1]

Dorothy is a little hard on Victoria. At thirty-three she would not have lost all traces of her once-admired beauty; and in any case Bartholomew Price would set more store by her wit and kindness which he could enjoy without his sight. He must have felt amply rewarded for all his years of devotion when he married her on 14 August 1653. After his death on 14 March 1680/1[2] Victoria kept her former name, living for a long time in London, and dying there in 1694 at the age of seventy-four. She was buried in St. James's Church, Westminster, in whose records her funeral inscription styles her 'Lady Victory Udall'.[3]

There is no further mention of Patrick's son John, who must have died in childhood, or of his daughter Susanna. But Edward Cary[4] has a place in the family records. Born under a luckier star than his father, he came to enjoy many advantages for which Patrick must have longed. He was fortunate to receive a university education, matriculating at Oxford, from Christ Church, on 27 June 1673 at the age of seventeen, and followed his father to Lincoln's Inn. He became a landed proprietor, falling heir to the considerable estates of his kinsman, John Cary of Stanwell, and married into a noble family through his wife Anne, daughter and coheir of Charles, Lord Lucas of Shenfield. In national and local politics he achieved no mean position, becoming M.P. for Colchester in 1688 in the Parliament of the Glorious Revolution, and High Bailiff of Westminster. For the latter part of his life he was resident there, as he is described as 'of St James's Westminster' on the administration of his estate by his widow on 24 November 1692. There he must surely have come into contact with his aunt Victoria, who outlived him by two years.

[1] Osborne, pp. 77, 78. [2] S.A.C. iii, p. 130.
[3] Ibid. iii, p. 131. [4] For Edward's career see Harrison, ii, 471-2.

Edward Cary's son, Lucius Henry,[1] born in 1687, succeeded at the age of seven his cousin Anthony, the fifth holder of the Falkland title, and son of that Henry of whom Hyde had written to Patrick 'only Harry is left'. Anthony, after a useful career in the service of James II and William and Mary—the Falkland Islands are named after him—died leaving only a daughter.[2] Lucius Henry, Patrick's grandson, thus became the sixth Viscount, and from him the line comes direct to the present Viscount, the fourteenth.

There is much worth relating in the subsequent history of the Falklands, including a link with Byron, who stood godfather for the son of the ninth Viscount, killed in a duel;[3] and a connection with William IV, whose daughter, Amelia FitzClarence, became the wife of the tenth Lord Falkland.[4] But it is not to my purpose to pursue it any further. Before leaving the Falkland story, however, one may stand and look back to the point in the seventeenth century where the family name and title were saved from extinction; and so doing, down a vista of more than three centuries, see the figure of the lad of Great Tew and Paris, the witty young man of Rome, the Benedictine novice, the gay guest of Wickham, the hard-working Dublin official—in short, the minor but individual Caroline poet, Patrick Cary.

A Note on Variant Spellings of 'Cary'

Some inconsistency will have been noted above in the spelling of the poet's surname: some writers use the form 'Cary', while others prefer 'Carey'. These are the main variants, although 'Carye' and 'Carie' are occasionally found. The origin of the family may be traced to Devon, where the manor of 'Kari' was to be found, according to Domesday Book. In the fourteenth century the name was in the process of changing through 'Kary' to 'Cary'; next it passed through half a dozen variants, all ending in -e, until in the sixteenth century it settled fairly uniformly to 'Carye', a form which seemed likely to crystallize. However, towards the beginning of the seventeenth century a separation arose between two groups within the family. The Bristol and Devon branches (the latter including the Falklands) dropped the -e and reverted to 'Cary', while the Hunsdon group began to transpose the final letters to 'Carey'. As the

---

[1] Ibid. ii, 472. [2] Ibid. ii, 461–64.
[3] Ibid. ii, 476–77. [4] Ibid. ii, 477.

Hunsdon branch was the more influential, its version of the name tended to be imposed on the rest of the family. The Falklands, however, usually styled themselves 'Cary', although Patrick tended to insert the –*e*. This slight confusion is reflected by those who have written about the Falkland family, Scott and Saintsbury, for example, preferring the form in –*ey*. For the sake of accuracy this spelling has been kept in quotations, but in the text 'Cary' is used, this being now accepted as the standard form. (For the historical details above, see Harrison, i, 10, n. 1.)

III. PATRICK CARY'S POETIC ACHIEVEMENT

Patrick Cary's poems are slender in bulk—only thirty-seven in all—but their range is considerable, their quality pleasing, their tone individual. His singing voice may be slight but it is his own. He has his own 'musical finesse': he is no mere warbler who has another man's tune by heart.

The verses, as has been said, fall into two parts. The first section, entitled in Cary MS. 'Triviall Ballades', opens with a dedication to the homely name of Mrs. Tomkins, in which the poet makes it clear he has no great opinion of his own work, 'these harsh Rimes'. There follow twenty-three items of secular verse: sixteen poems on topics connected with love, five political satires, a pastoral of thirteen stanzas, and the gay occasional piece, 'Come (fayth) since I'me parting', which I have already mentioned. These are all set to specific tunes, which are discussed in Appendix B (p. 115). The second group, which has a separate title-page in Cary MS. but no title except a text, consists of thirteen religious poems.

The dates of composition can be established with a fair degree of certainty from the title-pages in the manuscript and from internal evidence. The title-page of 'Triviall Ballades' has the date '1651, August the 20th'; that of the divine poems has 'Warneford, 1651'. Strictly speaking, of course, these references are only to the dates on which the poet was copying out his verse at 'M^{es}. *Tomkin's* commands'; but there is good reason for thinking that most, if not all, of the poems were composed within a year or so of this date. A curious point is that on the first title-page the date has been altered from 1650 to 1651, while on the second it has been changed from 1652 to 1651. The first date cannot possibly be 20 August 1650 as on 30

August of that year Patrick Cary was still in Douai, writing to Sir Edward Hyde a long letter from which I have already quoted.[1] This must be a simple mistake, corrected to the actual date, 1651. One can hardly, however, postulate two such mistakes in title-pages; therefore it seems likely that the second was correctly dated 1652 and for some reason, such as uniformity, later altered to 1651. The poet thus would have begun to copy out his verses, starting with the secular poems, in August 1651, and have continued into 1652. Some of the verses could not have been composed before 1652, judging by their topical allusions—e.g. 'A greev'd Countesse, that e're long' refers to an Act of February 1651/2. (See Commentary, p. 89.)

As to the dates at which the poems in general were composed, I suggest that the secular verses were mainly written between September 1650, when Cary returned from France to Wickham, and February 1651/2, when he began his studies at Lincoln's Inn; this is also the date of the latest identifiable allusion, mentioned above. The political events referred to—translation of the laws, prohibition of French wine, Act of Oblivion, and cancellation of patents of nobility—occurred between August 1649 and February 1651/2.[2] It is possible that some of the Ballades were written on an earlier visit to England; also that some were composed in Italy—several are set to Italian tunes. But they have in the main the light-hearted air of belonging to the interlude of ease and happy freedom which followed the poet's return to England after his brief stay in the Douai monastery. There is little to show in what order the verses were composed, nor does it greatly matter. The topical allusions link them with a fairly short period.

The religious poems were most probably written between May and August of 1650, during Cary's Benedictine novitiate. It is not impossible that some were written in Rome, but the whole tenor of his life there shows few signs of spiritual introspection. The first of the three triolets that open this section, 'Worldly Designes, Feares, Hopes, farwell!', evidently dates from about May 1650 and the poet's entrance into monastic life. It is interesting that the phrase 'wor[l]dly designe' occurs in Anne Cary's letter of 5 June 1650[3] informing Hyde of her brother's action, and a few lines further down is a passage strongly reminiscent of the third and fourth

---

[1] pp. xliii *et seq.*   [2] See Commentary, p. 83.
[3] MS. C.S.P. 40, 13–13ᵛ.

stanzas of the third religious poem in Cary MS. *Servire Deo, Regnare est*

... if he had not only an assurance of being favourite to the greatest King in Christendome, but that hee would resigne his Kingdome to him it would not move him one jot, hee having (by the great mercy of god) seene so much of the vanity of all earthly things.

This suggests either that Patrick had already written these verses and shown them to his sister, or, more likely, that the lines reflect ideas they had lately spoken of together.

Most of the poems in this section bear strong traces of being poetic records of systematic meditation. I believe them to be the fruit of Cary's daily periods of contemplative prayer in which as a novice he would be receiving instruction. Just as his mother, as a girl deprived of books and later as a woman deprived almost of means of subsistence, had shut herself in her room and lost herself in writing verses, so the son 'att quiett' in his 'peacefull Cell', found relief from the austerities of his new life in expressing in poetry the thoughts he had been turning over in prayer. I think one needs to use caution in applying to such verse in general the valuable yardstick Mr. Louis Martz has given us in *The Poetry of Meditation*. The Ignatian system of meditation was successful precisely because it applied to prayer a natural psychological process—the mind proposing to itself a subject, examining its various aspects, turning its conclusions or resolves into speech, voiced or silent, with itself or another. With very little ingenuity this process can be discerned in a vast number of religious or meditative poems; which is by no means to conclude that they owe their form and some of their content to the ascetic practices of the Counter-Reformation. However, in Patrick Cary's religious verse there is little doubt that this formal influence was at work, guiding him to develop a line of thought in three or more points and to sum it up in a final colloquy. This is clearly evident in such poems as *Crux VIA Caelorum*, with its four vigorous images of sailor, slave, soldier, and captive, dwelt on in successive stanzas and compactly linked in a fifth with the poet's spiritual state; or in *Crucifixus pro Nobis*, a contemplative triptych of Bethlehem, Gethsemane, and Calvary, beautifully epitomized and brought home to Douai in the last stanza. In these religious pieces as in the Ballades the order of composition cannot be fixed, but with so few items in so short a period it is of little importance.

Turning to the themes, and dealing first with the secular poems, we find the largest group exploring different aspects of love. These fall broadly into two divisions, the first, of seven poems, treating love from the standpoint of the dominant masculine figure, who is either sure of his lady's love or cares little if it is denied; the second, eight pieces with the rejected lover as their theme. Finally a single poem suggests the humble happiness of the lover accepted.

To the first group belongs 'Fayre-One! if thus kind You bee', where in something of Suckling's vein the masterful lover lays down conditions: 'I shall love you, whilst Y'are kind'; while 'There's noe Woeman, but I'me caught' pursues the same theme: it is no use blaming the poet for remaining heart-whole—the remedy is simple:

> Were I us'd but courteously
> I should soone becomme a Lover.

The lover's inconstancy is gaily avowed in 'I n'ere yett saw a lovely Creature', and explained away by the dexterous conceit of the mirror, receiving all reflections, retaining none. In 'Fayre Beautyes! if I doe confesse' infidelity is again the theme; but with an urbane metaphysical twist the poet protests he is more reliable than most men, for he is constant in his inconstancy. The debonair 'Surely now I'me out of danger' pays witty court to thirty different mistresses with fifteen different Christian names among them; and here incidentally, in the lines to young Victoria and Elizabeth, the poet's nieces, and to 'Amorous *Sophy*', nine years old, we note another motif not uncommon with the Caroline poets: what Dame Helen Gardner has called the 'Horatian theme of the charm of young girls to older men'.[1] To the same group belongs 'Some prayse the Browne, and some the Fayre', which contrasts a whimsical catalogue of the qualities most men look for in a mistress with the poet's own surprising stipulation, poverty:

> There's noe such Gagge, to still the Lowd;
> There's noe such Curbe, to rule the Proud:
> Itt never fayles to stint all strife;
> It makes one Master of his Wife.

The poems of the second group, eight in all, with considerable variety of mood ring the changes on the topic of unrequited love.

[1] *The Metaphysical Poets*, ed. H. Gardner, 2nd edn. (1967), p. xxx.

In 'O, permitt that my Sadnesse' the unhappy lover asks pardon for offending words, but not with passion—he argues too ingeniously that he is not responsible. Again, in 'Cease t'exaggerate your Anguish' he is despondent but not despairing; the lady's artificial name, the unromantic gout contrasted with the lover's pangs, hint at the deliberately correct posturing of the rejected suitor—every gesture laid down by amorous etiquette. Two poems with pastoral settings, '*Jacke!* nay prithee come away' and 'This Aprile last a gentle Swayne', set side by side the optimistic and the complaining lover; and in somewhat similar strain '*Ned!* She that likes thee now' shows a friend urging on the deluded swain the invincible inconstancy of the mistress. In 'Speake of somewhat else I pray;' the deluded lover is about to merge into the deluded husband, who cynically proposes a spirited counter-attack with his own unfaithfulness. With a refreshing difference of mood 'Poore Heart, retire!' sings its disenchantment with a lute-like cadence and a rare tenderness; and the same simple grace marks 'The Ermine is without all spott', which in the first stanza has every mark of a poem of humble contented love, but with a sense of rejection growing through the second and third till the last stanza, when with a deftly executed volte-face we are confronted not with the poet himself but with a charming pastoral pair, the disdainful shepherdess and the despairing lover, rising from his knees to throw away his pipe and sing no more.

To conclude these love poems there is the tuneful lyric ' ''Tis true. I am fetter'd', the only poem of happy affection: caught in the bright chains of his mistress's hair, the poet hopes, with romantic gallantry rather than passion, that life imprisonment will be his term.

Turning from these personal themes to the wider view of people and nation, we find a group of political satires of considerable verve and vigour, treating topical events and conditions with typical Cavalier nonchalance and, in comparison with many similar contemporary productions, only an occasional mild indecency. 'And can You thincke that this Translation' criticizes with robust good sense and persuasive good humour the proposal to translate the laws from Latin and Norman French into English; in 'Good People of England! come heare mee relate' the exclusion of French wine is linked with a spirited argument, very much *ad hominem,* satirizing Cromwell's most marked physical peculiarity. 'The Parliament ('tis sayd) resolv'd' shows how the proposed Act of Oblivion relieving the burden of fines and taxes on recusants has been allowed by the Rump Parliament to fall into the waters of Lethe; and Cromwell is besought with mock deference:

> Thou made'st them say They would forgett,
> O make them now remember!

All Royalist supporters have been bled white with sequestrations and compositions; but in 'And now a Figge for th' lower House' the poet asserts that he himself, being penniless, is rich in consequent freedom from their persecution. The recently ennobled are to be stripped of their prized titles: we see their reactions from an unusual point of view, the petulant anticipation of the 'greev'd Countesse', with an unexpected excursion into social as well as political satire, at the expense of the shallow, selfish lady who loves for its empty sound her 'sweet-noys'd Title'.

In addition to these poems there is one pastoral, 'The Country Life', a homespun affair contrasting rural delights with urban drawbacks. If it never brings us to the countryside, like Herrick, with a single vivid phrase, at least it resolutely refuses to be artificial:

> Sweet, and fresh our Ayre is;
> Each Brooke coole, and fayre is;
> On the Grasse wee treade:
> Foule's your Ayre, Streets, Water;
> And thereafter
> Are the Lives which there you leade.

As for the religious poems, for the most part they explore conventional ground, dealing in subjects familiar to the first half of the seventeenth century, with its profound and thoughtful attitude to religious experience.

A vast and august body of beliefs—the Christian religion—had survived with scarcely impaired authority into this philosophic century, together with all its associated imagery, its world-picture, its scale of values, its way of life.[1]

It is in this context that Patrick Cary writes verse that is Christian rather than Catholic, containing few specifically credal or sacramental elements except those common to most of the Christian

---

[1] Basil Willey, *The Seventeenth-Century Background* (1934), pp. 119–20.

churches. From this standpoint he chooses his themes, writing of the vanity of earthly things ('By Ambition raysed high'; *Nulla Fides*), mirrored even in the physical universe (*Fallax, et Instabilis*), and the helplessness and viciousness of man deprived of, or rejecting, grace ('What use has Hee made of his Soule'), for which death and divine justice will exact a terrible penalty (*EXPRIMETVR; Dies Irae*). Set against this grim picture is the call to the individual soul to repent (*Dirige vias meas Domine!*) and consecrate itself to God's service ('Triolets'), which by a tremendous paradox turns servitude into royal freedom (*Servire Deo, Regnare est*), and makes all hardships sweet and bearable (*Crux VIA Caelorum*). When the soul has learned from nature and grace to see its complete dependence on God ('Whilst I beheld the necke o' th' *Dove*'), it will share more and more in the consoling glory of Christ's redemption (*Crucifixus pro Nobis*) and the salvific action of the Trinity (*Nobis natus in Pretium*). The original emblematic sketches illustrating this section of the manuscript reinforce the poet's words with pictorial comment.[1]

This thematic variety of secular and religious verse is expressed in a corresponding variety of metrical forms. The secular poems, written as they are to specific tunes, have their form predetermined by the chosen melodies; but as these are drawn from the songs of four nations the range of form within them is considerable. The religious verse shows that rich originality of structure which is one of the great Caroline gifts, with stanzas and lines of varying length and varied rhyme schemes, many of which, with no apparent parallels in other poets, seem to have been dictated by the ebb and flow of the poet's meditative thought. Also included in the religious section are three triolets, one sonnet, and two poems in triplets, *Dirige vias meas Domine!* and *Dies Irae*. The first of these last is in the octosyllabic measure which Herbert uses beautifully in 'Trinitie Sunday', a form well suited to deliberative reflection; in the second the octosyllabic line of the Latin original is reduced by a syllable, avoiding feminine rhymes.

The triolets are particularly interesting. It would be pleasant to be able to claim that Cary was the first to write in this form in English, but the honour must go to Dunbar, whose curious 'Dregy'[2] or mock-dirge antedates him by a century and a half.

---

[1] See Appendix A, p. 102.
[2] Dunbar, *Poems*, ed. Mackenzie (1932), pp. 56–8.

Cary was, however, as far as I can discover, the first Englishman to use the triolet, and he manipulates skilfully this ingenious French measure with its repetitive harmonies. Almost anyone can handle it lightly, but it is something of a feat to write serious triolets in which the reiterated lines in so brief a compass ring gravely and true as in 'Worldly Designes, Feares, Hopes, farwell!', and 'Yes (my Deare Lord!) I've found itt soe;'.

The single sonnet, *EXPRIMETVR*, combines features of both Shakespearian and Petrarchan forms, the octave rhyming abababab and the sestet cdcdcd; but the break between them is finely made, with sober change of thought and sombre variation of imagery.

The metrical variety of Cary's poems, secular and sacred, is indicated by the fact that length of stanzas ranges from three to fifteen lines, and length of lines within the stanza from three syllables to eleven. Only four poems are written in quatrains, the longer stanza forms predominating, and especially in the religious verses carrying a wider sweep of thought.

These various metres he controls with ease, sureness, and fluency —according to some critics, such as Massingham,[1] a too facile fluency. This charge cannot altogether be refuted with regard to the secular poems, which mostly have the air of being written at pace, and in which the lines are sometimes inflated with meaningless words like 'troth', 'sooth', and 'alas', as the poet rapidly marshals his thoughts into the frame of the existing melodic line. Massingham also criticizes his 'lavish elisions' before consonants; but this censure seems due to a misinterpretation. Apart from such phrases as 'o' th'', 'i'th'' (where elision is a contemporary commonplace) the apostrophes merely indicate a very light stress and have no other metrical significance. Cary's ear is almost faultless, and the lines never limp awkwardly. In the sacred poems, where he is mainly devising his own forms, the metre for the most part bears the thought with precision and grace. A sad exception is the translation of the *Dies Irae*, which has the air of a task performed to order: the poet, with his heart not in it, has produced a bad translation and a poor poem. I agree with Saintsbury, who says: 'If I were not a really conscientious editor I should have felt much tempted to suppress it.'[2]

[1] *Seventeenth Century English Verse*, ed. Massingham (1920), p. 325.
[2] Saintsbury, p. 449.

In handling rhyme Cary shows similar inequalities. His rhymes are at times repetitive and unoriginal; at others they display considerable sophistication, as in 'Delinquent/Drincke went' ('The Parliament ('tis sayde) resolv'd'); or considerable fecundity as in 'And now a Figge for th' lower House', where he smoothly produces nine different rhymes for 'groat', and *Crux VIA Caelorum*, where he begins each of five stanzas with three interlacing rhymes in *o*. In his best verses, like 'Whilst I beheld the necke o' th' *Dove*', the rhymes are simple and unobtrusive, marking and conveying the movement of the thought without distracting attention.

The qualities of style displayed in this range of verse are well summed up by Saintsbury in two passages from his Introduction. In the first he speaks of Cary's 'varied, personal, actual touch'.[1] As to variety, I hope I have sufficiently shown to what an extent this is present in the subject matter, form, and treatment of this small group of poems. That they are highly personal and individual is evident to any attentive reader. Cary has been accused of being 'too fluently derivative'.[2] It is not difficult to catch hints and echoes of Wyatt and Suckling in the love poems, and of Southwell in *Fallax, et Instabilis* and *Crucifixus pro Nobis*; to trace imagery used by Jonson in 'Whilst I beheld the necke o'th'*Dove*', and Donne's abruptness in the beginning of *Nulla Fides*. But these resemblances are superficial not derivative. Cary stamps his own mark on what he writes, and the best of his verse, such as *Crux VIA Caelorum*, is quite unlike that of any poet of his own time. Saintsbury's third adjective, 'actual', describes an essential part of Cary's individuality. He writes with a vivid sense of occasion—*Comme je trouve*, as the Cary motto says.

This point is developed by Saintsbury a little further on in the same context, as he speaks of the poet's 'clear healthy common-sense, fully capable of keeping house with Fancy and even Imagination, as well as with Piety'.[3] Here he has hit very well what is Cary's most characteristic and distinctive trait—'clear healthy common-sense' marks everything he writes, invigorating rather than destroying the poetic quality. Whether he frames carefree love lyrics to divert and compliment, fluent *vers de société* merely to entertain, or robust political satire of protest or defiance, he contrives to keep cool touch with reality. His pastoral poems have an honest realism, resolutely avoiding conventional artificialities. The same

[1] Ibid., p. 450. [2] Weber, p. 326. [3] Saintsbury, p. 450.

attitude appears in his religious verse. In spite of his close contact with baroque culture in his formative years in Rome, he is almost untouched by its sensuous intricacies, which were foreign to his essentially English cast of mind. The nearest he comes to it is in *Crucifixus pro Nobis*, with its fusion of sense impressions and contrasts—cold, heat, sweat, blood, tears—with their mystical counterparts: rejection, spiritual agony, sacrifice, repentance. But for the most part his religious poetry is not marked by anything like Crashaw's inward glow of dedication or Herbert's sweet unction of devotion: it is rather a calm affirmation of central Christian truths, and a quiet girding of conscience and spirit to embrace them, expressed in terse, controlled language:

> Pray, when with Others; when alone:
> To Scorne, or Prayse bee as a stone:
> Forgett thy selfe, and all; but One.
>
> Remoove what stands twixt God, and Thee:
> Use not thy Fancy him to see:
> One with his will, make thy Will bee.[1]

Here as everywhere he is impatient of pose or sham, and refreshingly free from pretentiousness. This is shown in his consistent choice of diction which is, to use a phrase of his own, 'common, cleare, and pure'.[2] Thus in *Fallax, et Instabilis* the language is simple to the point of bareness:

> All Things below doe change
> The *Sea* in rest n'ere lyes;
> N'ere lay in rest, nor will:
> The *Weather* alters still,
> And n'ere did otherwise.

Yet the verse powerfully conveys the mutability of the natural world, which has always haunted man, reminding him of his own.

Cary's wit and clarity combine to give his poems a strong sense of structure. This can be illustrated from one of his most charming pieces, 'Whilst I beheld the necke o'th'*Dove*'. Here in five melodiously varied stanzas he frames symbols of the particular delights of the five senses: the iridescence of the dove's throat, the nightin-

[1] p. 61.   [2] p. 56.

gale's voice, the scent of the rose, honey from the bag of the bee, and the soft swan's-down. From each in turn he receives the message, which he takes to himself at the end of the poem, that all goodness, all loveliness, comes only from God. The images are perhaps trite: four of them occur in a very different context in a brief song of Jonson's.[1] Yet Cary integrates them into a lyric of individual beauty:

> Whilst I admir'd the *Nightingale*,
> These notes She warbled o're.
> *Noe melody*
> *Indeed have I,*
> *Admire mee then noe more:*
> *God has itt in his choice*
> To give the Owle or Mee *this voyce;*
> *'Tis Hee, 'tis Hee that makes mee tell my Tale.*
> Thus sang the *Nightingale*.

Notable is the technical expertise with which he manipulates the last line of each stanza through mounting, subtly varied inversions, over the deft rhythmical bridge created for the third: 'And thus reply'de the *Rose*', to the quiet and direct affirmation of the conclusion, with its emphatic normal word-order: 'I too, have all from GOD'.

This sense of form and completeness leads him to sum up and clinch the argument of many of his poems at the end. He does not need a stanza to do this. In *Nulla Fides* with chiastic brevity he compresses the first seventeen lines with their threefold imagery into three:

> That this poore *Fly*, this little *Sparckle*, this
> Soe much abhorr'd *Worme*, can
> *Honour* destroy; burne *Worlds*; devour up *Man*.

Saintsbury talks of Cary's 'clear healthy common-sense ... keeping house with Imagination'. He is indeed capable of effective imagery. A cursory analysis shows that images from the animal kingdom predominate, with contrasts such as those between the innocent dove and ermine, and the brutish goat and hog; the industrious ant and mole, and the rapacious worm and crow; the swan's soft down and the peacock's gaudy plume. Close behind

---

[1] See Commentary, p. 95.

these come images drawn from common, even homely, life, with its tools and mirrors, anchors and ploughshares, houses and tombstones. The background of nature is very much taken for granted, and images from weather, climate, and natural forces form a smaller group. The religious poems, as one might expect, make full and meditative use of Scripture; but in spite of Cary's sound education he rarely calls on the stock of classical allusions which provided rich associations for some of his contemporaries. If he has a favourite image it is that of light and its reflections: the impassive sun, spectator of mankind, or the 'ancient tapers' of the stars; the brief glint of a spark or a glow-worm; the dim phosphorescence of decay; the sheen of a silk dress or a girl's bright hair; the dull gleam of gold, 'but *guilt Clay*', or the brittle glitter of gems, 'but *Sparckling Froth*'; the opal tints of the pigeon's neck or the vanishing bubble. But in bringing together this group of images I have suggested an opulence that does not in fact exist in Cary's verse, which is deliberately spare. He can handle the extended metaphysical conceit with ease, but it is notable that he uses it more readily in prose, in his 'begging' letters, where he is exerting every artifice to make his impression:

My Lord, you see how my Boldness encreases: if you would have itt ebbe, your least Checke will make itt doe soe. Yett this I assure you that (although permitted to flow on) Itt shall never offer at any thing but your Recommendations....[1]

In his verse, apart from the looking-glass image (p. 8), it is seldom employed, for there he is writing to suit his natural self.

What this natural self of the poet is, as I see it, I have tried to show. There is little evidence as to what others think. Few critics have devoted much attention to Patrick Cary. Apart from Scott, who praised his 'playfulness, gaiety, and ease of expression, both in amatory verses and political satire',[2] and a few literary historians of later date, who have touched on him with fragmentary reference, only Saintsbury and Weber have given him any space in print. Their views are very different. Saintsbury's verdict errs on the side of enthusiasm, claiming that Cary can not only

... give a hand on one side to Lovelace and on another to Suckling for tender and for merry verse; he can in the other great division of Caroline poetry, the sacred, show things not unworthy of Herbert, if not even of

---

[1] MS. C.S.P. 41, f. 51ᵛ. [2] Scott, Introduction, p. iv.

PATRICK CARY'S POETIC ACHIEVEMENT   lxxxi

Vaughan, though of course he never touches any of the four at their very best.¹

Weber combines cool praise with regretful strictures on his 'ready imitativeness': 'he remains too fluently derivative' and 'hasn't . . . creative energy'.⁴ If I attempted to pigeon-hole him it would be somewhere between the two. But I can safely let him speak for himself, in the conviction that, minor poet though he may be, he is not undeserving of honour in his own country.

[1] Saintsbury, p. 449.
[2] Weber, p. 326.

Textual Introduction

I. THE MANUSCRIPT

The only extant manuscript of Patrick Cary's poems, which I refer to as Cary MS., is in Sir Walter Scott's library at Abbotsford (Press N, Shelf 5); it is in the form of a small, bound notebook. Through the kindness of Mrs. P. Maxwell-Scott, the present owner, and Dr. J. C. Corson, the honorary librarian, it was deposited temporarily in the National Library of Scotland, where Dr. T. Ian Rae examined it for me, and wrote the following account, which greatly supplemented, as well as corrected, my own description of it:

Though Scott in his Introduction to the edition of Cary's poems he published in 1819 describes it, in the manner of his period, as a small duodecimo, the vertical chain lines suggest it is a foolscap octavo, now, after trimming, measuring $5\frac{1}{2} \times 3\frac{1}{2}$ inches (138×90 mm). The volume is not foliated and is only partially paginated. It has been used from both ends and by at least one person other than Cary. At the beginning of the upper part are six leaves of religious aphorisms, the first written page headed with the date 1634. These are followed by Cary's secular poems, *Triviall Ballades*, written in his own hand. After the title-page bearing the date 20 August 1651, with the words 'writt here in obedience to M^{es}. Tomkin's commands', is a dedicatory verse followed by twenty-three poems including love poetry, political satire and occasional pieces, all set to existing tunes, most of which are named. These *ballades* are paginated 1–47. The notebook has then been reversed. The lower part begins with four leaves of an undated library inventory headed 'The names of the bookes'. On the next page Sir Walter Scott has written his signature with the word 'unique', and after this Cary's hand resumes, this time with the religious verse, thirteen examples in varying styles, with a title-page dated 'Warneford, 1651'. The religious verse is paginated 1–25, and is illustrated throughout with thirteen devotional drawings, presumably by Cary himself, separated from the text by rules in black ink. Between the two sets of poetical texts are nine leaves, blank except for some pencil scribblings.

Altogether there are 62 leaves of which the last two have only the upper halves left, having been cut across the middle; a number of pages have been cut or torn out, and several have been neatly patched, some of the missing leaves probably having been used for this purpose. All the leaves except the first two have been hand ruled with a border of thin double red lines about $\frac{1}{3}$ inch from the edge running round all four edges of each page; this rubrication, clearly executed before any of the users of the volume wrote in it, was probably done, before it was bound, by the stationer who supplied the volume. All the surviving watermarks are too incomplete for identification, and occur at the gutter end of the tail edge of the leaf. A full collation of the volume cannot be given because the tight binding hides many of the sewing threads; some threads, however, are visible in the first half of the book and these, together with the watermark positions, indicate the following partial make-up; none of the leaves has any signature after the manner of a printed book but for the purposes of description these have been supplied in relation to the ascertainable arrangement of the quires of the leaves within them: A^4 (A 3–4 stubs only) B^1 (no visible conjugate: this is the leaf bearing the date 1634) C^8 (parts of watermark on $C1$ and $C4$) D^8 (pp. 5–20: parts of watermark on $D1$ and $D4$) E^8 (pp. 21–36: parts of watermark on $E2$ and $E3$) F^8 (pp. 37–47 [48–52]: parts of watermark on $F2$ and $F3$). After F^8 come the following leaves, but it has proved impossible to collate them, and some torn-out leaves may have been overlooked: 1, 2 (stub), 3 (with watermark), 4, 5 (with watermark), 6 (stub), 7, 8 (with watermark), 9–13 (pp. [26] 25–17 of religious verse), 14–15 (pp. 16–13: with watermarks), 16–21 (pp. 12–1), 22 (title-page of religious verse with watermark), 23 (with watermark), 24 (stub), 25–27, 28 (stub), 29, 30–31 (upper halves only). The total, 68, comes to more than the 64 leaves of an eight-sheet octavo, but the difficulty of a detailed collation of the whole volume may throw some doubts on the reliability of the total.

The volume is bound in black morocco leather decorated with gold tooling; the style is not inconsistent with the date 1634 in the manuscript, though it may be slightly later. Scott, in his Introduction written in 1819, says it was by then 'stripped of its silver clasps and ornaments',[1] without mentioning how he knew the nature of these. Two holes on the horizontal centre line, 4mm and 23mm respectively in from the edge of one cover, and traces of similar holes on the other cover, indicate that the volume had a clasp fastening. The clasp anchorage was probably oval in shape and open in the centre. On the front cover a gilt letter L contemporary with the original tooling has been stamped where the centre of such an opening would be, and the freshness of the gilding of the decoration beside the anchorage holes suggests an oval shape; the point on the back cover where one might expect to find another initial has been

[1] Scott, Introduction, p. iv.

obscured by later repairs. A stamped initial in this position is unique in my experience. There are no signs of holes for fastenings of metal corner pieces, and the oval clasp was probably the full extent of Scott's 'ornaments'.

At the beginning of the nineteenth century the volume was repaired. It was rebacked, and the corners were repaired, with straight-grained blue morocco; the spine was divided by gold double fillets into six panels, the second top panel lettered in gold 'Carey's Poems', and the bottom panel with the date 1651. New end-papers, of wove paper coarser in texture than the rest of the leaves, were inserted. The style of rebacking suggests the date 1820–30 for this operation, but it could well have been done slightly earlier since Scott has written on the new end-papers two separate notes, one referring to his account of the manuscript in the *Edinburgh Register* for 1810, the other to his edition of 1819; if the repair work had been done after 1820 one note would have been adequate for both references. It is possible that John Murray would have had the volume repaired before he presented it to Scott. Both the original binding and the rebacking lack finesse, and it is probable that the nineteenth-century titling on the spine was done upside down (it is necessary to reverse the volume for the letter L already mentioned to appear correctly), although for the purpose of this description and collation it has been assumed that the titling is correct.

The volume was used by at least one other person as a notebook, but only Patrick Cary can be identified with certainty. Comparison with autograph letters preserved in the Bodleian Library places it beyond doubt that the entire manuscript of the poems is in the poet's own hand. One other hand may clearly be distinguished, the writer of the aphorisms, some of which appear under the date 1634. These take the form of short sentences such as: 'Cordialitie makes a commination of harts and minds which is the principall scope of amity'. The theme of amity and fidelity runs through all this section, and the passages may be notes taken from a book or a sermon. The same hand writes the first part of the library list. This list consists of the abbreviated titles of one hundred books, given without date of publication and in the vast majority of cases without authors. The titles are numbered from 1–60, followed by a group numbered 1–3 of which the third has been erased; these are all written in the same hand, probably all at the same time. The remainder of the list is numbered 61–97 and is written either in the same hand at a much later date or, possibly, in a second hand.

The books listed are entirely of a devotional or theological nature, and an attempt was made to identify a sample of them. Titles such as '56 A emanull of prayers' and '57 A emanull of meddetation' cannot be identified precisely, but suggest the Roman Catholic works of Richard

Broughton, *A manual of praiers used by the fathers of the primative church*, and *A new manual of old Christian Catholick meditations*. Other Roman Catholic works appear, such as St Augustine's *Meditations and Confessions*, Luis de Granada's *Of prayer and meditations*,[1] and Francis Meres's *The Sinner's guide* (a translation of works of Luis de Granada). But the majority of the titles identified were books written by Puritan divines; there are six works by Thomas Goodwin, three by Richard Sibbes, and two by John Preston, to name only the most prominent.[2] The dates of publication of these books are also interesting, ranging mainly over the latter part of the sixteenth and the first half of the seventeenth century (for this purpose, where a book appeared in several editions, the date of the first printing has been taken as the date of the book). It is clear that the first part of the library list, although written in the same hand as the aphorisms dated 1634, was written later than that date, as the following examples prove: '2 The vanity of thoughts' (Thomas Goodwin, *The Vanity of thoughts discovered*, 1637: STC 12043), '10 The golden septer' (John Preston, *The golden scepter held forth to the humble*, 1638: STC 20226), and '26 The honey-combe' (John Eaton, *The honey-combe of free justification by Christ alone*, 1642: Wing E 115). But, with the exception of one very doubtful attribution, none of the works identified in the first section of the list was printed after 1650. This is not the case with the second section, where works printed at a later date are to be found, especially towards the end of the list: '82 Jacobs wrestling' (either Francis Raworth, *Jacob's ladder . . . with Jacob's wrestling*, 1655: Wing R 373, or Thomas Taylor, *Jacob wrestling with God*, 1663: Wing T 555), '93 The mistical marriage' (Francis Rous, *The mysticall marriage*, 1653: Wing R 2024), and '97 Hamonds workes' (Henry Hammond, *The workes of*, 1674: Wing H 506).

This library list, although written in two different periods, is an obvious unity, the book collection of a person interested in theological writing of many hues, from the Catholicism of Granada to the Puritanism of Goodwin, with for good measure the Anglo-Catholicism of Hammond thrown in. The break in the compilation of the list apparently occurs round about 1650, the time at which Patrick Cary was inscribing his poems in the volume. It is therefore possible to put forward the following hypothesis about the history of the volume in the seventeenth century. The notebook, rubricated by a stationer, was acquired in 1634, used initially for a few pious notes and jottings, and subsequently for a list of theological books including works published in 1642. In 1651

---

[1] For these works see Allison and Rogers, *A catalogue of Catholic books in English* (1956), nos. 165, 166, 44, 45, 49, 50, 476.
[2] For these Puritan divines see William Haller, *The rise of Puritanism* (New York, 1938).

THE MANUSCRIPT

the notebook was given to Cary, who wrote his poems in it, and later returned it to the original owner, who continued the library list until 1674. If this is so, the presence of the initial L on the binding may identify the owner and compiler of the library list as Lucy Tomkins, at whose bidding Cary 'writt here' his poems.[1] It is, however, not clear when binding took place. The rubricated pages suggest that the notebook could have been an elaborate volume from the beginning, highly decorated and with its ornamental clasp an attractive possession for a lady. On the other hand, it could possibly have been bound and decorated after Cary had written in it and given the volume a greater value to the owner. Either possibility would fit the facts as they are known.

Cary's poems are written out carefully in a script which is small but perfectly legible, exceedingly neat and very graceful. There are only two or three emendations, the writing having evidently been done from a fair copy. Every poem is set precisely, as if printed, on its page; when a poem is not completed with the end of a page, catch-words are used as in printing. The verses fit line by line within the framework of the red border, only once or twice overlapping it; the size of the script is carefully adapted to the length of the line, and space is calculated meticulously, almost with a draughtsman's precision, even the longest lines fitting complete into the width of the page. The sense of the artist's eye persists, a handsome flourish filling the space left if a poem ends before the bottom of a page. A small but equally elegant flourish is set under most of the titles. Cary employs two types of script, a cursive and a non-cursive. The latter is used where a contemporary printer would use italic; but, since both his cursive and his non-cursive script are italic, I hesitate to distinguish the latter as 'italic', and have preferred to refer to it as his 'printed script'. He employs also other devices such as capitalization of whole words and variation in the size of letters to give special emphasis. The punctuation is also meticulous, and gives the impression of deliberate consideration. Another interesting feature, barely referred to by Scott in the Introduction to his edition, and not, as far as I know, taken into account by anyone who has written on Cary, is his use of emblematic sketches to illustrate the religious poems. These are fully discussed in Appendix A, p. 102.

For more than a century after Patrick Cary completed his last

---

[1] Weight is given to this tentative identification by evidence that Lucy Tomkins was born *c.* 1610 and died in 1677. (See p. 69.)

flourish and handed over the little volume to its 'onlie begetter', Mistress Lucy Tomkins, it disappeared from public view. However, far from being left to gather quiet dust on a library shelf, it was well thumbed and often handled. It was used as a song-book by candle-light as well as daylight, retaining traces of wax; it passed from hand to hand as men were drinking, not escaping an occasional stain. Favourite lyrics were marked in the margin; and pages with ballads written to the most popular tunes were turned so often that the edges became worn. Most often preferred were the verses written to the well-known tune 'Phillida flouts me', whose page is roughly trimmed at the outer edges, and has a tear which has been deftly patched. The religious poems were naturally read with less gusto, but their pages too are well worn.

At what point the book passed out of the keeping of the Uvedale circle we do not know. It next emerges from obscurity in 1771 in the possession of the Rev. Mr. Pierrepoint (or Pierrepont) Cromp, who at that date arranged for a selection of the poems to be published. I have not been able to discover how this gentleman came to own Patrick Cary's manuscript. I can only trace a few tenuous links and offer a conjecture, all centreing on the unusual name of Pierrepont. There are several slight associations between the Pierreponts and the Carys. As Royalist supporters they may have been friendly, and would at least have been acquainted: Robert Pierrepont, first Earl of Kingston, gave his life for the King in 1643, the same year as Patrick's brother Lucius, the second Viscount Falkland. That the families were not entirely strangers was evident in 1712, when the daughter of Evelyn Pierrepont, fifth Earl and first Duke of Kingston, married a connection of Walter Montagu, kinsman and benefactor of Patrick Cary (and incidentally became the famous Lady Mary Wortley Montagu).[1] The Rev. Pierrepont Cromp was rector of Holme Pierrepont,[2] the Kingston seat. Bearing the family name and holding the family living of Evelyn Pierrepont, second Duke of Kingston, he evidently enjoyed the ducal patronage, and would no doubt have access to the Pierrepont archives and library.

In 1806 comes a final slight but interesting link. In that year Charles (Meadows) Pierrepont, nephew of the second Duke, who had inherited his estates and assumed his name, was created Earl

---

[1] For the Pierreponts see *D.N.B.* xv, 1149, 1152.
[2] *Alumni Cantabrigienses*, I. i. 429.

Manvers;[1] and in the same year his son, the Hon. Henry Pierrepont, stood as godfather to Plantagenet Pierpont Cary, Patrick Cary's direct descendant, who later became the eleventh Viscount Falkland.[2] This would argue a family friendship of some standing.

At some time during this acquaintance the manuscript left the possession of the Uvedale circle. This may have occurred after 1696, when with the death of Elizabeth, Countess of Carlisle ('plump Besse' of Cary's poem, p. 78), the last surviving child of Sir William Uvedale, that branch of the family died out, and the Uvedale estate was divided and sold.[3] At all events, it seems possible that it was given, lent, or sold to the Pierreponts, in whose library it would have been found and acquired by the erudite Mr. Cromp. However that may be, reach him it did, and thus took a first tentative step towards literary recognition by venturing modestly into print.

II. THE EDITIONS

Patrick Cary's poems, which were not printed during his lifetime, or even during his century, have appeared in print, in whole or in part, four times. First in 1771, soon after the publication of Percy's *Reliques* had made popular a taste for literary antiquities, there was published a quarto pamphlet with the title *Poems from a Manuscript written in the time of Oliver Cromwell*, printed in London for 'J. Murray, No. 32, opposite St Dunstan's Church, Fleet Street'. It contains thirty-six pages including the title-page, from which pagination begins. The poet's name is not given with the title, but the 'Advertisement' bows to him in passing, although not so obsequiously as to the Rev. Mr. Cromp:

The following Poems are taken from a Manuscript Collection in the possession of the Rev. Mr Pierrepoint Cromp, a Gentleman whose taste, liberality and erudition at once serve and do honour to the cause of letters. They appear to have been written about the middle of the last century by one Carey, a man whom we now know nothing of, and whose reputation, possibly in his own time, never went beyond the circle of private friendship.

The omission of the poet's Christian name prevented the poems from being recognized as his until many years later.

Nine poems from Cary MS. are printed in this selection. First under the heading *SERIAE NUGAE* come four religious poems: 'Triolets', *EXPRIMETVR*, *Crux VIA Caelorum*, and

[1] D.N.B. xiii, 194.
[2] Information kindly supplied by the present Viscount Falkland.
[3] S.A.C. iii, 133.

'Whilst I beheld the necke o'th'*Dove*'. Then under *NUGAE LUSORIAE* follow five secular pieces: 'Surely now I'me out of danger', 'And can You thincke that this Translation', 'Good People of England! come heare mee relate', 'And now a Figge for th' lower House', and 'The Parliament ('tis sayd) resolv'd'. The spelling of the original verses was modernized, and some of the poems were given new titles. Comments on these and other relevant points, and on a number of variant readings, will be found under the individual poems in the Commentary. This slight production attracted little attention. The *Gentleman's Magazine* (xli (July 1771), 325) announced its coming publication, but did not honour it with a review. The *London Magazine* (xl (1771), 275) gave it a few lines which suggest that the reviewer had merely run a bored eye over the first few pages:

As the chief merit of these poems, which are of a serious cast, is the piety of their turn, we shall only say that a funeral sermon is likely to afford as much entertainment to our readers.

After its appearance the Rev. Pierrepont Cromp himself seems to have lost interest in his little manuscript volume, and left it with Murray's establishment, for some time before 1810 another John Murray presented it to Walter Scott.

Scott was charmed with his acquisition, and contributed to the *Edinburgh Annual Register* for 1810 a generous account of the unknown poet, from which it is evident that he was at the time unaware of the 1771 publication, for he says: 'It does not appear that Carey's poems were ever printed.' He was also ignorant as yet of the poet's real identity. Along with his eulogistic introductory notice he printed six of the poems. Four of these had appeared in the earlier section—'The Parliament ('tis sayd) resolv'd'; 'And now a Figge for th' lower House'; 'And can You thincke that this Translation'; and 'Whilst I beheld the necke o'th' *Dove*'. The other two poems chosen by Scott were the dedicatory Octave, and 'Come (fayth) since I'me parting'.

Unlike Mr. Cromp, Scott continued to show a lively interest in his discovery, as is evident from occasional references in his letters to 'my friend Patrick Carey'. By April 1819 he had decided to publish the verses as a whole, and dispatched them to James Ballantyne, his printer, with an Introduction dated 1 April 1819. For the next few months his letters contain allusions and requests of increasing impatience:[1] the engraver must be hurried with the coat of arms for the title-page, or the book printed without it; James is to send a copy by speediest conveyance to London to his brother John, who must arrange for disposal of the edition—it should be offered first to John Murray, who gave Scott the original manuscript. The reason for this urgency, when it appears in a letter to John Ballantyne, has a very human touch: Scott's elder son has just taken up a commission in the army; cash is short until *Ivanhoe* comes out, and 'Walter's rattle-traps' are 'abominably extravagant'.

The edition, duly published in London by John Murray of Albemarle Street, was ready by August 1819, a handsome quarto in boards, with the title *Trivial Poems and Triolets, written in obedience to Mrs Tomkin's Commands, by Patrick Carey, 20th Aug. 1651*. It has a short introduction, a summary of Scott's article in the *Register* of 1810, and 67 pages of text, including three pages of notes, mainly on allusions in the political verses. A number of copies have a small printed slip bearing the date 1820 pasted over the date 1819. The reason for this is a minor mystery, which reference to John Murray's archives does not completely solve. Murray's catalogue states that the book was published in 1820. However, the records also show that in August 1819 2,811 copies received Murray's 'acceptance' (which probably means his approval of the finished book), and that in the same month thirteen copies were sent to Scott. Murray's stock book records that copies arrived from the printer in October 1819, but that no copies went out (presumably to the Trade) until April 1820.[2] One possibility would be that all the copies were printed with the date 1819, that Scott received advance copies bearing this date, and that before the book was sent out for sale in 1820 the date was altered accordingly. Whatever the explanation of the altered date may be, the book was certainly in print in 1819, and Scott, who had reserved twenty copies for himself, was busy in September[3] sending some to his friends. This edition contained the text of all the poems, closely following the original spelling, although with inconsistent treatment of variations. There are a number of misreadings, which are noted in the Commentary, with other points of interest, under the poems concerned.

Scott's Introduction was not signed, but its dating from

---

[1] Scott, *Letters*, v, 345, 425, 427.
[2] For this information I am indebted to Mr. John Murray.
[3] Scott, *Letters*, v, 503.

Abbotsford was sufficient indication of its authorship. Referring to his previous account of the poems in the *Register*, he notes that his researches have not enabled him to add anything to that information, which he goes on to summarize:

> The reader is here introduced to a Bard of the seventeenth century, as staunch a cavalier, and nearly as good a poet, as the celebrated Colonel Lovelace.... Of the poems of this forgotten writer, only one manuscript copy is known to exist... and it is from this single copy that we can extract anything concerning the author, Patrick Carey, who appears to have been a gentleman, a loyalist during the civil war, a lawyer, and a rigid High-Churchman, if not a Roman Catholic.[1]

Then follows a description of the heraldic device on the title-page of the religious poems, in the hope, he writes, that these particulars may help some English antiquarian to discover the family of Patrick Cary. He mentions without further comment that the devotional verses are illustrated with 'small emblematical vignettes', and ends with a warm though balanced assessment of Cary's poetic achievement.

Even after this publication appeared Scott kept up interest in his poet. He encourages Surtees, as I have mentioned, to seek out his identity: after this has been discovered, he brings him gracefully and affectionately into *Woodstock*. He rewards a lady who has sent him a miniature of Patrick's famous brother Lucius, with one of his few remaining copies of *Trivial Poems and Triolets*.[2] His own copy of his edition in the Abbotsford library has a manuscript note in his own hand referring to the 1771 volume, the existence of which was not known to him at the time of his 1819 publication.

The last time Patrick Cary's poems appeared in print they assumed the form by which they are now best known, being included by Saintsbury in his *Minor Poets of the Caroline Period*, ii (1906).[3] Saintsbury reproduces the title-page of Scott's edition, contributes an Introduction of some four pages, explaining the discovery of the poet's identity and giving a somewhat roseate criticism of the verses, and includes pedigrees of the Cary and Uvedale families. He then reprints the poems from Scott's edition, modernizing the spelling, but not collating Scott's text in any way with Cary MS. His pages have a sprinkling of footnotes elucidating some allusions

---

[1] Scott, Introduction, p. iii. [2] Scott, *Letters*, viii, 390.
[3] Saintsbury, pp. 447–82.

and correcting conjecturally some of Scott's misreadings. He also reprints in full Scott's Introduction and the notes that close the 1819 edition. As the incomplete edition of 1771 and Scott's 1819 edition are now rare, Cary's poems have been up to the present accessible mainly in this collection of Saintsbury's, which for all its pleasantness has a number of inaccuracies and gives an inadequate reproduction of the text, as well as lacking the advantage, for biographical material, of a good deal of information that has since come to light.

III. THE TEXT

The text of Cary MS. presents little difficulty, as the unique manuscript appears to have been written out by the poet from a fair copy. There are very few emendations, and the whole text is set out very plainly and clearly. The punctuation of the original is careful but idiosyncratic. Rather than adopt complete repunctuation, I have kept closely to Cary's usage, apart from silently supplying missing full stops at the ends of lines, and making several slight adjustments in particular instances, which are noted in the Commentary.

I have preserved the original spelling, with all its variant forms, except for two points. The first is that I have followed modern practice in the treatment of *i/j* and *u/v* in both upper and lower case. In lower case Cary consistently uses *i* for both *i* and *j* and, with a single exception, *u* for both *u* and *v*. In upper case he uses two slightly different forms for *I/J* in his cursive script, and *I* for both capitals in his printed script. For *U/V* he usually employs U, but occasionally *V*. (A note on the incidence of *u/v*, *U/V* in Cary MS. is given on p. xcvi.) Since by the time Cary wrote modern usage had established itself in the printing house, it seemed best to standardize to modern practice. I have made two exceptions. The first is in the sonnet *EXPRIM-ETVR*, where Cary was plainly attempting to imitate a lapidary inscription (see Commentary, p. 99). The second is in the inscription *EX DOLORE, GAVDIVM* under the emblematic drawing on p. 54. The inscription is here part of the emblem, and again requires archaic lapidary style.

My only other departure from Cary's spelling is in the handling of the apostrophe in certain cases, where irregularities in Cary's usage have been regularized. Thus the forms 't'is', 't'were', 't'will', 't'has', 't'had', which occur almost invariably in the manuscript, have been altered to the more logical forms "'tis', "twere', etc. Also the forms 'n'ere', 'e'ene', which Cary habitually uses, have been employed throughout the printed text, replacing the occasionally occurring forms 'nere', 'eene'.

In dealing with titles, as distinct from the text, I have standardized their form. This has involved modernizing Cary's occasional use of y^e for *the*. I have also standardized the form of the scriptural references, which show a number of variations.

In transferring the poems from manuscript to print difficult problems arise, for which there can be no unquestionably right solution. The poems, except for the sonnet $EXPRIMETVR$, are written in a clear and graceful cursive script, throughout which variations occur. These are not haphazard. They are obviously employed with some deliberation, and the whole manuscript is so meticulously written and punctuated, and so lovingly set out, that such differences in presentation cannot be dismissed lightly. Cary evidently intended by these variations from his normal cursive script to give emphasis to certain words and phrases. But though Cary's intentions are clear enough his practice was not wholly consistent. An editor has to decide both how to represent Cary's range of devices in print and how to ensure that his inconsistencies do not interfere with his obvious intention to secure emphasis in the right places.

To indicate emphasis Cary uses four devices: initial capitalization; capitalization of entire words; a printed script both for single words and occasionally for passages; and variation in the size of letters in both cursive and printed script. The first three present no problem. I have followed Cary's use of initial capitals, although this shows frequent inconsistency, particularly in the matter of pronouns. Reference to the facsimile following p. xcvi might suggest that Cary was a lone pioneer in capitalizing the third person pronoun when it referred to the Deity, until one notices that it is similarly dignified when referring merely to a sailor. In general it is his practice to capitalize the nominative of personal pronouns; however, all cases of 'it' and oblique cases of other personal pronouns are rarely capitalized unless they bear particular emphasis.

When entire words are capitalized in the manuscript, this form has been mainly retained although the occasional appearance of a larger initial capital in such words has been ignored. Where Cary used a printed script for words, phrases, or lines occurring within passages written in his normal cursive hand, these have been rendered by italics. As all but a few proper names in Cary MS. are in printed script, I have italicized such names throughout. About these points there is little difficulty.

However, the fourth device—variation in size of letters in both cursive and printed script—presents more complications. In the first place, it is sometimes far from easy to decide whether Cary really intended to write a word larger, or whether he merely happened to do so by accident. After various attempts to convey the force of these apparent efforts at emphasis by the use of capitals of various sizes, I became convinced not only that this was impracticable, but also that the results were tiresome and misleading. Fussiness, over-emphasis, and falsification of emphasis, rather than clarification of the meaning, resulted; and I realized that what is charming, idiosyncratic, and revealing in a carefully written manuscript loses its quality and is positively ugly in print. I decided, therefore, to standardize to what was seventeenth-century printers' usage, which is to reverse the type for emphasis. Thus I have used italic for words written large when they occur in cursive script, and roman when they occur in printed script. This means that in passages in cursive script both words that Cary printed and words he wrote large are represented by italics; and in passages in his printed script words printed large are represented by roman type. More boldly, I have attempted to remedy his inconsistencies when he appears to have failed to carry out his own intentions.

These points may be illustrated by reference to the poem 'Whilst I beheld the necke o'th'*Dove*', of which a reproduction from the manuscript follows p. xcvi. The theme is, briefly, that objects which delight the five senses of man remind him that he owes all he has to God. The poem has six nine-line stanzas, of which the first five are constructed on the same pattern. The first, second, and last lines of each are in cursive script, the sense symbol being mentioned at the end of the first and last lines, where in seven cases out of ten it is in printed script. But at the end of stanzas 1, 3, and 5 the writer has, instead used large cursive for *Dove* and *Swan* and full capitals for *Rose*—this last being an obvious over-emphasis. I have standardized by giving all ten words in italic. The remaining six lines of these stanzas carry a message in direct speech, and are in printed script. I have italicized them. But, within these lines, in stanzas 1, 2, and 4, emphasis is placed, by larger printed script, on words that contrast with the sense symbol (*Raven, Owle, Gall*). Here again there is inconsistency, *Gall* being printed in full capitals. This is also an overemphasis, since it should not be more important than *Bee*. These words which are written large to give emphasis within the italicized passages I have given in roman type. But, though in most cases distinction is clearly intended, in some the distinction is slight, and it is difficult to tell whether Cary intended emphasis or was merely writing a word in a slightly larger script by accident. I have chosen to regard *Gall* and *Honny* in l.35 as intentionally larger, and *Prayse* and *Sent* in the preceding verse as accidentally so, the two lines in which they occur being in a slightly larger script than the following lines. But I am aware that another editor might have come to a different decision. The last stanza, which sums up the argument, is in cursive script for the first eight lines, with significant words (e.g. *Creatures, Senses, Mind*) in printed script. These words I have italicized. The whole of the last line of this stanza is in printed script in the manuscript, and has also been italicized. The last word, however, is in full printed capitals; and, as this is evidently meant to carry special weight, the name of God being used as the climax of the whole poem, I have shown it in roman capitals.

This poem and the sonnet *EXPRIMETVR* are the most difficult typographically; but similar problems occur in other parts of the text, and these I have dealt with also along the lines indicated above.

Note on incidence of *u/v* and *U/V* in Cary MS.

The following is a summary of the incidence of *u/v* and *U/V* in Cary MS.:

(1) *u* and *v* appear as *u* with one exception—*vias* (p. 60, title).
(2) *U* and *V* appear as *U* in all instances in the text except eight, where *V* is used, viz., *Vinter* (p. 12, l. 43); *Victoria* (p. 14, l. 17); VIA (p. 49, title); *Vidi* (p. 56, scriptural text); BVILDER'S (p. 63, l. 6); AVARICE (p. 64, l. 12); REVENGE (p. 64, l. 13); GVILT (p. 63, l. 14). In addition there are three examples in the titles of emblematic illustrations: GAVDIVM (p. 54, two instances); and EXPRIMETVR (p. 64), which also serves as a title to the sonnet that follows. For several changes involving *U* and *V* which I have made in printing the text of this sonnet, see Commentary, p. 99.

5. Who wishes then for Power, or Plenty craues,
O lett him Looke downe on them both from hence,
Heel see that Kings in Thrones, as well as Slaues
Are but poore Wormes, enslau'd to widest Sence:
Heel find that name are Poore who cant for nought,
But They who hauing much, for more haue sought.

6. Come Poore Selfed Wretch, climbe up to mee;
Thy naked Hermitage will teach all this:
I will teach thee too where truest Riches bee,
And how to gayne a neuer fading Blisse.
I will make thee see that truely None Doe raigne,
But Those who scorne our common Soueraign'ty.

The inuisible things of him from the
Creation of the World are cleerely
seene; being Understood by the
things that are made. Eph. 1: Rom. 1. 20.

1. Whilst I behold He neche o'th' Doue,
I pry'se and read these words.
This pretty Dye
Which takes your Eye
Is not at all the Birds.
The ducky Rauen might
Haue with these colours pleas'd your sight,
Had God but chose soe to ordayne aboue.
Thus behold more the Doue.
a. W. L. H.

2. Whilst I admire the Nightingale,
These notes She warbling me:
Noe melody
Indeed haue I,
Admire mee then noe more:
God has itt in his choice
To giue the Owle, or Mee this voyce:
Tis Hee, tis Hee that makes mee tell my Tale.
Thus sang the Nightingale.

3. I smelt and pray'd the fragrant Rose;
Blushing, thus answer'd She.
The Prayse you gaue,
The Sent I haue,
Doe not belong to mee:
This harmelesse Odour None
But onely God indeed does owne:
To bee his Keepers, my poore Leaues Hee chose,
And they reply'd the ROSE.

4. I tooke the Hunny from the Bee;
On th' Bagge thatwords more seeme.
More sweet then this
Perchance Nought is,
Yet GALL, it might haue beene:
If God itt should soe please,
He could still make itt such with ease;
And as well Gall to Honny change can Hee.
This learnt I of the Bee. I touch'd, &

Facsimile of pp. 4–5 of Cary MS.

5. I touch'd and lik'd the Downe, o'th' Swanne,
But felt these prooks there wrik.
Bristles, Thornes here
I soone should beare.
Did God ordayne but itt;
If my DOWNE to thy Touch
Seeme soft, and smooth, God made itt such;
Giue more, or take all this away, Hee can.
This may I taught by th' Swan.

6. All Creatures then, enforce to God
That th' loue him all, but J.
My Senses find
True what my Mind
Would still lift does Deny!
Hence Pride out of my fiule!
Oh, if Thou shalt nere more controule;
Ile leame thy Lesson, and escape the Rod.
I too, haue all from GOD.

What hast Thou
that Thou that
Thou did'st not
receaue?
I. Corinth.
C. IV. u. VII.
Now, if Thou did'st re-
ceaue it; why dost thou
glory, as if Thou hadst
not receaued it?

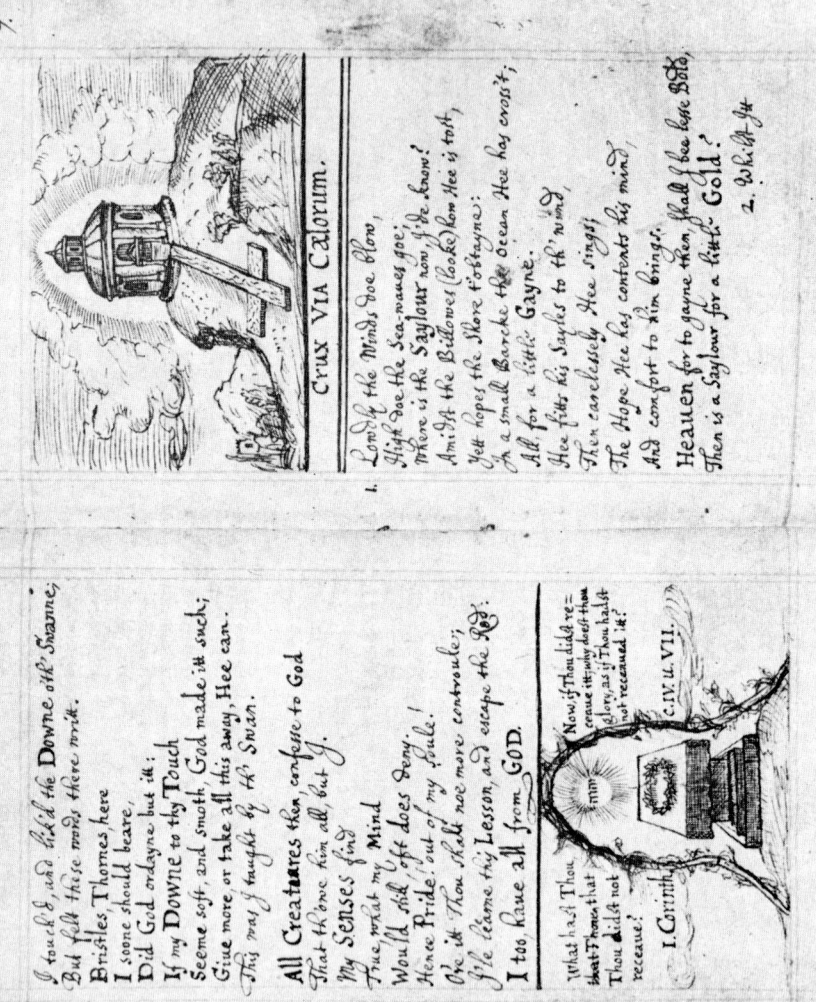

CRUX VIA CŒLORUM.

1. Lowdly the Winds doe blow,
High Goe the Sea-waues goe;
Where is the Saylour now, I'de know!
Am: Iff the Billowes (looke) how Hee is tost,
Yett hopes the Shore t'obtayne:
In a small Barcke the Ocean Hee has crost;
All for a little Gayne.
Hee fitts his Sayles to th' wind
Then carelessely Hee sings;
The Hope Hee has contents his mind,
And comfort to him brings.
Heauen for to gayne then shall bee bee Both,
Then is a Saylour for a little Gold?

2. Whilst y.

The Poems of
Patrick Cary

Triviall Ballades

writt here

in obedience to M^es. *Tomkin's* commands

by

J. Patr: Carey 1651

August the 20th

AN OCTAVE

Madame:
  I blush, but must obay. You'l have itt soe;
  And one such word of yours, stopps all excuse:
  Yett (pray) bee sure that You let Others know
  How *You,* not *Pride,* did mee to this induce;
  Else, when to Any these harsh Rimes you show,
  They'l suffer many a Flout; I, much Abuse:
      Since 'tis acknowledg'd that They *here* have place,
      Not for their *Worth,* but meerely through your *Grace.*

J. Patr: Carey

BALLADES

To the tune
Once I lov'd a Mayden Fayre &c.

1. Fayre-One! if thus kind You bee,
    Yett intend a Slaughter;
    Fayth You'll loose your paynes with mee,
    Else-where seeke hereafter:
    Though your Lookes bee sharp, & quicke,   5
    Thincke not (pray) to drill mee;
    Love, perchance, may make mee sicke,
    But will never kill mee.

2. Were my Mistresse n'ere soe browne,
    Yett, if kind, I'de prize her;   10
    Who's most fayre, if She but frowne,
    I shall soone dispize her:
    I love Kindnesse, and not Face;
    Who scornes mee, I hate her:
    Courtesy gives much more grace,   15
    In my mind, then Feature.

3. Red and White adorne the Cheeke
    Lesse by farre, then Smiling;
    That's the Beauty I most seeke,
    That Charme's most beguiling.   20
    Fayre-One! now you know my mind,
    See if th'Humour take you:
    I shall love you, whilst Y'are kind;
    When Y'are not, forsake you.

To the tune
I'le doe by Thee, as n'ere was donne

1.   The Ermine is without all spott,
    And harmelesse is the Dove;
    The Lambe is innocent, but not
    Like to my chastest Love:
    Soe pure a Flame did never shine   5
    From any Breast before;
    And (trust mee) such an One as Mine
    Thou'lt never meet with more.

2.   Hadst Thou accepted of my Heart,
    And us'd itt well awhile;   10
    Hadst Thou but sweetned all itt's smart
    With One poore word, One smile;
    Nay hadst Thou not, with angry scorne,
    Bid itt Thenceforth give o're;
    Itt would not then have thus forborne,   15
    'T had lov'd thee evermore.

3.   But since Thou didst my Love requite
　　With soe much coy disdayne,
　　Pretending that thy Honnour might
　　From thence receave some stayne,   20
　　My wronged Heart (being innocent)
　　Broke all the chaynes Itt wore,
　　And vow'd, to give thee full content,
　　Itt n'ere would love thee more.

4.   Thus to a cruell Sheppeardesse   25
　　A poore sad Shepheard sung;
　　Hee wept (such Greife could doe noe lesse)
　　His pipe away Hee flung:
　　Then rising, for her hand Hee strove,
　　Kiss'd his last kisse, and swore   30
　　That from that time, to Her of Love
　　Hee'd never speake word more.

To the tune
I would give twenty pound &c.

1.   There's noe Woeman, but I'me caught
　　Whilst She lookes with Kind eyes on mee;
　　If I love not then, the Fault
　　Is unjustly cast uppon mee:
　　They are to bee blamed, not I,   5
　　If with freedome still I hover;
　　Were I us'd but courteously
　　I should soone becomme a Lover.

2. Did I any one exclude
   For her Dye, or for her Feature, 10
   I should grant my selfe a rude
   Manner-lesse, hard-hearted Creature:
   But since I except gainst none
   By whom I am not contemned,
   If I can't find such an One 15
   Pray tell, Who's to bee condemned?

3. Not by Frownes, but Smiles, my Heart
   (I declare't) is to bee chained;
   On fayre termes with itt I'le part,
   But by foule 'twill n'ere bee gained: 20
   Take then other taskes in hand
   You, who loure, and scorne to crave itt;
   But Who's kind shall itt command,
   And for th'asking, She shall have itt.

To the tune
of
Bobbing Joane

1. I n'ere yett saw a lovely Creature
   (Were She a Widdow, Mayd, or Wife)
   But streight within my breast her Feature
   Was paynted, strangely to the life:
   If out of sight 5
   (Though n'ere soe bright)
   I straight-wayes lost her picture quite.

2. Itt still was mine, and Other's wonder
   To see mee court soe eagerly;
   Yett soone as Absence did me sunder 10
   From those I lov'd, quite cur'd was I.
   The reason was
   That my Brest has
   In stead of *Heart,* a *Looking-glasse.*

3. And as those Formes which lately shined
    I'th'glasse, are easily defac'd;
    Those Beautyes soe, which were enshrined
    Within my Brest, are soone displac'd:
    Both seeme, as They
    Would n'ere away;
    Yett last, but whilst the Lookers stay.

4. Then lett noe Woeman thincke that ever
    In absence I shall Constant prove;
    Till some occasion does us sever
    I can, as true as Any, love:
    But when that Wee
    Once parted bee,
    Troth I shall court the next I see.

To the tune
of
Troy-towne

1. Fayre Beautyes! if I doe confesse
    My selfe inconstant in my drincke;
    You ought not to love mee the lesse,
    I say but that which most Men thincke:
    And (troth) there is lesse hurtfull Art
    In a light Toungue, then a false Heart.

2. Some use to sweare that you will find
    Nothing but Truth, within their Brests;
    Yett waver more then does the Wind,
    When in a Tempest least Itt rests:
    Nought of my Thoughts I say to you,
    But what you'l find to bee most true.

3. More then I promise, I'le performe;
   They give you Oaths, but keepe them not:
   You build i'th'ayre, when as you forme
   False hopes on Vowes long since forgott.
      Leave, leave them then and deale with mee;
      Soe, you will n'ere deceaved bee.

4. Fayrely beforehand I declare
   That when I'me weary, I shall leave;
   Fore-warned thus, you'l bee aware,
   Whilst falser Men would yee deceave:
      Besides, in this I nothing doe
      But what I'de sweare you will doe too.

5. When of your Love I weary grow,
   Before I change, I'le tell you on't;
   Doe you the same when You are soe,
   And give mee time to thincke uppon't:
      Else-where I soone shall place my Heart;
      Then, kindly Wee'l shake hands, and part.

         To the tune
    But I fancy lovely Nancy &c.

1. Surely now I'me out of danger
   And noe more need feare my heart;
   Who loves thus to bee a Ranger
   N'ere will fix in any part;
   All the graces
   Of fayre faces
   I have seene, and yett am free:
   I like many,
   But not any
   Shall subdue my Libertee.

2. *Anne* was once the word, which mooved
    Most my heart, I'le itt avvow;
    Twelve att least, soe call'd, I've loved,
    But I care not for them now:
    Yett if ever 15
    I endeavour
    For a Mistresse, that's her Name;
    These are Fancyes,
    But with *Nancyes*
    Luckiest still hath beene my Flame. 20

3. With three *Bettyes* I was taken;
    Yett noe more, then whilst in sight:
    One of them is now forsaken,
    And her Sister has her Right.
    T'Other's pritty, 25
    But (what pitty!)
    In a Castle She is penn'd:
    The Third plenty
    Has for twenty,
    But She's courted by my Friend. 30

4. *Lucyes* there are two: for Beauty,
    Vertue, Witt, beyond compare:
    Th'One's too high for love, in duety
    I respect, but noe more dare:
    As for t'Other, 35
    Though a Mother
    (As I take't) to halfe a score,
    Had She tarryed
    To bee marryed,
    Shee'd have had one Suitour more. 40

5. I know two, and each a *Mary*;
   One's the greatest of this Land:
   Th'*Oxford-Vintner* made mee wary
   Least I should a gazing stand.
   Though I like her,   45
   Most unlike her
   Is the secound; and I sweare,
   Had her Portion
   Some proportion
   With my wants, I'de marry there.   50

6. *Katherne* has a lippe that's ruddy,
   Swelling soe, it seemes to poute;
   How to kisse her I did studdy,
   But could never bring't about.
   Beauteous *Frances*   55
   Loves Romances,
   But (alasse!) Shee's now a wife;
   She makes verses,
   And reherses
   With great grace *Primaleon's* life.   60

7. *Doll* has purest brests, much whiter
   Then their milck, but naked still;
   That's the reason why I slight her,
   For I've seene them to my fill.
   Jane is slender,   65
   But God send her
   Lesse opinion of her Race!
   Nell's soe spotted
   That Sh' has blotted
   Allmost out, her little face.   70

8. *Peg* is blith; but O She tattles;
   Nothing's soe demure as *Ruth*.
   Susan's head is full of rattles:
   Rachell preacheth well in truth.
   Were not *Tolly* 75
   Melancholly,
   She hath parts I most could prize;
   Amorous *Sophy*
   Reares noe trophy
   On my heart, with her gray Eyes. 80

9. Thus I still find somewhat wanting,
   Allwayes full of *Iffs* or *Ands*;
   Where there's Beauty, Money's scanting;
   Something still my choice withstands.
   'Tis my fortune; 85
   I'le importune
   With noe prayers, my destiny:
   If I'me scorned,
   I'me not horned;
   That's some Joy in misery. 90

To the Tune of *The Healths*

1. Come (fayth) since I'me parting, & that God knowes when
   The walls of sweet *Wickham* I shall see aghen;
   Lett's e'ene have a frolicke, & drincke like tall men,
       Till Heads with healths goe round. ❧

2. And first to S^r. *William*. I'le take't on my knee; 5
   Hee well doth deserve that a Brimmer itt bee:
   More brave Entertaynements None e're gave then Hee;
       Then lett his Health goe round. ❧

3. Next to his chast Lady, who loves him alife;
   And whilst wee are drincking to soe good a wife,   10
   The Poore of the Parish will pray for her life.
      Besure her Health goe round. ❧

4. And then to young *Will*, the Heyre of this place;
   Hee'l make a brave man, you may see't in his face;
   I onely could wish wee had more of the Race,   15
      Att least lett his Health goe round. ❧

5. To well-grac'd *Victoria* the next roome Wee owe;
   As vertuous Shee'l prove as her Mother I trow,
   And somewhat in Huswifry more She will know;
      O lett her Health goe round! ❧   20

6. To plump *Besse* her Sister, I drinck down this cup:
   Birlackins (my Masters) each man must take't up;
   'Tis foule play (I barre itt) to simper and sup
      When such a Health goes round. ❧

7. And now helter-skelter to th' rest of the house,   25
   The most are good Fellowes, and love to carowse;
   Who's not, may goe sneake-up; Hee's not worth a Louse
      That stoppes a health i'th'round. ❧

8. To th' *Clearcke*, soe hee'l learne to drincke in the morne;
   To *Heynous*, that stares when he'has quaft up his horne;   30
   To *Philip*, by whom good Ale n'ere was forlorne;
      These Lads can drincke a round. ❧

9. *John Chandler!* come on, here's some warm Beere for you;
   A health to the man that this liquor did brew:
   Why *Hewet*! there's for thee; nay take't, 'tis thy due,   35
      But see that Itt goe round. ❧

10. Hott *Coles* is on fire, and fayne would bee quench'd:
    As well as his Horses the *Groome* must bee drench'd.
    Who's else? lett him speake, if his thirst Hee'd have
       stench'd,
          Or have his Health goe round. ❧   40

11. And now to the Woemen, who must not bee coy.
    A Glasse, mistresse *Cary*, you know's but a Toy:
    Come come Mistresse *Sculler*, noe *Perdonnez moy*,
          Itt must, Itt must goe round. ❧

12. *Dame Nell;* soe you'l drinck, wee'l allow you a Soppe. 45
    Up with't *Mary Smith*; in your draught never stoppe.
    Law ther-now *Nan German* has left n'ere a droppe,
          And soe must all the Round. ❧

13. *Jane, Joane*, Goody *Lee*, great *Meg*, & the lesse,
    Yee must not bee squeamish, but doe as did *Besse*:   50
    How th'Others are named if I could but guesse,
          I'de call them to the round. ❧

14. And now, for my Farwell, I drincke up this Quart;
    To you, Lads, and Lasses, e'ene with all my heart:
    May I find yee ever, as now when wee part,   55
          Each Health still goeing round. ❧

To the tune
I'le tell thee Dicke that I have beene &c.

1. And can You thincke that this Translation
   Will benefitt att all our nation,
   Though fayre bee the Pretence?
   'Tis meet, you say, that in the Land
   Each One our Lawes should understand,   5
   Since Wee are govern'd thence.

2. But tell mee pray, if ever you
　　Read th'*English* of *Watt Mountague*,
　　Is't not more hard then *French*?
　　And yett That will much easyer bee　　　　10
　　Then the strange gibbring mish-mash, Wee
　　Shall hence-forth heare att th'Bench.

3. For from the Lawes whilst *French* wee'd banish,
　　Wee shall bring in *Italian, Spanish,*
　　And forty Nations more:　　　　　　　　15
　　Who'l then peruse the *Text*, must know
　　Greeke, Latine, Dutch, both High, and Low;
　　With *Hebrew* too, before.

4. Because i'th'*Greeke* ther's chang'd a Letter,
　　That They can understand itt better,　　　20
　　Fooles onely, will pretend;
　　As Hee, who did himselfe perswade
　　That Hee spoke *Latine*, cause Hee made
　　In *Bus* each word to end.

5. But had wee *English* words enough,　　　25
　　Yett ought wee never to allow
　　This turning of our *Lawes*:
　　Much lesse t'admitt that att the Barre
　　The *Merchand, Clowne,* or Man of *Warre*
　　Should plead (forsooth) his cause.　　　　30

6. Wordes may bee common, cleare, and pure,
　　Yett still the *Sence* remayne obscure,
　　And we as wise, as when
　　Wee should some long Oration heare,
　　Which in a new-found Language were,　　35
　　N'ere heard by us till then.

7. 'T was not the *Language*, 'twas the *Matter*
   (But that wee love our selves to flatter)
   That most times darcknesse brung:
   Some Questions in Philosophy,   40
   To puzzle Schollers would goe nigh,
   Though putt in any Toungue.

8. The *Shoe-maker*, beyond the Shoe
   Must not presume to have to doe,
   A *Painter* say'd of old: 45
   Hee sayd aright; for Each man ought
   To meddle with the Craft Hee's taught,
   And bee noe farther bold.

9. What th'*Anchor* is, few *Plough-men* know;
   Saylers can't tell what meanes *Gee-ho*;   50
   Termes proper hath each *Trade*:
   Nay, in our very sports, the *Bowler*,
   The *Tennis-player, Huntsman, Fowler,*
   New names for Things have made.

10. Soe Words i'th'*Lawes* are introduc'd   55
    Which common Talke has never us'd;
    And therfore sure ther's need
    That the *Gown'd Tribe* bee sett a part
    To learne by industry this Art,
    And that none else may pleade.   60

11. Our *Church* still flourishing w'had seene
    If th' *holy-Writt* had ever beene
    Kept out of *Laymens* reach;
    But when 'twas *English'd,* men halfe-witted,
    Nay, *Woemen* too, would bee permitted   65
    T'expound all *Texts* and preach.

12. Then what Confusion did arise!
    Coblers, Devines gan to dispise,
    Soe that They could but spell:
    This, *Ministers* to scorne did bring;   70
    Preaching was held an easy Thing,
    Each-one might doe't as well.

13. This Gulfe, *Church-government* did swallow;
    And after will the *Civill* follow,
    When Lawes translated are: 75
    For Ev'ry man that lists, will prattle;
    Pleading will be but *Twittle-twatle,*
    And nought but *Noyse* att Bar.

14. Then lette's e'ene bee content t'obay,
    And to beleeve what Judges say,   80
    Whilst for us, *Lawyers* brawle:
    Though Fower, or Five bee thence undonne;
    'Tis better have some justice donne,
    Then to have *None* at all.

To the tune
That we may row with my P. over the Ferry

1. Good People of England! come heare mee relate
   Some misteryes of our young *purse-sucking State*,
   Whereby Ev'ry man may conceave out of's pate
   A reason for things here ordayned of late.
   Heigh-downe, downe, derry derry downe,   5
   Heighdowne downe derry!
   What e're the State resolves, lett us bee merry.

2. French Clarret was banish'd, (as most doe suppose)
   Cause *Noll* would have nought here, soe red as his *Nose*;
   Or else cause Itt's Crimson from thence first arose: 10
   'T has tooke our wine from us, would't were in my Hose.
           Heigh downe, downe &c.

3. Since that, hee most bravely himselfe did entrench,
   Beleaguer'd, and tooke (as he thought) a Scotch *Wench*;
   But by th'tottring of's *Toter*, Hee has found She was
      French;   15
   And therfore that Toungue is now silenc'd att th'Bench.
         Heigh downe, downe &c.

4. His wrath gainst th'whole nation I cannot much blame,
      Since by't was endanger'd a *Nose* of such fame;
   That's England's great Standard, & doth more inflame 20
   You People, then e're did That att *Nottingham*.
         Heigh downe, downe &c.

5. *Noll*! e'ene turne to Hebrew the Lawes of our Land,
   For (howsoe're) wee never shall them understand;
   But th'Act of forbidding French wines counter-mand, 25
   Oddsniggs else wee'l pisse out thy fuming Fire-brand.
   Heigh downe, downe, derry derry downe!
   Heigh downe, downe derry!
   Till Clarett bee restor'd, lett us drincke Sherry.

        To the tune
       Will and Tom &c.

Dicke. 1. *Jacke!* nay prithee come away,
            This is noe time for sadnesse;
            Pan's cheife feast is kept to day,
            Each Shepeard showes his gladnesse:
            W'are to meet All on the Greene,   5
            To dance and sport together;
            O what Brav'ry will bee seene!
            I hope 'twill prove fayre weather.

2. Looke I've gott a new suit on;
   Say Man! how likes't the colour?
   Will't not take *Nell's* eyes anonne?
   All Greenes then this, are duller.
   Marcke how trim'd up is my Hooke,
   This Ribband was *Nell's* favour:
   Jacke the wench has a sweet Looke,
   I'le dye but I will have her.

Jacke. 3. *Dicke*, e'ene goe alone for mee;
   By *Nell* thou art expected:
   I noe Love have there to see,
   Of all I am rejected.
   Att my ragges each Mayd would flout,
   If seene with such a Shiner;
   Noe. I'le n'ere sett others out;
   I'le stay till I am finer.

4. Shall I goe to sitt alone,
   Scorn'd e'ene by *Meg* o'th'Dayry?
   Whilst proud *Tom* lyes hugging *Joane*,
   And *Robin* kisses *Mary*.
   Shall I see my Rivall *Will*
   Receave kind lookes from *Betty*?
   Both of them I'de sooner kill:
   Att thought on't, Lord, how frett I?

5. 'Cause Hee has a flocke of Sheepe,
   And is an elder Brother,
   'Cause (poore Hireling!) those I keepe
   Belong unto another,
   I must loose what's mine by right,
   And lett the rich Foole gayne her:
   I'le att least keepe out of sight,
   Since Hopelesse e're t'obtayne her.

Dicke. 6. Courage Man. Thy Case is not
    Soe bad, as Thou doest take itt:
    Yett 'tis ill; could I (God wott!)
    Much better would I make itt.
    Hee is Rich; Thou, Poore; 't were much   45
    Wer't Thou preferr'd by 'a Woeman;
    Woemen though keepe sometimes touch,
    But (sooth) 'tis not soe common.

    7. Thou, unto thy Pipe can'st sing
    Love-songs of thine owne making;   50
    Hee, nor that, nor any thing
    Knowes how to doe, that's taking.
    She did love thee once, and swore
    N'ere (through her fault) to loose thee;
    If She keepe her oath, before   55
    The Richer, She will choose thee.

Jacke. 8. Never, never. 'Lasse! such Oathes
    Have force but for few howers:
    If She lik'd once, now She loathes;
    And smiles noe more, but lowers.   60
    Scarce his suit had Hee apply'de,
    But She lov'd mee noe longer:
    Soone my Fayth She gan deride;
    For Wealth, then Fayth, is stronger.

    9. Farewell Shepeard then. Bee gonne;   65
    The Feast noe stay here brooketh:
    Prithee marcke *Besse* there anonne,
    If kind on *Will* She looketh.
    Who loves truely, loves to heare
    Tales, that encrease his Fier;   70
    I, alasse! bade tyding feare,
    And yett for Newes inquier.

To the tune
But that n'ere troubles mee Boyes &c.

1. And now a Figge for th'lower House;
    The Army I doe sett att nought:
    I care not for them both, a louse;
    For spent is my last Groat Boyes,
        For spent is my last Groate.   5

2. Delinquent I'de not feare to bee,
    Though gainst the *cause*, & *Noll* I'had fought;
    Since England's now a state most free
    For who's not worth a Groat Boyes,
        For who's not worth a Groate.   10

3. I'le boldly talke, and doe, as sure
    By Pursuivants n'ere to bee sought;
    'Tis a Protection most sicure,
    Not to bee worth a Groate Boyes,
        Not to bee worth a Groate.   15

4. I should bee soone lett loose againe
    By some mistake if I were caught;
    For what can Any hope to gaine
    From One not worth a Groate Boyes,
        From One not worth a Groate.   20

5. Nay, if some Foole should mee accuse,
    And I unto the Bar were brought;
    The Judges audience would refuse,
    I being not worth a Groate Boyes,
        I being not worth a Groate.   25

6. Or if some Raw-One should bee bent
    To make mee in the ayre to vault,
    The rest would cry; Hee's Innocent,
    Hee is not worth a Groate Boyes,
        Hee is not worth a Groate.   30

7. Yee Rich-men, that soe feare the State,
   This Priviledge is to bee bought;
   Purchase itt then att any rate,
   Leave not your selves a Groate Boyes
   Leave not your selves a Groate.   35

8. The Parliament which now does sitt
   (That all may have Itt, as They ought)
   Intends to make them for itt fitt,
   And leave noe man a Groate Boyes,
   And leave noe man a Groate.   40

9. Who writt this Song, would little care
   Allthough att th'end his name were wrought;
   Committee-men their search may spare,
   For spent is his last Groate Boyes,
   For spent is his last Groate.   45

The Country Life
To a French tune

1. Fondlings! keepe to th'Citty,
   Yee shall have my pitty;
   But my Envy, not:
   Since much larger measure
   Of true Pleasure,   5
   I'me sure's in the Country gott.

2. Here's noe Dinne, noe Hurry,
   None seekes here to curry
   Favour, by base meanes:
   Flattry's hence excluded;   10
   Hee's secluded
   Who speakes ought, but what Hee meanes.

3. Though your Talke, and Weeds bee
   Glittering, yett your Deeds bee
   Poore, wee them dispize: 15
   Silken are our Actions,
   And our Pactions,
   Though our Coats and Words bee Frize.

4. Here's noe Lawyer brawling;
   Rising Poore, Rich falling;   20
   Each is, what Hee was:
   That we have, enjoying:
   Not annoying
   Any Good, Another has.

5. There y'have Ladyes gawdy;   25
   Dames, that can talke bawdy;
   True, w'have none such here:
   Yett our Girles love surely,
   And have purely
   Cheekes unpainted, Soules most cleare.   30

6. Sweet, and fresh our Ayre is;
   Each Brooke coole, and fayre is;
   On the Grasse wee treade:
   Foule's your Ayre, Streets, Water;
   And thereafter   35
   Are the Lives which there you leade.

7. Not our time in Drenching,
   Cramming, Gaming, Wenching,
   Here wee cast away:
   Yett wee too, are Jolly: 40
   Melancholly
   Comes not neare us, Night, nor Day.

8. Scarce the Morne is peeping
   But wee straight leave sleeping;
   From our Beds wee rise: 45
   To the Field then hye wee;
   And there ply wee
   Wholsome, harmelesse Exercise.

9. Each comes back a winner;
   Each brings home his Dinner,   50
   Which was first his Sport:
   And uppon itt feasting,
   Toying, jeasting,
   W'envy not your Cates att Court.

10. Th' Afternoones wee loose not,   55
    Idleness wee choose not,
    But are still employ'd:
    Dancers some, some Bowlers,
    Some are Fowlers,
    Some in angling most are joy'd.   60

11. Th'Evening home-wards brings us,
    Whither Hunger wings us;
    Ready soone's our Food:
    Spare, light, sweet to th'Pallett,
    And a sallet   65
    To refresh our heated Blood.

12. Pleasantly then talking
    Forth wee goe a walking;
    Thence returne to rest:
    Noe sad Dreame incumbers   70
    Our sweet slumbers;
    Innocence thus makes us Blest.

13. Keepe now, keepe to th'Citty
    Fondlings! y'have my pitty,
    But my Envy, not:
    Since much larger measure
    Of true pleasure
    You see's in the Country gott.

75

To the tune
And will you now to Peace encline &c.

1. The Parliament ('tis sayd) resolv'd
    That, sometime ere They were dissolv'd,
    They'd pardon each Delinquent:
    And that (all past score to forgett)
    Good store of Lethe They did gett,
    And round about That Drincke went.

5

2. If soe; 'tis hard. For Th'have forgott
    All thought o'th'Act 'tis true; but not
    One Crime that can bee heard on:
    Soe that 'tis likely They'l constrayne
    Malignants to compound againe,
    In lieu o'th'noys'd out Pardon.

10

3. This comes of hoping to sitt still:
    By this wee find, 'twas not Good Will,
    But Feare, that caus'd their pitty.
    How sweet, how fayre, They spoke of late!
    What Benefitts both Church, and State
    Should reape from each Committy?

15

4. The Country for itts Fayth was prays'd;
    Noe more the great Tax should bee rays'd;
    Arrears should All be quitted:
    Our everlasting Parliament
    Would now give up itt's Governement;
    A new Mould should bee fitted.

20

5. Th'Act of Oblivion should come out,
   And wee noe longer held in doubt;
   Religion should bee stated:
   Goldsmithe's and Haberdasher's Hall
   Noe longer should affright us all,
   Nor Druery-house bee hated.

6. Feare made them promise this, and more;
   But now, They thincke the Storme is o're,
   Not one word is observed:
   The Souldier, full of discontent,
   To Ireland for's Arrears is sent;
   The Tax is still conserved.

7. Th'Act of Oblivion's layde aside;
   Sects multiply and subdivide;
   Gainst which noe Order's taken:
   And for th'new Representative,
   Fayth (for my part) I'de e'ene as live
   The Thought on't were forsaken.

8. Th'except gainst this, Th'except gainst that;
   They'l have us choose, but onely what
   Shall square with their direction:
   They doe soe straightly wedge us in,
   That if wee choose not them aghen,
   They'l make voyd our Election.

9. *Cromwell*! a Promise, is a Debt.
   Thou made'st them say They would forgett,
   O make them now remember!
   If They their Priviledges urge;
   Once more the House of office purge,
   And scoure out every member.

To a French tune
('Speake of somewhat else I pray;')

1. Speake of somewhat else I pray;
   This yeare, I'le not married bee:
   Lilly (*Joane*) fortells, They say,
   That hornes plenty wee shall see:
   This aspect of *Capricorne* 5
   I'le lett passe, for feare o'th'Horne.

2. Not that I pretend alone
   To goe free, since 't is i'th'Text;
   Cuckolds shall bee Every One;
   In this world, or in the next. 10
   I'de a while keepe out o'th'Heard;
   That's not lost, that is differr'd.

3. I've not Patience yett enough,
   All my Gelosye's not gonne;
   I'de stay, till my Fore-head tough 15
   Felt not, when that Capp's putt on:
   Quietly then, with the Rest,
   I shall beare the well knowne Crest.

4. When *Jove* th'European rape
   Did committ, large Hornes Hee wore; 20
   Though Hee reassum'd his shape,
   Those Hee ever after bore:
   Since the Gods doe weare them then,
   Why should They bee scorn'd by men.

5. 'Cause great Lords are crown'd, you guesse 25
   That their Heads noe Hornes doe beare;
   Yett, allthough wee see them lesse,
   Joane! assure thy selfe, Th'are there:
   Neither Learning, Strength, nor State
   Can secure us from that Fate. 30

6. For one Branch the Begger has,
   Forty can the Rich-man show;
   Whilst by Madame often was
   Th'Horner payde, to make them soe:
   Cuckold then who feares to bee,   35
   Meritts not good company.

7. From such Honour, yett awhile
   I'le bee kept, by my weake Head:
   But e're long (*Joane*) Thou shalt smile,
   Seeing how my fayre Hornes spread.   40
   For my comfort; Cuckolds (*Jone*)
   I'le make thousands; bee, but One.

To a French tune
('A greev'd Countesse, that e're long')

1. A greev'd Countesse, that e're long
   Must leave off her sweet-noys'd Title;
   A greev'd Countesse, that e're long
   'Mongst the Crowde for place may throng;
   In her hand that Patent holding   5
   Which perforce She must bring in,
   Oft with moyst Eyes itt beholding,
   Her complaynt thus did beginne.

2. Cruell Monsters! Doe you know
   What a Massacre y'have voted?   10
   Cruell Monsters! doe you know
   Th'harme you'l cause att one sad Blow?
   Dukes, Earles, Marquises, how many!
   'Las! how many a Lord, and Knight,
   Without pitty shewn to any,   15
   You'l cutt off, through bloody spight!

3. Fond Astrologers away,
   You that talke o'the sunnes thicke darcknesse;
   Fond Astrologers away
   Y'are mistaken in the day.   20
   Sure you calculate not duely,
   Th'Ephimerides else skippes;
   On the twenty fift more truely
   Y'ought to place the great Ecclipse.

4. Our deare-purchas'd Honours then   25
   Will by foggy mists bee clowded;
   Our deare-purchas'd Honours then
   Will (alasse!) n'ere shine aghen.
   All my Hopes are, that Those Vapours
   Which exstinguish now our Light,   30
   Will putt out too th'ancient Tapers;
   Since I'me Darcke, would All were Night!

To an Italian tune
('Poore Heart, retire!')

Poore Heart, retire!
Her Lookes deceave thee;
Sooth not thy Desire
With hopes Shee'l receave thee:
Thy selfe never flatter;   5
Her Smile, was noe Call:
'Lasse! Ther's noe such matter,
She lookes thus on all.
Mean't Sh'ought by her Smiling (poor Heart, creditt me)
Shee'd frown on thy Rivalls; Shee'd smile but on thee.   10

2. Thy flames extinguish,
   Noe more them feeding:
   Learne, learne to distinguish
   'Twixt *Love* and *good Breeding*.
   Fayre words are in fashion,   15
   Thou must not them mind;
   She spoke not with passion,
   To all She's as kind.
   Meant Sh'ought by those fayre words (poore Heart creditt
      mee)
   Shee'd speake that deare language to None but to thee.   20

3. Perhappes She granted
   Some few faynt Kisses;
   But ever They wanted
   That, which makes them Blisses.
   A Kisse has no savour   25
   If Love doe'nt itt owne;
   I count itt noe favour,
   'Lesse I kisse alone.
   Noe Kindnesse oblidges (poore Heart creditt mee)
   When t'others Itt's granted, as well as to Thee.   30

           To an Italian tune
        ("'Tis true. I am fetter'd')

   1. 'Tis true. I am fetter'd,
      But therein take pleasure:
      My Case is much better'd;
      This Chayne, is a Treasure.
      My Prison delights mee;   5
      'Tis Freedome, that frights mee;
      I hate Liberty:
      I'le not bee lamented,
      You'd All bee contented
      To have such Chaynes as I.   10

2. When (heretofore flying)
   My Loves oft I quitted;
   I then was a trying,
   And now I am fitted.
   I n'ere should have changed, 15
   If She (whilst I ranged)
   Had First strucke mine Eye:
   As soone as I mett her,
   Enchayne mee I lett her:
   Yee'd All doe, as I. 20

3. Soft Cords made of Roses,
   Then mine, would more gall mee:
   Her Bright Hayre composes
   Those Bonds which enthrall mee.
   Now, when She has proved 25
   How much her I've loved,
   My Hopes will soare high:
   Perchance, to retayne mee,
   Her Armes will enchayne mee;
   Then, Who'd not bee I? 30

To a Spanish tune called *Folias*

1. Cease t'exaggerate your Anguish,
   Yee, who for the Gout complayne!
   Lovers, that in absence languish,
   Onely know indeed, what's *Payne*.

2. If the Choyce were in my power, 5
   Sooner much the *Racke* I'de choose
   Then, for th'short space of an Hower,
   My deare *Stella's* sight to loose.

3. Sometimes *Feare*, sometimes *Desire*
   Seaze (by cruell turnes) my heart;   10
   Now a Frost, and then a Fire
   ('Las!) I feele in ev'ry part.

4. Horrid Change of Paynes! O leave mee,
   With my death else end your spight!
   Absence doth as much bereave mee   15
   As Death can, of her lov'd sight.

5. Thus (Deare *Stella*!) thy poore Lover
   His unlucky fate bemoanes;
   Whilst his parting Soule does hover
   'Bout his lippes; wing'd by sad groanes.   20

6. Yett Thou mayst from Death reprive him;
   Love such power to *Stella* gives:
   With thy sight Thou canst revive him;
   As Thou wilt Hee dyes or lives.

To the Italian tune
called *Girometta*

1. O, permitt that my Sadnesse
   May redeeme my offence!
   Lett not words, spoke in madnesse,
   Pregiudice Innocence!

2. 'Twas i'th'height of my passion,   5
   'Lasse! I rav'd all the time:
   Not thy Wrath, but Compassion,
   I deserv'd by my Crime.

3. Jealous Feares, with their thicknesse
   Had o're-clouded my Brayne: 10
   What I spoke in my Sicknesse
   N'ere remember agayne.

4. Franticke Men may talke treason,
   From all guilt They are free:
   Lawes, for such as want Reason,   15
   Noe chastisement decree.

5. Sure noe Tyrant did ever
   Call that Toungue to account,
   Which (in time of a Feaver)
   Tales of Plotts did raccount.   20

6. Then, since none can be heard on
   That e're punish'd such faults,
   O refuse not thy pardon
   To my past Words, or Thoughts!

7. Loe! as soone as I'me cured,   25
   I repent, I recant:
   Make mee too, once assured
   That my Grace has thy Grant.

To the tune
To Parliament the Queene is gonne &c.

1. This Aprile last a gentle Swayne
   Went early to the wood:
   His Businesse was, that Hee would fayne
   His Lott have understood.
   'Las, poore man!   5
   Sad, and wan
   Hee was growne, for love of *Nan*;
   'Twould him cheare,
   Could Hee heare
   The sweet Nightingale's Voyce here: 10
   Where-soe-e're Hee went,
   Still his Eare Hee bent
   Listning her to find.

2. His Friend (itt seemes) was better luck'd,
   And heard One in the Parcke; 15
   Whereatt by th'Sleeve Hee t'Other pluck'd,
   And cry'de, Harcke! there's One, Harcke!
   Th'honest Lad
   Was right glad,
   Thincking now good Newes t'have had: 20
   Whilst that Hee
   (Full of glee)
   Listning stood to ev'ry Tree,
   Not the Nightingall,
   But th'affrighting-all 25
   Ill-lov'd Cuckow sang.

3. What Tydings This may signify,
   I leave to Time to tell:
   But (if itt were mine owne Case) I
   Should hope, All would goe well. 30
   As I guesse,
   Faythfullnesse
   Well the Cuckow may expresse:
   Marcke your fill
   When you will, 35
   Him you'le find in One Note still.
   Though men feare him All
   When They heare him call,
   'Tis a lucky Bird.

4. Then cheare up *James*, and never sett 40
False comments on the Text:
If with th'one Bird this yeare Th'hast mett,
Thou'lte meete with t'Other next.
Doe not droope!
Nan shall stoope 45
To thy Lure, though the Cuckow Whoope:
The Bird sayth
That thy Fayth
Itt's Reward now neare-hand hath.
Never thincke on't Man! 50
Come; Lett's drincke to *Nan*,
She shall bee thine owne.

To the tune
I'le have my Love, or I'le have none

1. Some prayse the Browne, and some the Fayre;
Some best like Blacke, some Flaxen Hayre:
Some love the Tall, and some the Low;
Some choose, who's quicke; and some, who's slow.

2. If in all men one mind did dwell, 5
Too many would lead Apes in Hell:
But, that noe Mayd her Mate may lacke,
For ev'ry *Joane* there is a *Jacke*.

3. Thus, I have mine owne fancy too;
And vowe None but the *Poore* to woe: 10
My Love shall come (when e're I wed)
As naked to the *Church*, as *Bed*.

4. The Fayre, the Chast, the wisest Dame,
Though nobly Born, and of best Fame,
(By all the Gods) would n'ere enthrall 15
My Heart, if She were *Rich* withall.

5. I money count as great a Fault,
   As *Poorenesse* is 'mongst Others thought:
   With thousand Goods you'l find supply'de
   The want of *Portion* in a Bride. 20

6. There's noe such Gagge, to still the Lowd;
   There's noe such Curbe, to rule the Proud:
   Itt never fayles to stint all strife;
   It makes one Master of his Wife.

7. Should I reveale each good Effect, 25
   (Though *Poverty* now bring neglect)
   Suitours would throng about the Poore,
   N'ere knocking att the Rich-mayd's Doore.

8. Then, least that Some should surfitts vant,
   And Others sterve, the while for want, 30
   What rests (the Rich not to offend)
   I'le onely tell to some choyce Friend.

To the tune
of
Phillida flouts mee

1. *Ned*! She that likes thee now,
   Next weeke will leave thee!
   Trust her not, though She vow
   N'ere to deceave thee:
   Just soe to *Tom* She swore, 5
   Yett straight was ranging:
   Thus Shee'd serve forty more;
   Still Shee'l bee changing.
   Last Moneth I was the man;
   See, if denye't She can; 10
   Else aske *Francke*, *Jone* or *Nan*:
   Ned! fayth looke to itt.

2. Shee'l prayse thy Voyce, thy Face;
Shee'l say, Th'art witty;
Shee'l too cry up thy Race,   15
Thy State Shee'l pitty;
Shee'l sigh, and then accuse
Fortune of Blindnesse:
This *Forme* She still doth use,
When Shee'd show kindnesse.   20
Thou'lt find (if Thou but note)
That t'all She sings One note;
I've learnt her Arts by rote,
Ned! fayth looke to itt!

3. With scorne, as now on mee;   25
(Lesse may'st Thou care for't!)
E're long Shee'l looke on thee,
Thy selfe prepare for't.
The next new Face, will cast
Thine out of favour;   30
The Winds change not soe fast,
As her Thoughts waver:
If then Thou striv'st t'enchayne,
Thereby Thou'lt onely gayne
Thy Labour for thy Payne;   35
Ned! fayth looke to itt!

To the tune
of
Francklin is fled away

1. Alasse! long since I knew
   What would betide:
   My HOPES n'ere yett spoke true;
   My FEARES n'ere ly'de.
   False tales to please my heart,   5
   Those tell; These bring mee smart,
   But still the Truth Th'impart,
   N'ere flattr'ing mee.

2. Yett I was apt to heare
   Good newes, though made;   10
   And still would chide my Feare,
   When Itt gayn-sayde:
   This made mee entertayne
   Thoughts, which now prove most vayne;
   Beleeving, what soe fayne   15
   I'de have had true.

3. I fancy'de that thy Mind
   Was fix'd on Mee;
   But ('lasse!) my Love I find
   Contemn'd by Thee.   20
   'Cause I'de not *feare* before
   (Fond man!) I must therefore
   Despayre now ever-more.
   Sad is my chance.

4. But since thy *Kindnesse* had 25
   Part, in my fault;
   I know Thou wilt bee sad
   To see mee caught:
   And if Thou'lt not allow
   Thy *Love*; the next *Best* now 30
   Is that with *Pitty* Thou
   Looke on my Griefe.

I will sing unto

the

LORD

(Ps. xiii. 6)

Warneford
1651

[DIVINE POEMS]

Triolets

1. Worldly Designes, Feares, Hopes, farwell!
   Farwell all earthly Joyes and Cares!
   On nobler Thoughts my soule shall dwell,
   Worldly Designes, Feares, Hopes, farwell!
   Att quiett, in my peacefull Cell 5
   I'le thincke on God, free from your snares;
   Worldly Designes, Feares, Hopes, farwell!
   Farwell all earthly Joyes and Cares.

2. I'le seeke my God's Law to fullfill,
   Riches and Power I'le sett at nought; 10
   Lett Others strive for them that will,
   I'le seeke my God's Law to fullfill:
   Least sinfull Pleasures my soule kill,
   (By Follye's vayne Delights first caught)
   I'le seek my God's Law to fullfill; 15
   Riches, and Power I'le sett att nought.

3. Yes (my Deare Lord!) I've found itt soe;
   Noe Joyes but Thine are purely sweet:
   Other Delights come mixt with woe,
   Yes (my Deare Lord!) I've found itt soe. 20
   Pleasure att Courts is but in Show,
   With true content in Cells wee meete;
   Yes (my Deare Lord!) I've found itt soe,
   Noe Joyes but Thine are purely sweet.

> O that I had wings like a Dove;
> for then would I fly away, and bee at rest.
> (Ps. lv. 6)

1. By Ambition raysed high,
   Oft did I
   Seeke (though bruis'd with falls) to fly.
   When I saw the pompe of Kings
   Plac'd above,   5
   I did love
   To draw neare, and wish'd for wings.

2. All those Joyes which caught my mind
   Now I find
   To bee Bubbles, full of wind: 10
   Glow-wormes, onely, shining bright
   When that wee
   Blinded bee
   By darck Follye's stupid Night.

3. Looking up then I did goe   15
   Too and fro,
   When indeed They were below:
   For now, that mine Eyes see cleare,
   Fayre noe more,
   Small and poore,   20
   Farre beneath mee They appeare.

4. But a nobler Light I spy,
   Much more hye
   Then That Sun which shines i'th'Sky:
   Since itt's sight, all earthly Things   25
   I detest;
   There to rest
   Give, o Give mee the Dove's wings!

[DIVINE POEMS]

Servire Deo, Regnare est.

1. Are These the Things I sighed for soe, before?
   For want of These, did I complayne of Fate?
   Itt cannot bee. Sure there was Somewhat more
   That I saw then, and priz'd att a true rate;
   Or a strange Dullnesse had obscured my Sight,   5
   And even rotten wood glitters i'th'Night.

2. Mine Eyes were dimme; I could noe nearer gett;
   This Trash was with itt's most advantage plac'd:
   Noe mervayle then, if all my Thoughts were sett
   On Folly, since Itt seem'd soe fayrely grac'd.   10
   But now that I can see, and am gott neare,
   Ugly (as 'tis indeed) Itt doth appeare.

3. Now, were I putt on th'Erithrean sands,
   I would not stoope the choysest Jew'les to take:
   Should th'Indian bring me Gold in full-filled hands,   15
   I would refuse all offers Hee could make.
   Gemmes, are but *Sparckling Froth*; naturall *Glasse*:
   Gold's but *guilt Clay*; or the best sort of *Brasse*.

4. Long since (for all his Monarchy) that *Bee*
   Which rules in a large *Hive*, I did dispize: 20
   A *Mole-hill's* cheifest *Ant* I laughed to see,
   But any *Prince of Men* I much did prize.
   The *World* now seemes to mee noe bigger then
   Mole-hill, or *Hive*: *Ants, Bees*, noe lesse then *Men*.

5. Who wishes then for Power, or Plenty craves,   25
   O lett him looke downe on them both from hence!
   Hee'l see that *Kings* in *Thrones*, as well as *Graves*
   Are but poore *Wormes*, enslav'd to vilest *Sence*:
   Hee'l find that None are Poore who care for nought;
   But they, who having much, for more have sought.   30

[DIVINE POEMS]

6. Come Poore deluded Wretch! climbe up to mee;
My naked Hermitage will teach all this:
'Twill teach thee too where truest Riches bee,
And how to gayne a never-fading Blisse.
'Twill make Thee see that truely None doe raigne,   35
But Those who serve our Common Sovverayne.

The invisible things of him from the Creation of the World are cleerely seene; being Understood by the things that are made. (Rom. i. 20)

1. Whilst I beheld the necke o'th'*Dove*,
I spy'de, and read these words.
This pritty Dye
Which takes your Eye,
Is not att all, the Bird's.   5
The dusky Raven *might*
Have with these colours pleas'd your sight,
Had God but chose soe to ordayne above.
This Labell wore the *Dove*.

2. Whilst I admir'd the *Nightingale*,   10
These notes She warbled o're.
Noe melody
Indeed have I,
Admire mee then noe more:
God has itt in his choice   15
To give the Owle *or* Mee *this voyce;*
'Tis Hee, 'tis Hee that makes mee tell my Tale.
Thus sang the *Nightingale*.

3. I smelt and prays'd the fragrant *Rose*;
   Blushing, thus answer'd She.   20
    The Prayse You gave,
    The Sent I have,
    Doe not belong to mee:
    This harmelesse Odour, None
    But onely God indeed does owne;   25
    To bee his Keepers, my poore Leaves Hee chose.
   And thus reply'de the *Rose*.

4. I tooke the Honny from the *Bee*;
   On th'Bagge these Words were seene.
    More sweet then this   30
    Perchance Nought is,
    Yett Gall *itt might have beene:*
    If God itt should soe please,
    He could still make itt such with ease;
    And as well Gall *to* Honny *change can Hee.*   35
   This learn't I of the *Bee*.

5. I touch'd, and lik'd the *Downe* o'th'*Swanne*;
   But felt these words there writt.
    Bristles, Thornes, here
    I soone should beare,   40
    Did God ordayne but itt:
    If my Downe *to thy Touch*
    Seeme soft, and smoth, God made itt such;
    Give more, or take all this away, Hee can.
   This was I taught by th'*Swan*.   45

6. *All Creatures* then, confesse to *God*
That th'owe him all, but I.
My *Senses* find
True, what my *Mind*
Would still, oft *does* deny.
Hence *Pride*! out of my soule!
O're itt Thou shalt noe more controule;
I'le learne this *Lesson*, and escape the Rod:
I too, have all from GOD.

[DIVINE POEMS]

Crux VIA Cælorum.

1. Lowdly the Winds doe blow,
   High doe the Sea-waves goe;
   Where is the *Saylour* now, I'de know?
   Amidst the Billowes (looke) how Hee is tost,
   Yett hopes the Shore t'obtayne: 5
   In a small Barcke the Ocean Hee has cross't;
   All, for a little *Gayne*.
   Hee fitts his Sayles to th'wind,
   Then carelessely Hee sings;
   The Hope Hee has contents his mind,   10
   And comfort to him brings.
   Heaven for to gayne then, shall I bee less Bold,
   Then is a *Saylour* for a little *Gold*?

2. Whilst itt doth rayne, freeze, snow;
   Whilst coldest winds doe blow, 15
   How clad does the poore *Captive* goe?
   Noe Furres has Hee to wrappe his Body in;
   Nay more, Hee cares for none,
   But scornes all weathers in his naked Skin;
   Feare makes him make noe moane. 20
   Hee has uppon his Backe
   The marckes of many a wand;
   Yett (after stripes) Hee is not slacke
   To kisse his Master's hand.
   And shall I then for *Love*, repine to beare 25
   Less then a naked *Slave* endures for *Feare*.

3. The Scarres of many a Blow
   Can the maym'd *Souldier* show,
   Yett still unto the Warre does goe.
   Fame makes him watch many a winter-night, 30
   Hee sleepes oft on the ground;
   With Hunger, Thirst and Foes Hee oft must fight,
   And all but for a Sound.
   Whole long Dayes must Hee march
   When all his Force is spent; 35
   The scorching Sun his skinne doth parch,
   Yett is his Heart content:
   Shall then for *Fame* a *Souldier* doe all this;
   And I shrincke, suff'ring lesse for *Heavenly Blisse*.

4. In a darcke Cave below
   The Conquerour does throw
   His miserable vanquish'd *Foe*.
   Deepe is the Dungeon where that Wretch is cast,
   Thither Day comes not nigh;
   Dampish and nasty Vapours doe him blast,
   Yett still his Heart is high.
   His Prison is soe straight
   Hee cannot moove at will;
   Huge Chaynes oppresse him with their waight,
   Yett has Hee courage still.
   And can I thincke I want my *Libertee*,
   When in such *Thrall*, Hee keepes his *Mind* soe *Free*?

5. Itt shall not bee: Noe, noe.
   The *Saylour* I'le out-goe;
   The *Souldier*, *Slave*, & vanquish'd *Foe*.
   When Others *rage*, I'le thincke how I saw tost
   The *Seaman* in the Mayne:
   The naked *Slave* shall i'th'most pearcing *Frost*,
   Make mee beare any payne.
   The *Marche* I'le call to mind,
   When weary, and gett wings:
   Least I should thincke my selfe confin'd
   The *Pris'ner*, freedome brings.
   When e're *Restraint*, or *Greife*, or *Feare*, or *Cold*,
   Tempt mee; these Thoughts will then my Mind uphold.

        Man is borne unto Trouble.
            (Job v. 7)

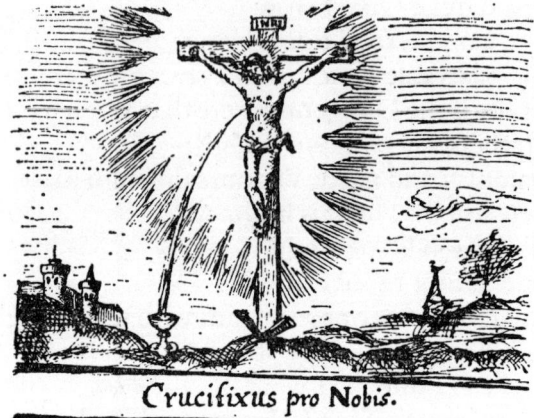

Crucifixus pro Nobis.

Christ in the Cradle
1. Looke, how Hee shakes for cold!
   How pale his Lippes are growne!
   Wherein his Limbes to fold
   Yett Mantle has Hee none.
   His pretty Feet, and Hands
   (Of late, more pure and white
   Then is the Snow
   That paynes them soe)
   Have lost their Candour quite.
   His Lippes are Blew,
   (Where Roses grew)
   Hee's frozen ev'ry where:
   All th'heate He has
   Joseph, alasse!
   Gives in a *Groane*; or *Mary* in a *Teare*.

Christ in the Garden

2. Looke, how Hee glowes for heate!
   What Flames come from his Eyes!
   'Tis *Blood* that Hee does *sweate*,
   Blood his bright Forehead dyes:
   See, see! Itt trickles downe: 20
   Looke, how itt showers amayne!
   Through every Pore
   His Blood runnes o're,
   And empty leaves each Vayne.
   His very Heart   25
   Burnes in each part;
   A Fire his brest doth seare:
   For all this Flame,
   To coole the same
   Hee onely breathes a *Sigh*, and weepes a *Teare*.   30

Christ in his Passion

3. What Bruises doe I see!
   What hideous Stripes are Those!
   Could Any cruell bee
   Enough, to give such Blowes?
   Looke, how They bind his Armes   35
   And vex his soule with Scornes:
   Uppon his Hayre
   They make him weare
   A crowne of pearcing Thornes.
   Through Hands, and Feete   40
   Sharpe Nayles They beate;
   And now the Crosse They reare:
   Many looke on;
   But onely *John*
   Stands by to *sigh*; *Mary*, to shed a *Teare*.

4. Why did Hee shake for *Cold*?
   Why did Hee glow for *Heate*?
   Dissolve that *Frost* Hee could;
   Hee could call backe that *Sweate*.
   Those Bruises, Stripes, Bonds, Tauntes, 50
   Those Thornes, which Thou didst see;
   Those Nayles, that *Crosse*,
   His owne Life's losse,
   Why, O why sufferr'd Hee?
   'Twas for thy sake. 55
   Thou, Thou didst make
   Him, all those *torments* beare:
   If then his Love
   Doe thy soule moove,
   Sigh out a *Groane*; *Weepe* downe a melting *Teare*. 6

EX DOLORE GAVDIVM.

[DIVINE POEMS]

Fallax, et Instabilis.

There is noe new Thing under the Sun (Eccl. i. 9)

1. 'Tis a strange Thing this World.
   Nothing but *Change* I see:
   And yett itt is most true
   That in't there's nothing new,
   Though All seeme new to mee.   5
   The Rich becomme oft Poore,
   And heretofore 'twas soe;
   The Poore man rich doth grow,
   And soe 'twas heretofore:
   Nor is itt a new thing   10
   To have a Subject made a King;
   Or that a King should from his Throne bee hurl'd.
   'Tis a strange Thing this World.

2. All Things below doe change
   The *Sea* in rest n'ere lyes;   15
   N'ere lay in rest, nor will:
   The *Weather* alters still,
   And n'ere did otherwise.
   Consum'd is many a Towne
   By *Fire*; how, none can tell: 20
   Playnes up to *Mountaynes* swell,
   While Mountaynes doe sincke downe.
   Yett ought Wee not t'admire
   The *Sea*, the *Ayre*, the *Earth*, or *Fire*:
   The *Sun* does thincke nothing of all this strange;   25
   Since all things here still change.

3. Lett None then fix his heart
   Uppon such trifling toyes;
   But seeke some object out,
   Whose change Hee n'ere may doubt;   30
   There, let Him place his Joyes.
   Since that our Soules are made
   For ever to endure;
   Of cheifest Greife w'are sure,
   If what wee love must fade: 35
   For Friends feele greatest payne
   When One must goe, t'Other remayne.
   With what I love then, that I n'ere may part,
   On *God* I'le fix my Heart.

*Vidi in omnibus vanitatem, & afflictionem
animi, & nihil* permanere *sub Sole*. (Eccl. ii. 11)

[DIVINE POEMS]

Nulla Fides.

1. For God's sake marcke that *Fly*:
   See what a poore, weake, little Thing itt is.
   When Thou hast marck'd, and scorn'd itt; know that This,
   This little, poore, weake *Fly*
   Has killed a *Pope*; can make an *Emp'rour* dye.   5

2. Behold yon *Sparcke of Fire*:
   How little hott! how neare to nothing 'tis!
   When thou has donne despising, know that this,
   This contemn'd *Sparcke of Fire*
   Has burn't whole Townes; can burne a World entire.   10

3. That crawling *Worme* there see:
   Ponder how ugly, filthy, vild Itt is.
   When Thou hast seene and loath'd itt, know that This
   This base *Worme* Thou doest see,
   Has quite devour'd thy Parents; shall eate Thee.   15

4. *Honour*, the *World*, & *Man*,
   What Trifles are they! Since most true itt is
   That this poore *Fly*, this little *Sparckle*, this
   Soe much abhorr'd *Worme*, can
   Honour destroy; burne *Worlds*; devoure up *Man*.   20

[*Stulte, hac nocte animam tuam repetunt a te.* (Luke xii. 20)]

1. What use has Hee made of his Soule
   Who (still on Vices bent)
   N'ere strove his *Passions* to controule;
   But, hum'ring them, his Life has spent?
   Pray tell mee, if I can   5
   Call such a very *Thing* as that is, *Man*?
   For since that just as *Sense* has bidde
   Itt *doe*, or *leave*; Itt *wrought*, or *ceas't*;
   And would not heare when *Reason* chidde,
   Or her commands reguard the least;   10
   Itt might have liv'd e'ene as Itt did,
   And yett have beene a *Beast*.

2. Had Itt a *Lyon* beene; Just soe
   Itt would roare out, and fume:
   Were Itt a *Peacocke*, Itt would goe
   Just thus, admiring itt's owne Plume:
   Or if Itt were a *Goate*;
   Thus, onely on base pleasures Itt would dote.
   More then this *Thing*, the ravenous *Hogge*
   Searches not, where his gutts to fill;
   Nor att a Stranger's Hound, the *Dogge*
   O'th'House more snarle or *envy* will;
   Then this odde *Thing* (though apt to cogge)
   Repine att Others still.
3. The *Crow*, that hoardes up all she finds;
   The *Ant*, that still takes paynes;
   Doe nothing more, then Hee who minds
   But how to fill his Baggs with *Gaynes*.
   The *Snayle*, & *Sluggerd* bee
   Within alike; tho' in shape They disagree.
   Call not that *Thing* then, *Man*; even as
   Thou wouldst not injure by the same
   MAN, who like *God* created was;
   GOD, who for *Man's* sake, *Man* became:
   But, since soe much o'th'*Beast* Itt has,
   Call Itt, by Itt's owne Name.

Accepit in vano animam suam.
(Ps. xxiii. 4)

Dirige vias meas Domine!

1. Open thy selfe, and then looke in;
   Consider what Thou mightst have bin,
   And what Thou art now made by Sin.
2. Asham'd o'th' State to which Th'art brought,
   Detest, and greeve for each past fault;
   Sigh, weepe, and blush for each foule thought.

3. Feare, but dispayre not, and still love;
   Looke humbly up to God above,
   And Him Thou'lt soone to *Pitty* moove.

4. Resolve on that which Prudence showes;
   Performe what Thou doest well propose;
   And keepe i'th'way Thou hast once chose.

5. Vice, and what lookes like Vitious, shunne;
   Lett Use make good acts eas'ly donne;
   Have Zeale, as when th'hadst first begunne.

6. Hope strongly, yett be humble still;
   Thy Good, is God's; what's thine, is ill:
   Doe thus, and thee *affect* Hee will.

7. Pray, when with Others; when alone:
   To Scorne, or Prayse bee as a stone: 20
   Forgett thy selfe, and all; but One.

8. Remoove what stands twixt God, and Thee:
   Use not thy Fancy him to see:
   One with his will, make thy Will bee.

9. Looke purely on God, when Thou doest well;   25
   But not on Heaven; much lesse, on Hell:
   Thou'lt gett Him thus in thee to *Dwell*.

10. Use-lesse our Master Wee doe serve;
    Our Labours noe reward deserve:
    Yett Happy, who these rules observe.   30

Nobis natus in Pretium: nobis datus in Præmium.

1. *Great God!* I had beene *Nothing* but for Thee;
   Thy all-creating Power first made mee *Bee*:
   And yett, noe sooner had I gott
   A *Being*, but I straight forgott
   That Thou (*Great God*) that Thou hadst given itt mee.   5
   My *being Somewhat* I did spend
   Onely, thy Goodnesse to offend;
   And, though chastiz'd, yett n'ere would mend.

2. *Christ!* but for thee, I had remayned soe;
   Thou didst redeeme mee, though I were thy Foe: 10
   And yett Thou hadst noe sooner spilt
   Thy Blood, to wash away my guilt,
   But my Ingratitude I straight did show.
   My Chaynes Thou kindly didst unloose;
   My Liberty, I soone did loose;   15
   And, to becomme a Slave, did choose.

3. *Blest Spirit!* (once agayne my soule to try)
   Thou didst her cleanse, renew, and sanctify.
   Scarce was She purged by thy Flame,
   But straight, more horrid She became   20
   Then, e're (*Blest Spirit!*) Thou didst her purify.
   All the *Three Persons* now in vayne
   Had try'de a perverse Soule to gayne,
   Who was resolv'd on her owne Bane.

4. Thus, though to save mee God strove ev'ry way,   25
   To Punishment I did my selfe betray.
   I greeve for th'Ill that I have donne;
   I weepe to see my selfe undonne;
   But, in excuse, have not one word to say.
   Yett (God!) since Thou didst mee create,   30
   Then ransome, then sanctificate;
   Save what th'hast *bought* att such a Rate!

Who, without Horrour, can that HOVSE *behold*
(*Though n'ere soe fayre*) *which is with* TOMBE-STONES
   made;
Whose Walls, fraught with INSCRIPTIONS *writt of old,*
Say still, Here underneath SOME-BODY's layde.

Though such translated CHVRCH-YARDS *shine with*
   GOLD,   5
Yett They the BVILDER'S SACRILEDGE *up-brayde;*
And the wrong'd GHOSTS, *there haunting uncontrol'd,*
Follow Each-one his Monumentall Shade.

But They, that by the POORE-MAN'S DOWNE-FALL
   rise,
Have sadder EPITAPHES *carv'd on their* CHESTS: 10
As Here, the WIDDOW; Here, the ORPHAN lyes.

Who sees their WEALTH, *their* AVARICE *detests;*
Whilst th'Injur'd, for REVENGE *urge* HEAV'N *with*
   CRYES;
And, through Itt's GVILT, *th'Oppressour's Mind n'ere rests.*

[DIVINE POEMS]

Dies Iræ, Dies illa.

1. A Day full of Horrour, must
   All this world dissolve to dust:
   Prophets say itt; w'are to trust.

2. What Heart will bee voyd of feare
   When our great Judge shall appeare,
   Strictly Each Man's cause to heare?

3. A shrill Trumpett there will sound;
   All must rise from under ground,
   And the Judge's Throne surround.

4. How astonish'd then will bee
   Death, & *Nature,* when They see
   From their Lawes each Body free?

5. A Booke, where Men's *Deeds* are writt,
   Shall bee read; the Judge to itt
   Will th'eternall Sentence fitt.

6. Att his sitting, 'twill bee vayne
   To conceale a secret Stayne;
   Nought unpunish'd shall remayne.

7. How shall I that day endure?
   What Friend shall I then procure,   20
   When the Just are scarce sicure?

8. My Request doe not reject,
   Thou that savest thine *Elect*;
   God! of mercy mee protect.

9. *Christ*! remember in that day,   25
   I'me thy Sheepe, (though gonne astray)
   Leave mee not, to Wolves a Pray.

10. Weary, oft mee sought Thou hast;
    For mee, nayl'd to th'*Crosse* Thou wast:
    Loose not all this paynes att last.   30

11. Though my Sinnes to vast Summes mount,
    Yett thy Mercyes them surmount:
    O n'ere call them to account!

12. I confesse my Guilt; Th'art meeke:
    Grant that pardon which I seeke!   35
    Loe, Shame's Blushes dye each cheeke.

13. *Mary*, and the Theife, scarce leave
    Sin, but Thou doest them receave;
    What Hopes hence may-n't I conceave?

14. True. My Pray'rs deserve not ought;   40
    By thy Passion Th'art besought:
    Keepe mee from the fiery Vault!

[DIVINE POEMS]

15. 'Mongst the *Sheepe* grant mee a stand;
    Drive mee from the *Goat's* curs'd Band,
    Placing mee on thy right hand.   45

16. This t'obtayne, my knees I bend;
    For this, all my prayers I send:
    Lord, take care of my last end!

17. O! that Day'le cause weeping Eyes,
    When to judgement Men shall rise: 50
    'Gainst then, *Mercy*! my Soule cryes.

Commentary

In the following Commentary I have noted substantial variations in previous editions (*Poems, 1771*, Scott, Saintsbury) not for their authority but simply to present a full critical picture. Cary MS. has no doubtful readings, and where previous editors differ from it, their text cannot be considered valid. I have not listed their variations in spelling or punctuation unless these affect the sense or interpretation of the text.

The illustrations in the original manuscript are discussed separately in Appendix A (p. 102), and musical settings of Cary's poems in Appendix B (p. 115).

In quoting words of the text at the beginning of each note I have italicized consistently, whatever type is used in the text itself, in order to make reading easier.

Title-page

Triviall Ballades. This is the wording in Cary's title for the first section of Cary MS., which contains secular verses. The word 'Ballades', which is printed carefully at the top of every page in this section, is presumably chosen because these poems are all written to specific tunes, most of which are named. The idea of song is implicit in the ballad as late as Johnson. See *O.E.D.*, 'ballad', 5. The spelling 'ballade' in this sense is found in the seventeenth century. There seems, therefore, no convincing reason for Scott to substitute 'Poems' in his title (*Trivial Poems and Triolets*); still less to incorporate in it 'Triolets', taken from the second section of Cary MS., which contains religious verse. See under *Triolets*, p. 92.

M[es]. *Tomkin's.* Mrs. Tomkin (Tomkins or Tompkins) was Lucy, daughter of Sir William Uvedale by his first wife, Anne Carey, who belonged to the Hunsdon branch of the Cary family. Lucy Uvedale (born *c.* 1610) had married first Thomas Neale of Warnford, and, after his death, Thomas Tomkins of Monington. She died in 1677. See p. 74.

1651. For a discussion of matters involved in this date see General Introduction, p. lxix.

COMMENTARY

An Octave

Scott prints the whole in small capitals with larger initial capitals, thus obscuring the emphasis laid on certain words by variations in size and style in Cary MS. Throughout the rest of the text Scott almost entirely ignores Cary's capitalization, apart from normal usage, and does not attempt to reproduce the other devices used in the manuscript to give emphasis.

l. 5. *Else, when to Any these harsh Rimes you show*. The poet makes it clear that he has a modest opinion of his own verse and is writing for a private audience only.

To the tune
Once I lov'd a Mayden Fayre &c.

('Fayre-One! if thus kind You bee')

Once I lov'd a Mayden Fayre &c. For this tune see Appendix B, p. 116.

ll. 2, 4. *Slaughter: hereafter*. As Cary also rhymes *Water: thereafter* (p. 24, ll. 34–5), it would seem that *Slaughter* has a pronunciation approaching its modern sound, and that *hereafter*, with silent *–f*, rhymes with this. See Dobson, ii, 519.

l. 13. *I love kindnesse, and not Face*. Cary here reflects in his own way a characteristic seventeenth-century attitude. Cf. the lines attributed, with some doubt, to Aurelian Townshend:

> 'Tis not how witty, nor how free,
> Nor yet how beautifull she be,
> But how much kinde and true to me.
> (*Poems and Masks*, ed. E. K. Chambers, 1912, p. 53.)

ll. 14, 16. *hate her: Feature*. Spenser and Shakespeare rhyme *feature: nature*. Cary has a similar rhyme, *Feature: Creature* (p. 8, ll. 10, 12). See Dobson, ii, 626. The ending *–ure* was regularly pronounced like the last syllable of modern *figure*. See Kökeritz, p. 271.

To the tune
I'le doe by Thee, as n'ere was donne

('The Ermine is without all spott')

I'le doe by Thee as n'ere was donne. For a discussion of this tune see Appendix B, p. 116.

COMMENTARY

To the tune
I would give twenty pound &c.

('There's noe Woeman, but I'me caught')

I would give twenty pound &c. I have been unable to trace this tune.
ll. 1, 3. *caught: Fault.* The seventeenth-century orthoepists regularly show *–l* to be silent in such words as *fault*. See Dobson, ii, 990–1. A similar rhyme, *caught: vault*, occurs on p. 22 (ll. 17, 27), and another, *besought: Vault,* on p. 66 (ll. 41, 42).

l. 10. *Dye*: 'hue', 'complexion', with no hint of the artificial. Cf. '*This pritty Dye*' 'Whilst I beheld the necke o'th'Dove' (p. 46, l. 3).

ll. 14, 16. *contemned*: condemned. It is clear from parallel lines that these are trisyllables. With Cary final *–ed* is pronounced separately in almost all cases where he does not indicate elision. Exceptions are: *blamed* (p. 7, l. 5); *tarryed: marryed* (p. 11, ll. 38, 39); *sighed* (p. 45, l. 1); *filled* (p. 45, l. 15); *killed* (p. 57, l. 5).

l. 24. *loure*. Cary MS. has 'lo'ure', obviously meant to indicate a monosyllable. (On p. 21, l. 60, Cary writes 'lowers' with two syllables.) However, the apostrophe is unnecessary, as 'loure' was a form in its own right. See *O.E.D.*, 'lour', v.

To the tune
Bobbing Joane

('I n'ere yett saw a lovely Creature')

Bobbing Joane. For the tune see Appendix B, p. 117, where Cary's verses are shown set to this well-known melody.

l. 14. *a Looking-glasse.* For a different application of the mirror-heart image, see Donne, 'The Broken Heart' (*Elegies, Songs and Sonnets*, ed. H. Gardner, 1965, p. 51).

To the tune
Troy-towne

('Fayre Beautyes! if I doe confesse')

Troy-towne. For the tune see Appendix B, p. 118.
l. 30. *Then, kindly Wee'l shake hands, and part.* Saintsbury (p. 457, n.).

draws attention to the difference in contemporary temper and spirit between this and Drayton's late sonnet in *Idea* (1619):

> Since ther's no helpe, come let us kisse and part,
> . . . . .
> Shake hands for ever, cancell all our vowes.

Cf. also Cary's own lines in 'Poore Heart, retire!':

> Learne, learne to distinguish
> 'Twixt *Love* and good *Breeding*.
> (p. 31, ll. 13–14.)

To the tune
But I fancy lovely Nancy &c.

('Surely now I'me out of danger')

But I fancy lovely Nancy &c. For the tune see Appendix B, p. 119. *Poems, 1771*, begins its second section, of secular poems, under the title *NUGAE LUSORIAE* with these verses.

While the poem is in some ways reminiscent of Cowley's catalogue of successive idols in 'The Chronicle' (*Poems*, ed. Waller, 1905, p. 39), and possibly of Herrick's in 'Upon the losse of his Mistresses' (*Poems*, ed. Martin, 1956, p. 15), it has its own individuality and interest. The latter springs largely from its strongly autobiographical element. It is a pleasant, entertaining tribute to the group of ladies in whose society the poet gratefully found himself in the autumn of 1650. Although Cary talks as airily about 'Twelve att least' by name of Anne as Suckling does of 'A dozen dozen', he is quick to add: 'These are Fancyes'; and the groups of three and two and single names which follow have distinct marks of authenticity. Three families, those of Sir William Uvedale and his brothers, Francis and Richard, lived within a few miles of one another in Wickham, Bishop's Waltham, and Droxford in Hampshire. There was no lack of feminine members in each household, and the same Christian names often recurred. Patrick Cary, with a sister and a 'patroness' from one family and a wife or a sweetheart from another, weaves their names and those of other women relatives and, no doubt, friends, into a deft example of *vers de société*. Although I cannot suggest identities for all thirty ladies named, it seems unlikely that the poet would introduce imaginary heroines among so many demonstrably real characters.

COMMENTARY

ll. 8-9. Saintsbury prints these as one line, which affects his numbering.

l. 10. *Libertee*. Sainsbury (p. 457, n.) was attracted by this form and kept it in his modernized edition. It was a perfectly legitimate seventeenth-century spelling (see *O.E.D.*, 'liberty', sb.) which Cary uses again on p. 51, l. 51. A different form, 'Liberty', appears on p. 31, l. 7.

l. 11. *Anne was once the word*. Cary may not have known twelve Annes, but he could have been acquainted with at least four, besides his eldest living sister, Dame Anne Clementia Cary, whose letters to Edward Hyde, quoted in the General Introduction, pp. xxxviii, *et seq.*, are witness to the strong affection between her and her brother. They were: Anne Uvedale, cousin to Mrs. Tomkins, and sister to Patrick's wife, Susan; Susan's mother, still living in 1661, whose maiden name was Anne Hearst; Anne Tomkins, daughter of Thomas Tomkins by his first wife, Mary Pye: born after 1636, she would very likely, at fourteen or so, be living with her stepmother in 1650; there was also twenty-year-old Anne Griffin, baptized at Wickham in 1630, whose mother was Lady Frances Griffin, Mrs. Tomkins's sister. (The biographical details given for this and the following poem are based on: the Falkland pedigrees in *H & G* iii, 39 *et seq.*; the Uvedale pedigrees in *S.A.C.* iii, following p. 183; and 'Pedigree of Tomkins of Herefordshire', privately compiled by Rev. Henry A. Colthurst Tomkins, 1926, a manuscript in the archives of the Society of Genealogists, London.)

l. 21. *three Bettyes*. There is no lack of candidates for this title. Apart from Cary's sister, Dame Elizabeth Augustina Cary (like her sister Anne, a nun at Cambrai), there were three Elizabeth Uvedales: the eldest sister of Mrs. Tomkins; Patrick Cary's niece, daughter of his sister, Victoria ('plump *Besse*' of the drinking song, p. 14, l. 21); and Susan's elder sister. For good measure there was also Elizabeth Dowse, who married William Uvedale, Susan's eldest brother, and could be the lady 'courted by my Friend' (l. 30).

l. 31. *Lucyes there are two*. Patrick's sister, Dame Lucy Magdalena Cary, had died at Cambrai in November 1650; but there were two 'Lucyes' in his intimate circle. The first is Lucy Uvedale, another elder sister of Patrick's wife, Susan, and unmarried in 1660, who perhaps gets a gallant apology for not being wooed. (Another possibility for the first Lucy is Lucy, Countess of Carlisle (d. 1660), whose beauty was celebrated by poets of the Great Tew circle, Waller, Suckling, and Carew.) The second is undoubtedly Mrs. Tomkins herself: with two children from her previous marriage to Thomas Neale, the four children of Thomas Tomkins by *his* first marriage, and her son, Uvedale Tomkins (aged two or three in 1651), she was well on the way to being mother '(As I take't) to halfe a score'. As the subject of the dedication she receives a special tribute of chivalry, not undeserved if we may credit the description of a descendant of her first husband: 'the sometimes most accomplisht both by the beautiful embellishments of mind and body, the Lady Lucie Uvedale'. See Payne Fisher, *The Tombes, Monuments etc. ... in St Paul's* (1685), p. 79.

l. 41. *two, and each a Mary*. The first is obviously Queen Henrietta Maria, to whose patronage Cary owed the benefices on which he lived in Rome. (See General Introduction, p. xxxiii.) The other may be Mrs. Tomkins's cousin, eldest daughter of Sir Richard Uvedale, who, born in 1619, died unmarried in 1686; but it is more likely to be Mary Uvedale, Susan's eldest sister, who would be about twenty-six at the time of the poem.

l. 43. *Th'Oxford-Vintner*. This puzzling reference baffled previous commentators (Saintsbury, p. 458, n.; Weber, p. 323). Dame Veronica Wedgwood in a letter to me suggested that the allusion was possibly to Sir William Davenant. He was certainly devoted to the Queen, and widely regarded as her poet. She acted in his masques, and as a result of her influence he was made Poet Laureate in 1638. Through his involvement in the disastrous Army Plot, as one of her special coterie, he was arrested and imprisoned in 1641. Eventually escaping, he joined her on the Continent, and continued as an active agent in her strategical moves until, starting off on an abortive expedition to Maryland (of which Charles II had appointed him lieutenant-governor) he was again arrested and imprisoned. (See Arthur H. Nethercot, *Sir William D'avenant* (1938), pp. 17–20, 74–5, 186 *et seq.*, 257 *et seq.*) Davenant's second imprisonment took place in February 1650—not very long before Cary began to write his poems. There are two links between Davenant and the Cary–Uvedale circle. In 1641, shortly before his arrest, he received a warrant for £40 for his services in the Bishops' Wars, from the

Treasurer at Arms, Sir William Uvedale, who, if I am right in identifying him with the knight of Wickham, was Patrick Cary's brother-in-law. Davenant would also be well known to Sir William's wife, who as Mistress Victoria Cary took part in two of his Court masques. See General Introduction, p. li. He was thus known to both the Uvedales, with or near whom Cary was staying when he wrote these verses. The title 'Oxford-Vintner' could easily be a term applied to Davenant, either in teasing or opprobrium, as he had succeeded with his brothers and sisters to the ownership of their father's Oxford tavern in the Cornmarket, later known as the Crown. If this identification is correct, it is easy to see how his several imprisonments for loyalty to the Queen could well make our poet 'wary'; and 'a gazing stand' may be interpreted as 'show public admiration for the Queen'. It is more likely that the allusion would refer to a well-known Royalist figure than to some obscure incident involving an actual Oxford tavern-keeper during the Queen's residence in Oxford in 1643-4.

l. 51. *Katherne*. She may be Sir Richard Uvedale's second daughter, who would be young enough at thirty to qualify for the flattering description given to her. *Poems, 1771* reads 'Catherine'.

l. 55. *Beauteous Frances*. This romantically minded lady is surely Mrs. Tomkins's sister Frances, who married Sir Edward Griffin, and is mentioned in her father's will, proved in 1652.

l. 60. *Primaleon's life*. Primaleon is the hero of the first book of the *Palmerides*, chivalric romances describing the exploits and loves of Palmerin de Oliva, Emperor of Constantinople, and attributed to the Portuguese Francisco de Moraes (*c.* 1500-72), or the Spaniard, Luis Hurtado (1530-79). Primaleon's name was associated with the whole series, as 'Amadis' was with its Gallic counterpart. Anthony Munday between 1580 and 1590 produced English versions of the Amadis and Palmerin cycles; thus *Palmerin of England* and *Amadis of Gaul* were examples of the sort of romances beauteous Frances might find so absorbing. Was she trying her hand at a metrical adaptation of the first book of the *Palmerides*?

ll. 61, 65. *Doll* and *Jane* I cannot trace, although Jane was a family name with the Uvedales, given at baptism to one of Sir William's sisters.

l. 68. *Nell's soe spotted.* I regret I cannot identify young Nell, with the fashionable patches on her face. Spots or patches to adorn the face, and sometimes to hide blemishes, were being used by English ladies at least as early as 1611, and were variously shaped like stars, half-moons, lozenges etc. A number of contemporary poems deal with the subject, including Kenelm Digby, *Musarum Deliciae* (1655), pp. 76, 95, and *Wits Interpreter* (1655), p. 87; also Lovelace, *Poems*, ed. Wilkinson (1953), pp. 129, 130; and Suckling, 'Upon the Black Spots worn by my Lady D.E.' (*Poems*, ed. Thompson, 1910, p. 53). I owe these references to the kindness of Mrs. Anne Pratt, who collected them while annotating a long poem on black patches by Clement Paman (1611–64), MS. Rawlinson Poet. 147. See also *O.E.D.*, 'patch', sb. 2; 'spot', sb., II.4.b.

ll. 71–2. *Peg is blith . . . demure as Ruth.* The high-spirited Peg and the sedate Ruth also eluded my search.

l. 73. *Susan's head is full of rattles.* This is Patrick Cary's only mention in verse of his wife's name.

l. 74. *Rachell preacheth well.* Rachel Hungerford was married to Patrick's nephew, Henry Cary, the fourth Viscount Falkland, in 1653. It is not impossible that Patrick had met her before that. He was on cordial terms with his relatives at Great Tew, the Falkland seat, as is shown by a letter from Henry Hammond, dated 7 January (1651?), which speaks of him as being 'planted' at Great Tew. See Harleian MS. 6942, No. 116.

ll. 75–6. *Were not Tolly/Melancholly.* 'Tolly', as Saintsbury suggests (p. 458, n.), probably stands for 'Victoria', for which 'Tory' is a known abbreviation. The transition to 'Tolly', perhaps as a childish nickname, is not difficult to accept. Since she is 'Melancholly', it is no doubt serious, housewifely Victoria, his niece, rather than her mother, his sister, that the poet is saluting here. See note on 'well-grac'd *Victoria*', p. 76. *Poems, 1771* amends the name uncompromisingly, and unjustifiably, to 'Polly'.

l. 78. *Amorous Sophy.* The honour of concluding the catalogue may well have fallen to Anna Sophia Neale, daughter of Mrs. Tomkins by her previous marriage. She would be only nine at the time the poem was written, but is a far more likely candidate than the only other Sophy I can find: Mrs. Sophy Cary, who acted with Victoria

COMMENTARY

Cary and other ladies of the Queen in Aurelian Townshend's masque, *Tempe Restor'd*, in 1631. See Townshend's *Poems and Masks*, ed. Chambers (1912), p. 100. There is no record of this Sophy in any of the pedigrees: she may belong to a different branch of the family.

l. 87. *With noe prayers, my destiny*. Scott, with a slip that evaded proof correction, printed: 'With noe my prayers my destiny'. He was followed by Saintsbury, who, however queried (p. 458, n.) the correctness of the reading.

ll. 88, 89. *scorned: horned*. These are obviously disyllables. See note on *contemned*, p. 71.

To the tune
The Healths

('Come (fayth) since I'me parting')

Like the preceding poem this is not an exercise of fancy, but an attractive occasional piece, here expressing before the poet's departure gratitude for hospitality, and dexterously embodying the names of actual people, including all the members of the family and many of the servants. Poems on the various aspects of parting were favourites at this period, which saw so many national, domestic, and spiritual cleavages.

The Healths. See Appendix B, p. 120, for this popular tune, with a version of Cary's words set to the melody.

l. 2. *sweet Wickham*: Sir William Uvedale's seat at the village of that name in Hampshire. See the General Introduction, p. lii. *aghen*: an unusual spelling in the seventeenth century, when according to O.E.D. 'againe' predominated, with 'agen' occasionally found, especially in poetry.

l. 4. A symbol ∻ after each stanza in Cary M S., represented in the test thus: ∻, indicates that the refrain is repeated.

l. 5. *S^r. William*: Cary's brother-in-law, here acclaimed the prince of hosts. For Sir William Uvedale, see the General Introduction, p. lii.

l. 9. *his chast Lady*. See the General Introduction, pp. l, *et seq.*, for the unusual story of Patrick's sister, Victoria, who was affianced to

William Uvedale the younger, married his father, and finally, left a widow, bestowed her hand on her faithful blind admirer, Bartholomew Price. *alife*: dearly. See O.E.D., 'alife', adv.

l. 13. *young Will, the Heyre*. Cary's wish for his nephew was not fulfilled. Young Will died, *s.p.*, before 1663. There is some confusion about Sir William Uvedale's sons called William after him. The Uvedale pedigree accounts for two: an infant who died in 1617, and young Will, Victoria's son. This does not explain William the younger, who was engaged to Victoria Cary and died in 1638. Either this latter was William II, born between the other two—in that case perhaps his death abroad caused the lack of a funeral record; or the William Uvedale who was buried at Wickham in 1617 was not Sir William's son, and the first William lived to court Victoria. The family is a confusing one to follow, and the name William recurs in various branches.

l. 17. *well-grac'd Victoria*: Cary's elder niece, probably the 'Tolly' of the preceding poem (see p. 76). She married in 1663 Sir Richard Corbet of Lognor, Salop, and died before 1683. It was this mention of her name that contributed to the discovery of the poet's identity. See the General Introduction, p. xv.

l. 21. *plump Besse*: Elizabeth Uvedale, Victoria's younger sister, who was about five at this time. She did well for herself in later life, marrying first Sir William Berkeley, Governor of Portsmouth, and after his death becoming Countess of Carlisle.

l. 22. *Birlackins*: By our Ladykin, by our little Lady (i.e. the Virgin Mary).

l. 27. *goe sneake-up*. Chappell (i, 289, n.a.) suggests this should be 'sneck-up', a common verbal expression meaning 'go and be hanged': it is found in this sense in *Twelfth Night*, II. iii. 90. There may be a punning suggestion of the substantive 'sneak-up' (or 'sneak-cup') found e.g. in *1 Hen. IV*, III. iii. 84, 'a cowardly worthless fellow' or perhaps 'one who shirks his liquor'. See O.E.D., 'sneak-up', sb. and v.; and 'snick', v. [1] (obs.) b.

l. 29. *To th'Clearcke*. It is worth noting that according to the custom of the time the chaplain is ranked not with the family but with the senior servants. Cf. Carew, 'To my friend G.N. from Wrest':

COMMENTARY 79

    Some of that ranke, spun of a finer thred
    Are with the Women, Steward, and Chaplaine fed
    With daintier cates ...
                  (*Poems*, ed. Dunlap, 1949, p. 87.)

l. 38. *drench'd*. One earlier sense of 'drench', make to drink, is now restricted to administering a draught of medicine forcibly to an animal. See *O.E.D.*, 'drench'. A similar use is found p. 24, l. 37.

l. 39. *stench'd*. Saintsbury's dismissal of this (p. 460, n.) as a 'liberty' though dialectal is unwarranted. 'Stench' is an obsolete form of 'stanch' or 'staunch', in its obsolete sense of 'quench, allay' (of thirst etc.). See *O.E.D.*, 'stench', v., and 'stanch', v., 3.

l. 42. *mistress Cary*. This lady's identity is a puzzle. She cannot very well be, as Saintsbury suggests (p. 460, n.), one of Patrick Cary's four unmarried sisters, who were all Benedictine nums at Cambrai, unless she is the one who, according to a letter from Henry Hammond (Harleian MS. 6492, No. 73) dated only 'Nov. 9', had come over by pass from Parliament to London to 'take Physick'. I assume this refers to Dame Anne Clementia Cary, who is recorded as having gone to Paris in 1651 for cure of an illness. See Guilday, *The English Catholic Refugees on the Continent*, 1558–1795 (1914), i, 281. Another possibility is the 'Mrs. Faith Cary' who was buried at Wickham in 1652. She does not seem to have any place in the Falkland pedigrees, but was perhaps a relative of Sir William's first wife, Anne Carey, to whom he may characteristically have extended hospitality after Anne's death.

l. 43. *Mistresse Sculler*. I cannot trace Mistress Sculler, who is perhaps teased for affectation in being given a French excuse. If Mistress Cary in the preceding line should indeed be Dame Clementia, Mistress Sculler could conceivably be a travelling companion, who had acquired a Gallic turn of phrase from residence in France.

l. 45–8. *Dame Nell ... a Soppe*. etc. Dame Nell is the housekeeper, head of the female servants. She is addressed with some circumspection, and out of consideration for her abstemious tastes is to be allowed to dip her bread in the drink. See *O.E.D.*, 'sop', sb. 1. (Saintsbury's suggestion, p. 460, n., of 'sup' or 'sip' is superfluous.) Mary Smith, and Nan German, with her habitual exclamation 'Law ther-now!', sharing her stanza as they share her position at table, must be in the upper circles of the household staff. *wee'l allow you a Soppe*. Scott omits 'you', which Saintsbury conjecturally restores.

ll. 49–51. *Jane, Joane, Goody Lee* etc. The lower ranks too receive a genial salutation. 'Goody', a shortened form of 'Goodwife', was a term of civility formally applied to a woman, usually married, in humble life, often prefixed as a title to the surname. See *O.E.D.*, 'Goody', sb. 1. Is Meg the less the same as '*Meg* o'th'Dayry' (p. 20, l. 26), who seems at the nadir of domestic prestige? In any case she closes the list of names in the song, although the rest of the verse shows that there are still more servants in Sir William's hospitable household.

To the tune
I'le tell thee Dicke that I have beene &c.

('And can You thincke that this Translation')

I'le tell thee Dicke that I have beene &c. For this well-known tune see Appendix B, p. 121.

Poems, 1771 prints these verses, supplying a title: 'On the TRANSLATION of the LAWS into ENGLISH'.

l. 1. *this Translation.* On 22 November 1650 the Rump Parliament passed a law that all law-books were to be translated, and new ones printed in English; and that all writs, processes, proceedings of courts, statutes, patents, etc. were to be in the English tongue only, and 'not in Latine or French or any other Language then English'. See Henry Scobell, *A collection of Acts and Ordinances of General Use* (1658), Part II, pp. 148–9. Scott (Note II, p. 66) points out that this was done 'to intimidate the lawyers, by threatening not only to unveil, but to destroy the mysteries of their profession; and to gratify the Independents ... who had got it into their heads that the common law was a badge of the Norman Conquest'. He adds: 'It is scarce necessary to say that the act was never put into force.' Cary argues with wit and common sense that the Act could lead only to confusion. His concern for the law led Scott to suppose that he was 'bred to it'. In fact he was not admitted to Lincoln's Inn till the following year—10 February 1651/2. See the General Introduction, p. lviii.

l. 2. *our nation*. *Poems, 1771* reads 'the nation'.

COMMENTARY 81

l. 8. *Watt Mountague*. Walter Montagu, a kinsman of the Falklands, was the second son of the first Earl of Manchester. He was employed to negotiate the marriage of Henrietta Maria with Charles I, subsequently became a Catholic, and was one of the Queen's favourite courtiers. He wrote for her the pastoral play, *The Shepheard's Paradise*, in which she and her ladies, including two of Patrick Cary's sisters, acted. The Queen found her part lengthy and tedious, and the obscurity of the piece was a frequent subject for friendly satire. Cf. Suckling, 'Session of the Poets', where Apollo asks Montagu if he understands his own pastoral. (*Poems*, ed. Thompson, 1910, p. 11.) Exiled from England in 1649, Walter Montagu became abbot of Pontoise, and continue his service to the Queen. It was through him that Patrick Cary gained Henrietta Maria's recommendation to Cardinal Barberini, which won him the preferments he enjoyed in Rome. See *H & G* iii, 55, n.; Agnes Strickland, *Lives of the Queens of England* (1845), viii, 69.

ll. 19–24. Scott's note, cited above, makes a shrewd comment on the 'absurdity of this innovation, which, like the translation of botanical classifications, could only tend to substitute a barbarous vernacular jargon of dubious import, instead of the technical language of law-Latin and law-French to which time and the course of practice had given an exact and discriminate meaning'.

ll. 25, 26. *enough*: *allow*. The rhyme shows the confusion in sound and spelling still existing in the seventeenth century between *enough* and *enow*, the latter being given by Johnson as the plural form.

l. 39. *That most times darcknesse brung*. The sense of the passage in which this phrase occurs is: 'It is not the difficulty of a foreign language but the abstruseness of the subject matter that in most cases causes obscurity, although we are reluctant to acknowledge this.'
brung. O.E. had a rare past participle 'brungen'; otherwise the form is not given by *O.E.D.* except for the dialectal 'brung', dating from the nineteenth century. See *O.E.D.*, 'bring', v. *Poems, 1771* has a misreading: 'doubts has brung'.

ll. 43–5. *The Shoe-maker, beyond the Shoe* etc.: a reference to the proverb, 'A cobbler should stick to his last', based on Pliny: *Ne supra crepidam sutor iudicaret* (*Hist. Nat.*, Loeb edition, 1952, XXXV. xxxvi. 85). Pliny recalls the story that Apelles on the advice of a cobbler corrected a fault in a shoe-fastening in one of his paintings, but when the criticism was extended to the legs replied, 'Keep to your trade'.

l. 47. *meddle*. Cary M S. has *medde*, which must have been written in error. *Meddle* with the meaning 'to concern oneself (with)' was well established by the seventeenth century. *O.E.D.*, under 'meddle', v., cites: 'R. Harris, Serm. 8: "Happie that State wherein the Cobler meddles with his last, the Tradesman with his shop." 1622.'

l. 55. *Soe Words* etc. *Poems, 1771* reads 'For words' etc.

ll. 61–6. From these lines Scott, ignorant at the time of the poet's identity, concluded that Cary was a Roman Catholic. Saintsbury's suggestion (p. 460, n.) that they might have been written by a 'very good *Anglo*-Catholic (especially just after chipping the shell)' reads somewhat quaintly in the light of Cary's career, in which there is nothing to suggest that his deviation from Catholicism was due to any particular enthusiasm for the Church of England. In 1650–1 his family was still sufficiently Catholic for him to speak of 'our Church'.

To the tune
That we may row with my P. over the Ferry

('Good People of England! come heare mee relate')

That we may row etc. For a discussion of the tune see Appendix B, p. 122.

Poems, 1771 prints this piece supplying a title: 'On CROMWELL'S Red Nose being the Occasion of prohibiting the Importation of CLARET'.

l. 2. *State*: Republic, as contrasted with 'Kingdom'.

l. 3. *out of's pate*. *Poems, 1771* reads 'out of his pate'.

ll. 5–7. *Heigh-downe* etc. *Poems, 1771* omits this refrain from all stanzas.

In l. 6 a symbol ∻ occurs in Cary M S. to mark repetition; so with l. 28. This is represented in the text as ∻ .

COMMENTARY

l. 8. *French Clarret was banish'd*. During the second Civil War the Royalist sympathies of France led first to a raising of the existing duty on French wines, then to a total prohibition, imposed on 28 August 1649. See Scobell, *Collection of Acts*, Part II, pp. 86–7; Maurice Ashley, *Financial and Commercial Policy under the Cromwellian Protectorate* (1962), p. 60.

l. 9. *soe red as his Nose*. Cromwell's bulbous nose, dominating his reddish face, was a prime target for abuse from his opponents, and even a source of witticisms for his supporters. See Maurice Ashley, *Oliver Cromwell* (1940), pp. 193–4.

l. 14. *a Scotch Wench*. Cromwell was waging a victorious campaign in Scotland even as Cary was writing out these lines, and in August 1651 had captured Perth. See Ashley, *Oliver Cromwell*, p. 178.

l. 15. *th' tottering of's Toter* etc. 'Toter' for 'tooter', something that projects; hence, a prominent nose. See *O.E.D.*, 'tooter', sb.[1] (obs.), 2. Cromwell's Scotch wench is 'French', i.e. has the 'French disease', which causes the 'tottering' ('tettering') of his nose.

l. 16. An allusion to the topic of the previous poem.

ll. 20–1. *England's great Standard . . . att Nottingham*. Charles I set up his standard at Nottingham on 22 August 1642, the decisive moment that marked the beginning of the first Civil War.

l. 24. *Wee never shall* etc. *Poems, 1771* reads awkwardly 'we shall never' etc.

l. 26. *Oddsniggs* etc. For 'God's nigs', a form of oath, with a substantive not found in other contexts, and probably corrupt or fabricated. See *O.E.D.*, 'God', 14 b. The mild indecency of these verses is in notable contrast with the coarseness of some contemporary political pieces, e.g. *The Rump Poems*.

l. 29. *Till Clarett bee restor'd, lett us drincke Sherry*. The suggestion that Spanish wine will do as well is given point by the fact that ministers of Charles II had recently been soliciting aid from Spain. The two wines are thus symbolic of their countries. As if in ironic compliance with Cary's injunction to countermand the Act, Parliament in 1656 removed the tax on French wine. Soon after, during the Spanish war, the same policy of taxing was adopted in regard to sherry and other Spanish wines, which were duly raised £2 per tun. See Ashley, *Financial Policy*, p. 61; Scobell, *Collection of Acts*, Part II, p. 388.

To the tune
Will and Tom &c.

('*Jacke*! nay prithee come away')

Will and Tom &c. For the tune see Appendix B, p. 122.

l. 16. *but I will have her*. Saintsbury inexplicably reads 'but what I' etc.

l. 22. *Shiner*. Saintsbury (p. 463, n.) quotes several possible meanings from *Dial. Dict.*: clever fellow (ironic); knave; sweetheart. He further suggests 'one whose clothes are worn and shiny'. I prefer his final suggestion, that Dick with his new green suit ('All Greenes then this, are duller'), is the Shiner beside whom Jack's poverty would be accentuated.

l. 34. *And is an elder brother*. The phrase has a haunting ring for Patrick Cary, who in his fleeting appearances in seventeenth-century documents, and even in much later references, is seldom introduced as a personality in his own right, but rather as the 'great Lord Falkland's brother'.

ll. 46, 48. *Woeman*: *common*. A clue to this rhyme is perhaps afforded by the fact that Elisha Coles (1674) gives the phonetic spelling *wum-man*; and that Shakespeare puns on *common* and *Come on* (also spelt *Com' on*). See Dobson, ii, 722. The spelling *woe-*, invariable in Cary, is more commonly found in the plural form.

l. 47. *keepe sometimes touch*. 'Keep touch' (obs.): to keep faith or promise; perhaps from the practice of striking hands, or touching something sacred, in making agreement. See *O.E.D.*, 'touch', sb., 24 a.

l. 57.*'Lasse*! From the context and from comparison with line 71 below, this is obviously an abbreviation of 'alasse'. Cary uses this form several times as an expletive (p. 30, l. 7; p. 33, l. 6; p. 39, l. 19). A variant form is ''Las!' (p. 29, l. 14; p. 33, l. 12). Both these forms appear in Cary MS. without an initial apostrophe: I have supplied this to avoid ambiguity.

COMMENTARY

To the tune
But that n'ere troubles mee Boyes &c.

('And now a Figge for th'lower House')

But that n'ere troubles mee Boyes &c. I have been unable to trace this tune.

Poems, 1771 prints this poem with a title: 'NOT WORTH A GROAT'.

ll. 2, 5. *nought*: *Groate*. Eight other words in this poem rhyme with *Groate*: *fought, sought, caught, brought, vault, bought, ought, wrought.* The pronunciation of 'groat' made clear from this list is recorded as widespread by phoneticians writing between 1643 and 1700. See Dobson, ii, 530; i, 165, 266.

l. 3. *For spent is my last Groat Boyes. Poems, 1771* omits 'Boyes' in this line, and the whole of the following line, in all stanzas.

l. 6. *Delinquent.* This term, defined by an Order of 27 March 1643, was applied by the Parliamentary party to all who supported the Crown between 1642 and 1660. In practice it included all Royalists, and came to be synonymous with 'Cavalier'. See *O.E.D.*, 'delinquent', sb., 2.

l. 7. *Though gainst the cause, & Noll I'had fought.* Scott surmised from this line that Cary was a loyal Cavalier soldier, and, describing the militia he was helping to raise in 1819, adds: 'They are all practized marksmen, and full of a sort of spirit which would have pleased old Carey.' See Scott, *Letters*, vi, 68. In fact Cary is here expressing an unrealized condition.

l. 10. *Poems, 1771* reads 'For who's not worth a groat?' The meaning is obviously 'For one who is not worth a groat'.

l. 12. *Pursuivants*: royal or state messengers with authority to execute warrants. See *O.E.D.*, 'pursuivant', sb., 2.

l. 13. *sicure.* *O.E.D.* does not record this spelling, which Cary repeats on p. 66, l. 21. It seems to be influenced by Italian *sicuro*, which would be familiar to him after twelve years in Italy.

l. 19. *From One. Poems, 1771* reads 'From me'; other misreadings in this poem are: l. 22, *were brought* ('was brought'); l. 24, *I being not* ('I not being'); l. 42, *wrought* ('wrote').

l. 26. *Raw-One*. 'Raw': uncultivated, uncivilized, brutal. See *O.E.D.*, 'raw', a. 3. If 'in the ayre to vault' (l. 27) means 'to be hanged', 'Raw-One' would seem to be a contemptuous reference to the common executioner.

l. 43. *Committee-men*. See note on *Committy*, p. 87.

The Country Life

To a French tune

The Country Life. This is the only poem in this section of the manuscript to which the poet himself has given a title.

l. 11. *secluded*: ostracized.

l. 17. *Pactions*: bargains, agreements; now chiefly Scottish.

l. 18. *Frize*: frieze, a coarse woollen cloth with nap usually on one side only.

l. 35. *thereafter*: in accordance, i.e., foul like the 'Ayre, Streets, Water'. For the rhyme see p. 70.

To the tune
And will you now to Peace encline &c.

('The Parliament ('tis sayd) resolv'd')

And will you now etc. For this tune see Appendix B, p. 123.

Poems, 1771 prints this piece with a title, 'The ACT of OBLIVION'. It omits stanzas 2, 3, 6, and 7.

ll. 1–3. *The Parliament ('tis sayd) resolv'd* etc. As Cary wrote these lines in 1651 the Long Parliament was renewing discussions on attempts made several times before to repair its reduced popularity by granting an amnesty for Royalist acts of treason. The Act of Oblivion was finally passed at Cromwell's instigation on 24 February 1652. However, so many exceptions were added that it brought little relief to the hard-pressed Cavaliers. See Gardiner, *History of the Commonwealth and Protectorate, 1649–1656* (1903), ii, 81.

l. 5. *Lethe*. The waters of the river of forgetfulness flowing through the underworld of Greek mythology are identified with liquor in a neatly insulting accusation of intemperance: Parliament has thus become oblivious of its own Act of Oblivion.

COMMENTARY

ll. 9, 12. *heard on*: Pardon. The pronunciation of *heard* as *hard* was a current colloquial form in educated society up to the eighteenth century. See Wyld, *Rhymes*, p. 122.

l. 11. *Malignants to compound.* 'Malignant': one ill disposed towards rightful authority, used by the Parliamentary party against Royalists. *compound*: to pay (also, to accept) terms of settlement in lieu of prosecution, especially of Royalists under the Commonwealth. See O.E.D., 'malignant', sb., B., b.; 'compound', v. 15, b.

l. 18. *each Committy*. To administer moneys amassed from Royalist fines and property the Long Parliament set up special funds with offices situated in London. In 1650 there were ten such departments, most of their business being controlled by special committees, with one or other of whom Royalists under penalty would have to deal. Under the Protectorate the funds were united in one exchequer and the Committees gradually ceased to function. See Ashley, *Financial Policy*, p. 40.

ll. 28–30. *Goldsmithe's and Haberdasher's Hall . . . Druery-house*. The Committee at Goldsmith's Hall (in Foster Lane) assessed fines paid by Royalists to avoid sequestration or total forfeiture of property. As soon as this 'composition' had been settled, the delinquent was sent to Haberdasher's Hall (in Gresham St.) to pay his fine. Drury House was the office for the sale of confiscated Royalists' lands. The point of the reference is that the three names were hated symbols for successive stages of Parliamentary prosecution. See Ashley, *Financial Policy*, p. 39; Saintsbury, pp. 465–6, n.

ll. 34–5. *The Souldier . . . to Ireland* etc. The Parliamentary forces were engaged in the bitter task of subduing Ireland until the surrender of Galway in May 1652. The pay of soldiers employed in this campaign was provided by confiscation, subdivision, and distribution of estates of Irish landowners. This policy of turning soldiers into small farmers in a foreign land instead of paying them in their own, seldom successful in history, was calculated to make the Parliamentary troops indeed 'full of discontent'. See Charles Firth, *Oliver Cromwell* (1906), p. 265.

l. 40. *th'new Representative*. In February 1649 a petition from 'many Christian people' of the county of Norfolk and the city of Norwich was presented to Parliament, proposing the establishment of a Fifth Monarchy (to succeed the four of the ancient world)—the rule of 'Christ and his Saints'. The Church was to be the sole source and control of civil authority, which would operate through church assemblies. On 15 October 1651 *A Model of a New Representative* revived the proposals of the Fifth Monarchy, submitting that the new Parliament should be elected by the 'Churches of the Saints'. See Gardiner, *History of the Commonwealth*, i, 29; ii, 71. Most Royalists probably shared Cary's view that the existing Government, pernicious as they thought it, was preferable to this.

l. 41. *I'de e'ene as live*. 'live': lief, i.e. soon. 'I'd just as soon'.

l. 49. *A Promise, is a Debt*. For the origin of this saying see Tilley, *Dictionary of the proverbs in England in the sixteenth and seventeenth centuries* (1950), p. 603.

ll. 53–4. *House of office*: a privy. On 20 April 1653 Cromwell unwittingly followed this excellent advice and dissolved the Long Parliament.

To a French tune

('Speake of somewhat else I pray;')

l. 3. *Lilly*: William Lilly, the astrologer (1602–81), who was then at the height of his reputation. He did not impress Dorothy Osborne when he told her fortune in 1654. See Osborne, p. 175. (*Joane*.) There is no clue to the identity of this lady. The '*Joane*' mentioned in another poem (p. 15, l. 49) is obviously one of the Uvedale servants.

l. 5. *Capricorne*: the tenth (strictly the eleventh) sign of the zodiac (21 December–20 January). In classical mythology Capricorn was Pan, who, having changed himself into a goat for fear of the giant Typhon, was made by Jupiter one of the signs of the zodiac. See Brewer's Dictionary, p. 468.

l. 6. *fear o' th' Horne*. To wear the horn: to be a cuckold. The phrase has borne this meaning for over four centuries in many European languages. Several explanations, none very convincing, have been offered. See *Brewer's Dictionary*, p. 468.

ll. 19–24. *When Jove th' European rape* etc. Jove took the form of a beautiful bull to attract and carry off the maiden Europa; and as

Jupiter Ammon he was worshipped under the form of a ram, and portrayed in the Graeco-Roman world as Zeus with ram's horns.

l. 38. *my weake Head*. Scott, followed by Saintsbury, has an inexplicable misreading, 'stead'.

To a French tune

('A greev'd Countessse, that e're long')

ll. 1–6. *A greev'd Countesse* etc. One gesture of revenge made against peers who had supported Charles I was the deprivation of the titles he had conferred. On 4 February 1651/2 Parliament passed an Act nullifying all titles of honour given by him since 4 January 1642. All patents of nobility were to be brought in and cancelled under penalty of £50 fine. To continue to use such a title, or even call another by it, was to incur heavy penalty. The Act was stringently applied, to the chagrin of the nobles and of course their wives, one of whom figures in Cary's poem. See Scobell, *Collection of Acts*, Part II, p. 178. The dating of the Act, early in 1652, implies that this poem was written later than the date on the title-page of Cary MS., 20 August 1651. See p. lxix.

l. 2. Note that the second line in each stanza has no matching rhyme.

ll. 17–18. William Lilly published his *Annus Tenebrosus*, noting calculated dates of eclipses, in 1652. See Saintsbury, p. 467, n.

l. 22. *Th' Ephimerides*: the tabulated positions of a heavenly body for a series of successive days—hence a determinant of dating astronomical phenomena. See *O.E.D.*, 'ephemerides'.

l. 23. *the twenty fift*. The Act of 4 February 1652 appointed 25 March of that year as the latest day for compliance. See Scobell, Part II, p. 178.

To an Italian tune

(''Tis true. I am fetter'd')

l. 1. *'Tis true. I am fetter'd*. This, the only poem Cary writes of happy fulfilment in love, may date from the time of his engagement to Susan Uvedale. See the General Introduction, p. lv.

COMMENTARY

To a Spanish tune
called *Folias*

('Cease t'exaggerate your anguish')

Folias. For a discussion of this tune, see Appendix B, p. 124.

l. 8. *Stella.* This appears to be the only occasion Cary chooses an artificial name for his supposed mistress. The gloomy Petrarchan tone, so different from his usual airy gallantry, is consciously adopted with wry detachment.

To the Italian tune
called *Girometta*

('O, permitt that my Sadnesse')

Girometta. For a discussion of the tune, see Appendix B, p. 125.

l. 4. *Pregiudice.* This unusual spelling not given by O.E.D. suggests Italian influence. In a letter quoted on p. 1 Cary writes 'pregiudiciall'.

l. 20. *raccount.* Perhaps this form is due to influence of Fr. *raconter*.

To the tune
To Parliament the Queene is gonne &c.

('This Aprile last a gentle Swayne')

To Parliament etc. For a discussion of the tune, see Appendix B, p. 125.

l. 13. Note that the last line of each stanza has no corresponding rhyme.

l. 16. *Hee t'Other pluck'd.* Scott, followed by Saintsbury, reads 'her t'other' etc., a strange association of pronouns in the context.

ll. 24–6. Various superstitions of ill luck are associated with hearing the first cry of the cuckoo. As it occupies the nest and ousts the eggs of other birds, it is regarded as a symbol of marital infidelity. The nightingale is a natural emblem of love's felicity. Cf. Milton:

> Thy liquid notes that close the eye of Day,
> First heard before the shallow Cucoo's bill
> Portend success in love . . .

COMMENTARY

Now timely sing, ere the rude Bird of Hate
Foretell my hopeless doom in som Grove ny.
(Sonnet i, *Poems*, ed. Darbishire, 1958, p. 428.)

l. 33. *Well the Cuckow* etc. Scott, followed by Saintsbury, reads 'With the cuckow' etc.

ll. 45-6. The metaphor is from falconry; 'stoop': swoop down; 'lure': the device used to recall the falcon to its master.

To the tune
I'le have my Love, or I'le have none

('Some prayse the Browne, and some the Fayre')

I'le have my Love etc. For a discussion of the tune, see Appendix B, p. 125. Scott and Saintsbury read 'have on[e]'.

ll. 1-4. *Some prayse the Browne* etc. One cannot help recalling Donne: 'I can love both faire and browne' ('The Indifferent', *Elegies, Songs and Sonnets*, ed. H. Gardner, 1965, p. 41). But a closer resemblance is seen in Thomas Stanley, 'Love's Heretick':

> Black or fair or tall or low,
> I alike with all can sport . . .
> (*Poems*, ed. Crump, 1962, p. 34.)

. 6. *lead Apes in Hell*: the doom of old maids. Cf. *Much Ado*, II. i. 34. For the origin of the expression, see *Brewer's Dictionary*, p. 39.

ll. 9, 10. *too*: *woe*. *Woe* is a regular seventeenth-century spelling of *woo*; hence the rhyme would be accurate. See *O.E.D.*, 'woo', v.; and Dobson, i, 412.

l. 29. *surfitts vant*. Scott, followed by Saintsbury, reads 'surfeitts want', which duplicates the rhyme and makes poor sense; 'vant': vaunt, boast.

To the tune
Phillida flouts mee

('*Ned!* She that likes thee now')

Phillida flouts mee. For this popular tune, see Appendix B, p. 125.
l. 11. *Francke*. Saintsbury (p. 470, n.) points out that this could be

92   COMMENTARY

short for Frances as well as Francis. Cromwell's daughter Frances was sometimes called Frankie. The context requires a feminine name.

l. 31. *not soe fast*. Scott misreads 'soe aft', which Saintsbury amends.

To the tune
Francklin is fled away
('Alasse! long since I knew')

Francklin is fled away. For this tune, see Appendix B, p. 126.

l. 8. Note that the last line in each stanza does not rhyme. The original song ends each with a refrain, 'O hone, O hone'.

l. 10. *made*: 'invented, fictitious'. See *O.E.D.*, 'made', past part., I. 1. b.

Title-page of Part II, Cary MS.

The title-page of this section of the manuscript, which contains religious poems, is headed by the text, 'I will sing unto the LORD' (Ps. xiii. 6). Cary uses the wording of the Authorized Version for this and all English biblical quotations. Below the text is a coat of arms, a Tudor rose, and the inscription, 'Warneford, 1651'. Scott (*Letters*, ii, 427) describes this rose as red, but there is no trace of colour now: he may have made a slip in describing from memory. He transferred an engraving based on this coat of arms etc. to the first title-page of his own edition. I have reproduced on the second title-page in the text (p. 41) an impression of the original design. For a discussion of this illustration and the problem of the date, see the General Introduction, pp. xiv, lxix, *et seq*.

Triolets

Triolets. This word is clearly printed at the top of the first page of this section of Cary MS., and only on that page. It obviously refers only to the three triolets which come under this heading. Scott takes it as the title for all the religious verses, printing it at the head of each page in this section of his edition, and incorporating it into his title, *Trivial Poems and Triolets*. Saintsbury (p. 472, n.) observes that 'Triolets' is not an appropriate title for the whole section. He was

COMMENTARY

not aware that Cary never intended it as such. For a discussion of Cary's handling of the triolet, see the General Introduction, p. lxxv. *Poems, 1771* has for the heading of its first section, containing four of the religious poems, the title *SERIAE NUGAE*, and begins with 'Triolets'.

l. 1. *Worldly Designes, Feares, Hopes, farwell!* This was obviously written just before or just after Cary's entrance into the Benedictine Order. See the General Introduction, pp. lxix *et seq.*

> 'O that I had wings like a Dove
> for then would I fly away, and bee at rest'
> (Ps. lv. 6)
> ('By Ambition raysed high')

l. 4. *the pompe of Kings.* Saintsbury justly observes (p. 472, n.) that this is not mere 'copy-book morality'. At the court of Pope Urban VIII Cary had indeed seen the 'pompe of Kings'.

l. 10. *Bubbles, full of wind.* Cf. William Drummond:

> This life which seems so faire,
> Is like a Bubble blowen up in the Aire,
> By sporting Childrens Breath.
> (Madrigal i, *Poems*, Part 2, 1616.)

Servire Deo, Regnare est

Servire Deo etc. The title appears to be taken from a phrase hallowed by Christian devotional tradition, occurring in the post-communion prayer of the Votive Mass for Peace, in the Roman rite: *Deus... cui servire regnare est.*

l. 6. *rotten wood glitters.* This expressive image recalls a poem attributed with some doubt to Raleigh:

> Say to the Court it glowes
> and shines like rotten wood...
> ('The Lie', *Poems*, ed. Latham, 1951, p. 45, ll. 7–8.)

The idea of the phosphorescence of rotten wood finds support in Pliny: *quin et in tenebris multorum piscium [oculi] refulgent, aridi sicut robusti caudices putresque vetustate* (*Hist. Nat.*, ed. Loeb, 1947, XI. lv. 151).

ll. 13–14. The Erithrean sands were the shores of the Red Sea. For the belief that jewels were found on sea-shores, including the Red Sea, and the banks of rivers, see *Batman upon Bartholme* (1582), ff. 261^r–62^r.

ll. 15–17. The Indies seemed to Cary's age a fabulous source of wealth. Cf. Carew:

> I'le trade with no such Indian foole as sells
> Gold, Pearles and pretious Stones, for Beads and Bells.
> (*Poems*, ed. Dunlap, 1949, p. 86.)

l. 18. *guilt clay*. Cf. Herbert's 'Frailtie': 'I surname them [riches etc.] guilded clay' (*Works*, ed. Hutchinson, 1941, p. 71). In Cary there may be a suggestion of a pun. Cf. *Macbeth*, II. ii. 56–7.

ll. 19–21. The idea of the miniature kingdom of the beehive, ruled by a king rather than a queen, was familiar from Pliny (*Hist. Nat.*, ed. Loeb, XI, xvii) and Virgil (*Georgics*, iv. 21). The bee as a symbol of pomp would have been a common sight to Cary in Rome, from the three in the coat of arms of Urban VIII. In these lines of his poem the tiny communities of hive and ant-hill mirror and mock at man's busy, pretentious world.

ll. 29–30. An echo of the Pauline paradoxes in 2 Cor. vi. 10. Underneath this poem in Cary M S. are three small sketches—skull, crown, hour-glass—the first of Cary's emblems, discussed in Appendix A, p. 103.

> The invisible things of him from the Creation of the World
> are cleerely seene; being Understood by the things that are made.
> (Rom. i. 20)
> ('Whilst I beheld the necke o'th'*Dove*')

For a discussion of textual problems and other aspects of this poem see the General Introduction, p. lxxviii, and the Textual Introduction, pp. xcv *et seq. Poems, 1771* prints this piece with a different title, 'The Senses'.

l. 18. *Thus sang* etc. Scott, followed by Saintsbury, reads 'This sang etc.'

COMMENTARY

ll. 19–45. The images in these lines are reminiscent of elements of Ben Jonson's well-known stanza, 'Have you seene but a bright Lillie grow' (*The Devil is an Ass*, II. vi. 104–13, included in 'The Triumph of Charis', *Underwoods*, 1640). However, Cary's handling of them is individual. After this poem in Cary MS. is Emblem (2), altar and wreath. See Appendix A, p. 103.

Crux VIA Cælorum

Above this poem in Cary MS. is Emblem (3), temple with cross as pathway. See Appendix A, p. 103. The poem is a commentary on both title and emblem.

Crux VIA Cælorum. If this is a quotation I have not found the exact source; but I suspect it is the poet's own summary of some such passage as: *Non est alia via ad vitam . . . nisi via sanctae crucis.* (*Imitation of Christ*, II. xii. 6). *Poems, 1771* prints this poem under a somewhat clumsy Latin title of its own: *QUICQUID PATIATUR HOMO, IN REBUS DIVINIS OPTIME PATIATUR.* I can find no classical or theological source for this—it seems merely a Latin summary of the theme.

l. 29. *Warre. Poems, 1771* reads 'wars'.

l. 56. *I saw tost.* Scott and Saintsbury misread 'I am tost'.

Crucifixus pro Nobis

Above this poem is Emblem (4), a crucifixion scene. See Appendix A, p. 104.

Crucifixus pro Nobis. The title recalls the Nicene Creed: *crucifixus est etiam pro nobis.*

Christ in the Cradle. These lines inevitably suggest comparison with Southwell's 'The Burning Babe', with their associations of cold, heat, and the infant Christ. See *Poems*, ed. McDonald and Brown (1967), p. 15.

l. 5. Note that the fifth line in each stanza is left without a rhyme.

l. 7. *Then is the Snow.* Scott reads 'show', which Saintsbury corrects.

l. 9. *Candour*: in the classical sense of 'whiteness'.

96 COMMENTARY

ll. 46, 48. *Cold*: *could*. *Could* owes its – *l* to analogy with *should* and *would*; but it seems that this – *l* was not always merely graphic. Spenser and Drayton rhyme *could*: *behold*; and Owen Price (writing 1665–70) links the sounds of *could*: *cold*: *cool'd*. See Wyld, *Rhymes*, p. 130.

l. 50. *Stripes*. Scott has 'strippes', silently amended by Saintsbury.

Beneath the last stanza of this poem is Emblem (5), roses from thorns. See Appendix A, p. 104.

A choral setting of the poem was composed by Dr. D. Mews, University of Auckland, 1970.

Fallax, et Instabilis

Above the heading of the poem is Emblem (6), a mermaid. See Appendix A, p. 105.

Fallax, et Instabilis. If this is a quotation I have not been able to trace it. There is a hint of Virgil's *varium et mutabile* (*Aen.* iv. 569); but the phrase is more likely to have been formed from some passage in *The Imitation of Christ*, e.g. *Infirmi sumus et instabiles, cito fallimur et permutamur* (*Imit.* III. xlv. 1). In their general temper the verses recall Southwell's 'Times goe by turnes' (*Poems*, ed. McDonald and Brown, 1967, p. 57) but the concepts emphasized are somewhat different.

There is noe new Thing etc. Cary MS. gives Eccl. i. 10 for this text. In fact the Authorized Version, which he is quoting, gives it as verse 9, although the Vulgate, which he uses for the Latin texts, gives verse 10.

ll. 14–26. Mention in these lines of earth, air, fire, and water recalls the ancient philosophical theory that all matter was composed of these four elements in a state of union or division.

Vidi in omnibus etc. Scott, followed by Saintsbury, reads the imperative *Vide*. The Vulgate text Cary is quoting, Eccl. ii. 11, has the indicative *Vidi*.

Nulla Fides

Above the title of this poem is Emblem (7), Fortune on her wheel. See Appendix A, p. 106.

COMMENTARY 97

Nulla Fides. The phrase looks like an abbreviation of some scriptural or devotional text, e.g. *Quam saepe non inveni fidem ubi me habere putavi?* (*Imitation of Christ,* III. xlv. 1.)

l. 1. *For God's sake.* The explosive opening suggests a deliberate imitation of Donne, the more so as the rest of the poem is in quieter, more reflective vein.

l. 5. *Has killed a Pope.* If Cary is referring to a specific case, it can only be that of Hadrian IV (Nicholas Breakspeare), the only English Pope, who died on 1 September 1159 of quinsy, as he was preparing to excommunicate the Emperor Barbarossa. The improbable rumour spread that he was choked by swallowing a fly which had lodged in his throat as he was drinking at a well. Some attribute this tale to the Emperor's supporters, who claimed the death as an act of divine vengeance. See F. M. Steele, *The Story of the English Pope* (1908), p. 173.

l. 12. *vild Itt is.* 'Vild' is a variant, now obsolete, of 'vile', the consonantal ending being more apt before the vowel of 'Itt'. Elsewhere Cary uses 'vilest' (p. 45, l. 28).

[*Stulte, hac nocte animam tuam repetunt a te.* (Luke, xii. 20)]

('What use has Hee made of his Soule')

Above this poem is Emblem (8), the Fool on a pedestal. See Appendix A, p. 107.

[*Stulte, hac nocte* etc.] As this is the only poem in Cary MS. without a title of any kind, I have ventured to provide one from the Vulgate, combining the elements of the fool, his misused soul, and the penalty awaiting him.

ll. 13–29. The catalogue of animals taken here as typifying the lowest instincts and passions of man's nature suggests the poet may have been turning over the pages of one of the emblem books which inspired his illustrations. I have suggested (p. 103) that Cary was familiar with the emblems of J. Camerarius. In the latter's *Symbolorum et Emblematum ex animalibus quadrupedibus desumtorum centuria altera* we find a number of examples each of the lion, the goat, the boar-hog, and the hound. In the next division (*Centuria Tertia*) appear the crow and the peacock; and in the last book

COMMENTARY

(*Centuria Quarta*) the snail. While it is obvious that these creatures are part of the stock-in-trade of fable-writers and moralists, their association here is at least interesting.

l. 23. *cogge*: 'cheat, deceive'. The origin of the verb in this sense seems to be a cog or device for loading dice. See *O.E.D.*, 'cog', v.³

Accepit in vano etc. Cary MS. quotes these words as Ps. xxiii. 4, giving the Vulgate text and numeration. In the Authorized Version the passage appears as Ps. xxiv. 4. Because of a variation in grouping the psalms of the Massoretic text, the Vulgate numbering is one behind that of the Authorized Version for the greater part of the psalter. It is perhaps worth noting that the poet wrests the words somewhat to his own purpose. The Vulgate reads *qui non accepit in vano animam suam*; A.V. renders, 'who hath not lifted up his soul unto vanity'.

Dirige vias meas Domine!

Above this heading is Emblem (9), the choice of ways. See Appendix A, p. 108.

Dirige etc. The title seems based on Ps. v. 8, which in the Vulgate reads *dirige in conspectu tuo viam meam*.

l. 18. *affect*: 'love, show preference for'. See *O.E.D.*, 'affect', v.,¹ 2.

ll. 19–20. Scott's punctuation, kept by Saintsbury, distorts the sense:

> Pray, when with others; when alone,
> To scorne, or prayse bee as a stone;

Obviously a strong pause is needed at the end of the first line; 'when alone' balances 'with Others': prayer is to be both communal and private.

l. 28. *Use-less our Master* etc. This was perhaps suggested by Luke xvii. 10: 'So likewise ye, when ye shall have done all those things which are commanded you, say, We are unprofitable servants: we have done that which was our duty to do.'

Nobis natus in Pretium: nobis datus in Præmium

Above the title is Emblem (10), monogram I H S with infant Christ. See Appendix A, p. 109.

Nobis natus etc. This seems a composite title, formed from two hymns of the Roman Breviary Office of Corpus Christi:

> *Nobis datus, nobis natus*
> *Ex intacta virgine;* (*Pange Lingua*)

> *Se nascens dedit socium,*
> *Convescens in edulium,*
> *Se moriens in pretium,*
> *Se regnans dat in praemium.* (*Verbum Supernum*)

l. 31. *sanctificate*: a rare usage as a verb; the earliest instance given by O.E.D. is from a sermon of Barrow (1671).

EXPRIMETVR

EXPRIMETVR. The title is here included within the frame of the Emblem (11) of a winepress, which heads the poem. Without the sketch the title is practically meaningless: Saintsbury (p. 479, n.) was baffled by it. See Appendix A, p. 110.

Poems, 1771 gives this piece a title: 'The EXTORTIONER'S Epitaph'. This is Cary's only example of the sonnet. The unusual rhyme scheme—ababababcdcdcd—was used by Sidney, the *Old Arcadia*, Sonnet 53 (*Poems*, ed. Ringler, 1962, p. 80).

The text presents special problems in typography. In the Textual Introduction, p. xciii, I have explained the general principles I have adopted in dealing with Cary's variations between cursive and printed script, and the varying size of letters employed. This sonnet is an exceptional case: alone of all the poems in the Cary MS. it is in printed script throughout. Alone, too, it has a large number of words in capitals: twenty-one in fourteen lines, fourteen of which are further emphasized by large initial capitals. In two of these words (BVILDER'S and GVILT) the capital V (for U) is carefully printed, as it is in the title printed above the emblem: EX-PRIMETVR. The central image of the poem is tombstones, and the whole effect of the sonnet is to recall funerary inscriptions. These retained the use of V for both V and U longer than printed books.

The general principle I have adopted is to render Cary's ordinary cursive script by roman type and his printed script by italic. Therefore the whole of this sonnet is shown in italic, except for some words in ll.4 and 11, for which see (3) below, and the words in capitals. These last, for the sake of special emphasis, I have printed in roman capitals, but I have ignored the fact that Cary has dignified fourteen of them by large initials. I have also taken the following liberties with the text:

(1) The words shown in this edition as 'HOVSE' (l.1) and 'HEAV'N' (l.13) appear in Cary MS. with initial capitals, and the remaining letters in lower case but as large as capitals in other words. Cary plainly meant to emphasize them and I have treated his failure to put them wholly in capitals as an inconsistency.

(2) To carry out what I believe to have been Cary's intention (to produce a lapidary effect), I have printed V for U in all cases where this letter occurs, except 'underneath' (l.4), for which see (3) below. This involved printing V instead of U in 'HOVSE' and 'HEAV'N', as above, and also in 'CHVRCH-YARDS' (l.5).

(3) ll.4 and 11 give the actual wording of two inscriptions. In Cary MS. they read:

l. 4. '*Say still,* HERE UNDERNEATH SOME-BODY's *layde.*'

l. 12. '*As, Here, the* WIDDOW; *Here, the* ORPHAN *lyes.*'

It seemed desirable to standardize the form of these two inscriptions, and also to keep the emphasis placed on 'SOME-BODY' 'WIDDOW', and 'ORPHAN' by their having words in smaller printed script beside them. The simplest way to do this seemed to be to employ small roman type for the inscriptions with the emphatic words in roman capitals:

l. 4. '*Say still*, Here underneath SOME-BODY's layde.'

l. 11. '*As*, Here, the WIDDOW: Here, the ORPHAN lyes.'

l. 2. Cary MS. has 'wrought', which has been crossed out, with 'made' in printed script above it in Cary's hand. With such exquisite care is the manuscript written out that this instance, and another in *Dies Irae, Dies illa*, for which see below, are the only examples of emendations made by the poet in his text, apart from two words ('hast Thou') duplicated and lightly deleted in the Scripture text

COMMENTARY

which forms part of the design in Emblem (2), reproduced in the text on p. 48, and described in Appendix A, p. 103.

Dies Iræ, Dies illa

Above the title is Emblem (12), Christ the Judge. See Appendix A, p. 109. In the right-hand margin of the manuscript are the words 'This is a Translation'.

l. 8. *under ground*. Here the poet apparently wrote 'undergroun', crossed out the last five letters and wrote 'ground' separately.

ll. 22–7. It is hard to see how Cary, or anyone else, could render *Rex tremendae maiestatis* by 'My Request doe not reject'; or why he should have complicated with sheep and wolves the noble simplicity of *Quod sum causa tuae viae*. The sonorous rhyming Latin of the *Dies Irae* has allured over two hundred translators to try turning it into English, an almost impossible feat to accomplish successfully. One can only regret that Cary wished, or was persuaded, to add to their efforts a singularly bad translation.

l. 30. *this paynes*. Scott misreads 'this pray'rs'. Saintsbury follows him but correctly notes (p. 480, n.) it should be 'pains' from Latin *labor*. After this poem is the last Emblem (13), the Blessed Virgin enthroned. See Appendix A, p. 112.

Appendix A

PATRICK CARY'S USE OF EMBLEM

An interesting and significant feature of Cary MS. is the use made by Patrick Cary of the emblem. This has not been noted by any previous editor or writer apart from a short sentence in Scott's Introduction (p. iv): 'These devotional pieces are ornamented with small emblematical vignettes, very neatly drawn with a pen.' Apparently Scott did not regard these sketches as anything more than ornament: he made no attempt to consider their relationship with the poems they illustrate, or the link they establish between Cary and the emblem-writers.

The quality and appeal of these 'emblematical vignettes' are considerable. There can be no doubt that they are Cary's own work: the delicacy of the pen-and-ink drawing points to the writer who executed the exquisitely neat text and described the intricate flourishes that here and there decorate it. The printed script of the wording that forms part of some of the sketches is identical with that used in the text. The designs cannot be dismissed as mere ornament, but must be considered in the light of the verses associated with them, and of the emblem tradition in general.

Reproductions of these illustrations, in natural size, will be found in their places in the text of this edition. It is unfortunately not possible to reproduce the precision of detail and shading, or to convey the warm toning of sepia ink against paper deepened in tint by time and handling. In spite of a number of artistic flaws the drawings have to my mind both merit and significance.

It may be assumed that Patrick Cary in the cultivated ecclesiastical society of Rome, as well as in the Benedictine monastery of Douai, would have had access to a good many English and European emblematists as sources of inspiration. Urban VIII, his patron, was himself a dilettante poet, according to Herbert's epigram: *Pontificem tandem nacta est sibi Roma poetam*,[1] and encouraged poets and emblem-writers by personal interest.[2] Cary would thus have had a wide range of models to draw on. In the following comments the drawings are numbered, according to their order in the text.

[1] *Works*, ed. Hutchinson (1953), p. 417.
[2] See M. Praz, *Studies in Seventeenth-Century Imagery* (1939; 2nd edn. 1964), p. 201, n. 1.

PATRICK CARY'S USE OF EMBLEM

(1) A skull, a crown, and an hour-glass (p. 46). These small separate sketches on the same horizontal plane occur at the end of the verses *Servire Deo, Regnare est.* That they are not just space-fillers is shown by the fact that similar spaces at the end of other poems are taken up with flourishes of the pen. They are established symbols, relating specifically to the verses above them. The skull is a *Memento mori*, suggested by '*Graves*' and '*Wormes*' in ll. 27–8. The crown, an emblem of heavenly reward, catches up the notions of earthly monarchy in '*Prince of men*' (l. 22), '*Kings*' and '*Thrones*' (l. 27); and of divine kingship in the title and in 'Sovverayne' (l. 36). The hour-glass, an accepted symbol of passing time, is always with the emblematists a silent reminder that notice should be taken of their words before it is too late. This idea of time runs through the poem itself—time past: 'before' (l. 1), 'then' (l. 4); time present: 'Now' (l. 13); future: 'Hee'l see' (l. 27), 'will teach' (l. 32); and finally the timeless eternal present: 'doe raigne' (l. 35).

There is no need to list sources of these symbols, which are commonplaces among the emblem-writers, as well as in many forms of art.

(2) An altar with laurel wreath (p. 48). This sketch occupies about a third of the page on which end the verses 'Whilst I beheld the necke o'th'*Dove*'. The altar, seen through an arch of foliage, with its laurel wreath of praise offered to God, whose presence is signified by the sun bearing Hebrew lettering, is a clear representation of the lesson taught in the last line of the poem, '*I too have all from* GOD'. This is reinforced by the Pauline text set about the emblem: 'What has Thou that Thou didst not receaue?' etc.', which summarizes the message emphasized by varying images through the stanzas.

The most likely source for this design is G. Rollenhagen, *Nucleus Emblematum* (1611), which shows (ii, 1) an altar with a laurel wreath upright above it and (ii, 7) the sun with Hebrew lettering representing the divine presence. The same combination of altar and laurel wreath is seen in *Symbolorum et Emblematum ... centuria una* (No. 50) of J. Camerarius, whose emblem books were first published 1590–1604. A leafy or thorny arch similar to that in Cary's sketch appears in Georgette de Montenay, *Emblèmes ou Devises Chrestiennes* (1571), p. 47.

(3) A temple on a hill, with a cross as pathway to it (p. 49), above the poem *Crux VIA Cælorum*. The round, pillared temple, in classical style, is a familiar emblem for heaven, or for the Church that leads man there. The most suggestive model for Cary's sketch is perhaps one from Hieronymus Ammon, *Amoris divini et humani antipathia* (1629), facing p. 8. Here are the temple and cupola, the hill, the pathway, the distant landscape with its towers. The title, too, is suggestive, 'Hierusalem Amoris'. A similar emblem appears in Georgette de Montenay, *Emblèmes*

Chrestiennes, p. 12, where only the façade of the temple is seen, and a sturdy figure in cape and short cloak is preparing to tackle the steep ascent. Cary has no human figure in his sketch; he has given it an original touch by making the cross itself serve as pathway to the heavenly Jerusalem. This reinforces the message of the lettering below, *Crux VIA Cælorum*, which is also the title of the poem.

(4) A crucifixion scene, above the poem *Crucifixus pro Nobis* (p. 52). A special feature of Cary's drawing is that blood from the wound in Christ's side is flowing into a chalice at the foot of the cross, recalling Herbert:

> Love is that liquor sweet and most divine,
> Which my God feels as bloud; but I, as wine.
> ('The Agonie', *Works*, ed. Hutchinson, p. 37.)

In the distant background, one on either side, are a castle and a church—a suggestion of St. Ignatius's meditation on the Two Standards in his *Spiritual Exercises*. Strictly speaking, the illustration has relevance only to the third and fourth stanzas of the poem, which refer directly to the passion of Christ; although theologians would be quick to argue that the actual crucifixion was only the culminating point in Christ's redemptive mission, which began in his infancy and continued throughout his life on earth.

A scene that strongly suggests Cary's illustration appears in Rollenhagen, *Selectorum Emblematum Centuria Secunda* (1611), No. 20, which shows in the foreground a pelican, a common eucharistic symbol, feeding its young with blood from its own breast; while in the left background is a crucifixion scene, with blood spurting from Christ's side into chalices upheld by a number of palm-bearing figures. The inscription reads:

> *Dux vitam bonus et pro lege et pro grege ponit,*
> *Haec veluti pullos sanguine spargit avis.*

Although Rollenhagen's crucifixion is a secondary element in his picture, the similarities are very marked, even to the blaze of light that surrounds the cross. I believe Cary may have used Rollenhagen as a source for other emblems, and it is quite possible he may have noted this one. Rollenhagen's plate was used by G. Wither, *A Collection of Emblems* (1635), p. 154, where the inscription is simply *Pro lege et pro grege*.

(5) A hand with roses, emerging from thorns (p. 54), at the end of the poem *Cruxifixus pro Nobis*. This little scene occupies about half a page of the manuscript. The bare arm, somewhat plump, is stretched out from

behind a stylized section of a tree-trunk covered with thorns, holding out a bunch of roses. They are Tudor roses of the type that appears on the title-page of the religious poems, under the Uvedale arms, and on Patrick Cary's own coat of arms, which bore on a bend sable three roses argent, barbed and seeded. In the middle distance are hilly slopes, and in the left background a cluster of buildings with castles and churches. Underneath in bold capitals is the legend *EX DOLORE, GAVDIVM*. Here the illustration gives point and meaning to the Latin phrase, which Scott and Saintsbury merely print at the end of the poem, to which its reference is not clearly apparent without the picture: the verses are all *dolor* with no suggestion of *gaudium*.

Disembodied arms and hands holding a variety of things are one of the commonest conventions of the emblem books. J. Camerarius (i, No. 51) has a flowering rosebush and (i, No. 52) a hand from the clouds holding a flowering rod with the motto *Insperata floruit*. In combination these two might have suggested Cary's emblem. His backgrounds are very like Camerarius's, with their tiny landscapes, distant hills, and buildings. In G. Whitney, *Choice of Emblems* (1586; facsimile reprint 1866), p. 165, a man is plucking a rose from a bush, with the motto *Post amara dulcia*, which conveys the sense of Cary's phrase. However, the most likely source seems to be Georgette de Montenay, *Emblèmes Chrestiennes*, p. 66, in which a robed figure with bare arm outstretched is gathering a rose from a bush which looks very like Cary's stylized bouquet. The motto reads *EX MALO BONVM*—a precise grammatical and antithetical parallel to *EX DOLORE, GAVDIVM*.

(6) A mermaid with two tails, floating on the sea (p. 55) above the poem *Fallax, et Instabilis*. Occupying the top half of the page on which the poem begins is this very unusual sketch of the mermaid, a large and carefully drawn figure, with long hair, crowned and wearing bracelets. Two scaly tails curve up, one on either side, of her erect figure, the tips lightly held in her hands. This double-tailed mermaid has a long history. She appears, for example, in a fifth-century mosaic in Ravenna (which could well have been seen by Cary); and was discovered by a correspondent of mine on a flowerpot at the Villa d'Este in Tivoli. However, an almost exact model for Cary's sketch is seen in J. Camerarius, iv, No. 64. Camerarius's mermaid, crowned, is between two pillars on a choppy sea; she is holding a tail in either hand, her fingers curving about the tips. Camerarius in his turn probably derived his design from Paolo Giovio, whose *Dialogo dell' Imprese militari et amorose*, 1562 (p. 137), shows the mermaid between two pillars, crowned and with two upcurving tails, her arms, however, by her sides. Both Camerarius and Giovo have the motto *Contemnit tuta procellas*. For them, the mermaid safely riding a stormy sea between her two protecting pillars is a symbol of security.

APPENDIX A

Cary, while retaining the symbol, has reversed the symbolism. Presumably the combination of the ever-changing sea—'The *Sea* in rest n'ere lyes'—and this double-shaped figure dominating it suggested to him the twofold concept of deceit and fickleness, qualities which he imputes to the world in the three stanzas of the poem. This connection of deceit with a double tail may perhaps owe something to Peacham's *Minerva Britanna*, p. 47, where deceit is shown as an old man wearing a golden coat, with a pious expression and two intertwining tails. Peacham also has the double-tailed mermaid (p. 141), but, her scales sprinkled with stars and her coils forming two unbroken rings, she symbolizes eternity. Peacham based both of these on similar emblems in the *Iconologia* of Cesare Ripa, which as the work of a protégé of Pope Urban VIII, was probably known to Patrick Cary. In fact the eternity image was brought to Ripa's notice by Urban himself, as Cardinal Maffeo Barberini.[1] Cary has treated his mermaid imaginatively, omitting the pillars, an emblem of stability, and bringing her forward to occupy almost the whole foreground, with a homely little coastal landscape behind her. He has given her bracelets—'trifling toyes'—and set at her waist a curious little medallion with a sad fool's face, as if to suggest that man, left to himself, is the plaything of ruthless ambiguous forces.

(7) Occasion or Fortune on her wheel, floating on the sea (p. 57) above the poem *Nulla Fides*. This small sketch, occupying about a quarter of its page, shows a scene that appears frequently in the emblem books: a woman's form with flying hair, poised on a wheel, often on the sea. In one hand Cary's figure holds a small scourge and with the other she lifts aloft a sail, the lower end of which is bunched and draped about her naked body. The wind is swelling the sail, although it appears to be blowing her hair in the opposite direction. In the left background is a country scene with a distant church spire amid trees; to the right a city view with a tall tower, perhaps a lighthouse at the harbour entrance, and other buildings. To the left of the figure on the wheel a sailing-ship fully rigged is ploughing through the waves; while on the right rides a small boat with a single sail. They represent perhaps man in society and man alone; or more simply, the wealthy and the poor. In the top left-hand corner the sun with a human face looks down, suggesting a line from the preceding poem on the opposite page in the manuscript—'The *Sun* does thincke nothing of all this strange'.

This figure, Occasion or Fortune, is a favourite with the emblematists. The closest likeness to Cary's sketch appears in G. Whitney, *A Choice of Emblems*, p. 181; but there are others in Alciati, *Emblemata* (1567), p. 185;

---

[1] See Ripa, *Iconologia* (1611), pp. 151-2; also p. 424 for another double-tailed mermaid, this time a siren attending Pleasure.

Rollenhagen, *Nucleus Emblematum*, No. 4; and G. Wither, *Collection of Emblems*, p. 4. Cary's figure has a sail trailing around her naked body instead of the scarf-like drapery of the three just mentioned. The sail is also found in J. Boissard, *Emblematum Liber* (1593), p. 103, where Fortune is in an elaborate gondola-shaped boat; also in S. de Covarrubias, *Emblemas Morales* (1610), p. 134. Patrick Cary is original in giving his Fortune a scourge instead of the razor she is usually shown holding. With most of the emblem-writers the motto emphasizes the fleeting nature of Fortune's bounty and the need to seize her, as the old proverb says, by her long forelock as she whirls past. Cary prefers to stress the fickleness of her favours, which can so quickly change to penalties. In this he is like Covarrubias, whose motto is *Mutatur in Horas*; and his final message is contained in the last stanza of the poem below the picture:

> Honour, the World & Man,
> What Trifles are they!

(8) The Fool on a pedestal (p. 58), above the poem 'What use has Hee made of his Soule'. This interesting and rather puzzling sketch, occupying nearly two-thirds of its page, shows a man's figure standing on a pedestal. He wears kirtle, hose, short cape, and, covering all his head except the face, a cap from which protrude fools' or asses' ears. In front of him he holds a large circular object, shield or picture, on which is seen in profile a face, somewhat feminine in feature. Around this face is a crescent-shaped curve, and in the sky, right, a small crescent moon. In the left background is a group of buildings of a type familiar in Cary's sketches, the pointed turrets of a castle, with a tall pillared arcade. At the right slope low hills with the suggestion of a small village below. To the right of the figure in the foreground is a lopped-off tree-trunk, with bare branches cut short on either side. The pedestal on which this strange form stands is set on a plateau below which the ground falls away to a lower level, where a few palings inadequately fence off a dangerous-looking gap. After this is a further drop, beyond which appears the distant background scene.

This figure by its dress reminds one of the Vice in the morality plays, with his rascalities as well as his buffooneries, and the suggestion, whatever the origin of his name, of his identification with human frailty. The shield or picture with its feminine traits hints at the feminine *Anima*, a conventional character in the emblem books, representing the human soul. Considering the first line of the poem beneath the sketch, it suggests to me a man holding his soul in his hands, responsible for its choice of good or evil. This impression is reinforced by the withered trunk with its scriptural connotation of the barren tree destined to be cut down and cast into the fire (Luke, xiii. 7); and further strengthened by the opening lines of the poem:

APPENDIX A

>What use has Hee made of his Soule
>Who (still on Vices bent)
>N'ere strove his Passions to controule...

The theme of man's submission to the bestial impulses of his lower nature is brought out by the closing lines:

>But, since soe much o'th'*Beast* Itt has,
>Call Itt, by Itt's owne Name.

Finally, point is given to the argument by the scriptural text that follows the poem: *Accepit in vano animam suam*.

I can find no direct model for this sketch in the emblem books, and I suggest that Patrick Cary created it out of elements he found in various emblematic pictures. Individual constituents of his design are to be found in many places; e.g. in Bellini's 'Allegories' in the Accademia at Venice is a painting showing a nude figure on a pedestal, holding a circular mirror with elaborate border, reflecting a human face, and variously interpreted as prudence or ill-fame. However, a likely source in which all the elements are found closely associated, though not synthesized, is Rollenhagen, whom I think Cary used for the altar and wreath emblem (1), and the crucifixion scene (4). Rollenhagen also has an emblem of Fortune in which as in Cary's sketch (7) the figure's hair and drapery are blowing in opposite directions. In a single book of Rollenhagen (*Centuria Secunda Emblematum*) the following are to be found: the crescent moon in a circle, with a human face, suggesting the portrait or mirror Cary's fool is holding, and also the actual crescent moon in his sky (Rollenhagen, No. 48); the fool's face and cap, with its long grotesque ears (No. 53); a pedestal with the ground falling away to three or four levels (No. 54—there are many such pedestals in Rollenhagen, also strong similarities in backgrounds of buildings, distant cities etc.); the fool, full figure this time, in cap, cape, and kirtle, very like the clothing of Cary's figure (No. 67). Cary may well have created his picture imaginatively out of these or similar elements.

(9) The choice of ways (p. 60), above the poem *Dirige vias meas Domine*! The top half of the page centres interest on a carefully tiered tower, a sort of ziggurat, in front of which are two groups of travellers with staves, setting out on a journey. To the right two groups of smaller figures are disappearing in different directions in the background. In the immediate foreground a larger band, sketched with some precision, wearing wide-brimmed hats and costumes vaguely of the period, are disputing which way to go. A figure on the right is firmly stepping eastward; beside him a man stands reflecting, hand on hip, while on the left another gestures urgently towards the west. The other members of the group are obviously

hesitating which direction to take; hence the title *Dirige vias meas*. The picture thus illustrates the choice of a way of living either conformable or contrary to the law of God. In the first line of the poem the soul is invited to examine its position: 'Open thy selfe, and then looke in'; and after that to decide its future course.

The distinctive tower which is the main feature of Cary's drawing may be traced here and there among the emblematists. Quarles, *Emblemes*, v, 5, has a slender, more elongated form as a subsidiary element in a picture illustrating the text, 'My soul melted whilst my beloved spake'. Set on a rocky shore, it appears to be a sort of lighthouse, with a lantern suspended from the top. In Georgette de Montenay's *Emblèmes Chrestiennes* (1635), p. 23, is shown an elaborate staged tower of the same type as Cary's. It is obviously the Tower of Babel, and above it is the motto *QVID SVPEREST*, a symbol of man's pride. However, the model for Cary's sketch is undoubtedly the picture that appears in a title-page decoration in Richard Verstegan's *Restitution of Decayed Intelligence* (1605, and later editions 1628 and 1636), with the title *Nationum Origo*.[1] On this, the tower, the central group of figures, and four smaller groups are almost exactly as Cary has drawn them; but there are four other bands, all setting off in different directions. The title *Nationum Origo* makes it clear that the building in the Verstegan engraving is the Tower of Babel, and the groups represent the development of national groupings in the human family. The building itself recalls Brueghel's *Tower of Babel* (1563). It is all the more likely that Cary had seen this engraving, since Verstegan was also a Catholic exile. Cary adapts the design to his moral purpose, using it to illustrate his theme of choice, which encourages perseverance in a right resolution:

> Resolve on that which Prudence showes;
> Performe what Thou doest well propose;
> And keepe i'th'way Thou hast once chose.

(10) The symbol IHS with the infant Christ (p. 62), above the poem *Nobis natus* etc. Half the page is taken up with the monogram IHS, enclosed in a blaze of light. Beneath the H are three nails arranged crossing one another in a fan-like cluster. The letters are a frequent liturgical symbol for Christ: they are the first three in the Greek form of JESUS, although popular etymology later interpreted them as *In hoc signo* (i.e. in the sign of the Cross) or as *Jesus Hominum Salvator*. On the cross-bar of the H stands the infant Christ, a muscular little boy, naked except for a loin-cloth, with an orb surmounted by a cross in his left hand, and a cross with pennant attached in his right. A serpent coiled about his legs is crushed under his foot, and around his head is an aureole, which is

---

[1] I owe this reference to the kindness of Professor Norman Davis.

repeated on a larger scale by the sunlike halo framing the whole design. The association of the child Christ with emblems of his future passion points to the redemption motif in the first part of the title, *Nobis natus in Pretium*. This is underlined by the serpent trodden under his feet, symbolizing his victory over Satan. This child in triumphant glory, holding in one hand the standard of the Cross, and in the other the orb of the world he has redeemed, bridges the history of the human race from the creation to the parousia; a thought expressed in the second part of the title: *nobis datus in Præmium*.

This is a purely theological concept, and the emblematists for the most part prefer moral themes. It was not to be found in any of the emblem books I examined. I suspect that Cary may have seen something similar in some work of devotion. The design appears in a small *Neujahrsbild* engraving produced by Joseph Carmine in Augsburg (see A. Spamer, *Das Kleine Andachtsbild*, 1930, Tafel clxxxix). It shows among other pious emblems an elaborate IHS with the child Christ standing on the crossbar, and the nails of the passion arranged fan-like below. This could not have been Cary's model—it belongs to the next century—But it shows that the convention he followed became well established.

(11) A winepress, with juice pouring into a vat (p. 64). Above it, within the frame of the picture is the word $EXPRIMETVR$, and below the sketch is a sonnet on the iniquity of oppression. The winepress, which occupies the greater part of the illustration, is very finely drawn, with the graining of the wood clearly defined and contrasted. With the cheerful disregard for realism shown by the emblematists in general, it is improbably placed at the edge of a stream, with a wooded landscape beyond.

This illustration is a good example of the relationship of these emblem drawings to an understanding of Cary's text. Scott ignored the emblem, and printed the sonnet with the title *Exprimetur*. Saintsbury, following him, added (p. 479, n.) a note on the title: 'This must have had a special meaning; but what, who shall say?' The accompanying sketch pictorially answers his question and alone explains the title, which otherwise has only a tenuous link with the text and no bearing on the imagery of the sonnet. The verse, with powerful images drawn from death and funeral monuments, condemns the oppression of the poor and helpless. In the context of the winepress from which juice is being relentlessly crushed out, I should translate $EXPRIMETVR$ as something like 'To the last drop'. The title thus has a double application: while proclaiming the shameful fact that the weak are, and will continue to be, oppressed, it suggests with its grim future tense that the oppressor will himself one day be 'expressed', crushed by the wrath of God. The symbol of the winepress (cf. Isa. lxiii. 3) stands in Scripture for both the passion of Christ and the divine vengeance on unrepentant sinners. This combination of an emblematic sketch and title apparently dissociated from the text accompanying it reminds one of Herbert's verses 'The Pulley' where the title, as Dame Helen Gardner has said, 'provides us with an image analogous to the image of the poem, but entirely distinct and unhinted at in the poem' ('The Titles of Donne's Poems', *Friendship's Garland,* 1966, i, 191.)

The winepress is hardly a favourite subject with the emblematists, but it occurs in a few instances. Christopher Harvey's *Schola Cordis* (1647), using the emblems, and an English version of the text, of Benedictus van Haeften (1635), shows (No. 15) the heart crushed in a press, and (No. 47) a winepress with circular vat at which the heart is being filled with wine from grapes trodden by Christ. On the title-page of *Quarleis,* included with Quarles's *Emblemes* (1635), is a small representation of a winepress, but it is only one element in a large and complex design, together with angels, bees, flowers, and musical instruments. More prominence is given to the press by Johann Mannich in his *Sacra Emblemata,* 1624 (p. 50). Here it is the centre of the design and is drawn with great care in a rural setting. However, the winepress, like the one in *Quarleis,* is drawn from a side elevation; moreover, the text of the emblem links it with the trials of married life, to be endured and overcome by faith, hope, and charity, whose symbols are also shown. Wherever Patrick Cary derived his emblem from, he gave it an unusual and individual application.

(12) Christ in Judgement (p. 65). Above the translation of the *Dies Irae* fully half the page is taken up with this picture of Christ as judge of mankind. He is shown surrounded by clouds, seated on a rainbow or a single arc of light, his feet (which look disproportionately small) resting on the globe. His left hand bears a cross with a pennant marked I H S; his right is raised with two fingers uplifted in blessing or warning, or both. His face is grave but not terrifying. In the lower right-hand corner a vigorous angel is blowing a trumpet.

This scene is not often chosen by the emblematists, and where it does occur it is not central. In J. David's *Paradisus Sponsi et Sponsae* (1618), for example, it is seen in the first section, 'Messis Myrrhae et Aromatum', facing p. 6, where it is subsidiary to the main emblem, Christ's agony in the garden. In the top left-hand corner is a contrasting vignette of Chiist glorious and sitting in judgement, enthroned on a rainbow, surrounded by clouds. In H. Hugo's *Pia Desideria* (1624) is an emblem reproduced by Quarles, *Emblemes,* iii, 14: *Anima,* the soul, seeking union with Christ, her beloved, sees him, above the grim skeleton of death, seated on a rainbow between two trumpeting angels. Strictly this emblem belongs to theology and devotion, and Cary may have taken his inspiration from some illustrated book of piety, or some representation in art remembered from Rome.

(13) The Blessed Virgin holding a cross, with the Holy Ghost as a dove hovering over her (p. 67). This, the last of Cary's sketches, is found at the end of the *Dies Irae*. Our Lady sits on a low pedestal with the clouds of heaven around her and the hills of earth below. In her right hand is a large cross, while with her left she gestures to the right of the picture, towards the Holy Ghost, represented in the conventional form of a dove, shedding rays of light.

As with (10) and (12), I think it likely Cary found his model not in the emblem books but in some manual of devotion or work of art. In J. David's *Paradisus*, mentioned above, is a section devoted to Mary, 'Pancarpium Marianum', in which No. 36 (facing p. 148) shows her seated on a throne, with the divine dove over her head. She is holding her child, not the cross, and the setting is indoors; but the general similarity is sufficiently pronounced to indicate the sort of picture from which Cary could have devised his sketch.

This illustration cannot be said to have much to do with the *Dies Irae*, and is probably meant as a companion drawing to that of Christ at the beginning. Such a balancing of images of Christ and his mother is a common feature of liturgical art. I think it probable that Cary did not relate it to the poem, but chose it to conclude his whole collection of religious verse. He leaves us with the Mother of God bidding us cling to Christ's cross and follow the promptings of the Holy Spirit.

It will be seen that Cary can claim considerable originality in the use of emblem. Of what I might call the professional English emblematists—the writers who set out to produce emblem books proper—only Henry Peacham in his *Minerva Britanna* can be said to have devised his own illustrations, and a number of these he borrowed from Cesare Ripa's *Iconologia* (see R. Freeman, *English Emblem Books*, 1948, p. 79). Those among English emblematists who can lay claim to some independent reputation as poets, such as Quarles, Harvey, and Wither, all derived their emblems from plates already engraved for continental emblem-writers, or prepared by English engravers. Of poets who have made casual use of emblem, Crashaw is the outstanding figure, with twelve engravings illustrating *Carmen Deo Nostro*. Thomas Car in his dedicatory poem for this work (*Poems*, ed. Martin, 1957, p. 235) speaks of 'the pictures in the following Poemes which the Authour first made with his owne hand admirably well, as may be seen in his Manuscript dedicated to the right Honorable Lady the L. Denbigh'. This manuscript of Crashaw's has never been found, and there is no means of knowing what the pictures in it were. However, in the 1652 edition of *Carmen Deo Nostro*, which is all we have to go on, most of the engravings are not Crashaw's, but clearly the work of professionals (signed 'J. Messager'; 'I.G.'). It is generally agreed that only two are likely to represent Crashaw's own drawings: the locked heart heading the poem addressed to the Countess of Denbigh, and the head and shoulders of Magdalen above 'The Weeper'. These are not entirely original in conception: the first is taken from *Imago primi saeculi S.J.*; while the second finds parallels in Hugo's *Pia Desideria* and Ammon's *Amoris divini et humani antipathia* (see M. Praz, *Studies in Seventeenth-Century Imagery*, 1939, 2nd edition 1964, p. 227).

This leaves Patrick Cary, slight though his poetic reputation may be, in an unusual position among English emblem poets, with thirteen emblems from his own hand, few, if any, of them slavishly copied, many showing creative originality. Artistically the drawings may have flaws of perspective and other defects, but they are still of considerable merit, and the impression they make in the setting of the original manuscript is one of charm and dignity.

How far may Patrick Cary's drawings be strictly regarded as emblems? Rosemary Freeman (*English Emblem Books*, 1948, p. 238, n.) formulates four distinctive features of an emblem book: it must be a collection of moral symbols; it must have pictures, or at least postulate the existence of pictures; each picture should have a motto or brief *sententia* to interpret it; and there should be a passage in verse or prose explaining the moral or religious significance of the emblem.

Patrick Cary's sketches mostly fulfil the first three of these requirements, although occasionally, as in emblem (5), the roses from thorns, they make a final rather than a preliminary comment. However, the verses he associates with the drawings rarely confine themselves to explaining or interpreting the illustrations. For example, in (8), the Fool or Vice on a pedestal, the true emblematist would perhaps crowd into his picture all the creatures mentioned in the verses (pp. 58–9) as typifying the shameful qualities of man; or, more likely, present a series of separate sketches as Quarles does in his *Hieroglyphiques* (1638; x, xi, xii, xiii), where he lingers in turn over the peacock, the goat, the boar, and the lion. With Cary, almost always, the emblem sketch comments on or illustrates only a general view, or one, or at most several, aspects of the topic he expands in his verse.

I am not sure how far or how rigidly Miss Freeman's fourth requirement should be applied: whether for a true emblem the explanatory verse or prose passage should be exclusively or mainly about the picture. Quarles and Harvey are often general and diffuse, and continental emblem-writers frequently collect every conceivable view of their subject, and pile or piece these together for the edification of their readers.

I think, however, that Patrick Cary did not set out to create emblems. His original notebook gives the impression that he did not start with the emblem, but wrote the verses and then found or devised the emblematic sketches to illustrate them, finally combining verses and drawings in a finished and graceful manuscript.

Appendix B

MUSICAL SETTINGS OF PATRICK CARY'S POEMS

Twenty-three of Patrick Cary's poems, all his secular verse, are written to existing tunes, eighteen of which are named. The bulk of these are English, but some are derived from Italian, French, and Spanish.

In thus writing poetry to specific airs, Cary is following a convention, technically known as musical parody, which was long established by the seventeenth century. The tunes used are of the kind which Dr. F. W. Sternfeld describes as 'wandering melodies', those airs that 'hover in a poet's ear before he feels impelled to create a new text to an old song'. Dr. Sternfeld continues:

> There may exist a mood, an atmosphere that is impatient for expression, but its crystallization into verbal form has not taken place. Not until the poet hears a tune, one that is exactly right, its lilt and sing-song the inevitable carrier for what needs saying, does the poem take definite shape. The melody which brings it to life has 'wandered' from its old text and its past associations into a new context to which it conveys not only its properties of rhythm and pitch but also some aspects of its original mood and content.[1]

This technique had been used effectively by a long line of poets before Cary. A good deal of Renaissance verse was written to existing tunes, following a practice that extended, particularly in the sphere of ecclesiastical music, back to the Middle Ages. Many of the Elizabethan court poets wrote to popular tunes; Marlowe set his famous lyric 'Come live with me' to a tune that served many ballads, and was probably already old when he chose it; the same melody may well have been lingering in Raleigh's memory when he wrote his reply, and in Donne's when he composed his parody 'The Bait'. Sidney, who has left a song to the air known as 'Greensleeves', set verses to several Italian tunes, and one to a Spanish air.[2] Lord Herbert of Cherbury has left a record of two Italian tunes to which he wrote verses.[3] So Patrick Cary was in good company when he inscribed in his precise hand at the head of so many of his poems the phrase 'To the tune of ---', which is most often their only title.

---

[1] *Sound and Poetry*. ed. Northrop Frye (1957), pp. 16-17.
[2] Sidney, *Poems*, ed. Ringler (1962), pp. 136, 139, 155, 156.
[3] Edward Herbert, *Poems*, ed. Moore Smith (1923), p. 26.

APPENDIX B

I give below musical settings and notes for all the tunes I have been able to trace. Three have eluded me altogether; about several others I can offer only conjecture. In these cases I have not supplied musical settings. I have given words with the tunes only when Cary's verses have actually been set to the melodies.

Once I lov'd a Mayden Fayre &c.

This tune, sometimes called simply 'Maiden Fair', is found in the first ten editions of *The Dancing Master* (1651–98); in *A Booke of New Lessons for the Cithern and Gittern* (1652); in Playford's *Brief Introduction to the Skill of Music* (1660); and in a number of later collections. In D'Urfey's *The Fool Turned Critick* (1678), IV, ii, 'Maiden fair' is praised as a fine old tune, as contrasted with the 'lowsy lamentable' airs in current fashion. The tune takes its name from the opening line of a ballad 'The Reuolted Louer', licenced in 1629, found in *The Roxburgh Ballads*, ii (1874), 404. See Chappell, i, 257, and Simpson, pp. 556–7. I give here Simpson's version of the melody, which is slightly different from Chappell's:

Original is unbarred

I'le doe by Thee, as n'ere was donne

I have been unable to trace a tune with this title, but a likely source is a song sometimes called from its refrain 'I'll never love thee more'—words that find echoes in the last line of each stanza of Cary's verses. His words exactly fit the melody, and the construction and rhyme scheme of the stanzas of this song are similar to his. Usually appearing under the title of 'My dear and only love, take heed', it is thought to belong to the time of James I. Part of the text with the air is found in *Wit and Drollery* (1656), and several ballads in the *Pepys Collection* are set to the tune, which enjoyed wide popularity: Montrose was among many who set words to it. See Chappell, i, 380, and Simpson, pp. 355–7. The resemblance seems strong enough to warrant reproducing the air, which I give in Simpson's version:

MUSICAL SETTINGS OF PATRICK CARY'S POEMS

Bobbing Joane

The tune 'Bobbing Joe', sometimes called 'Bobbing Joan', is found in every edition of *The Dancing Master*, beginning in 1651, in *Musick's Delight on the Cithren* (1666), and various later collections, many ballads being sung to it after the Restoration. See Simpson, pp. 46-7, and Chappell, i, 290-1. I give Chappell's version, as it shows Patrick Cary's words, though in a modernized form, set to the music:

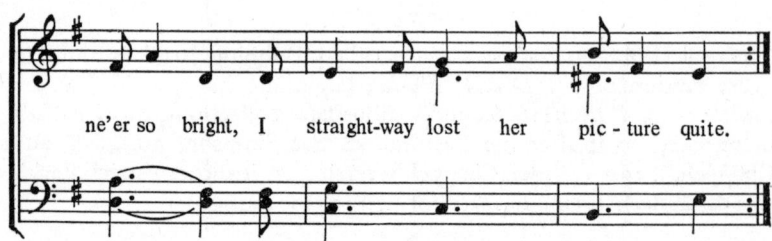

Troy-towne

A ballad to this tune, usually called 'Queen Dido' or 'The Wandering Prince of Troy', was entered on the Register of the Stationers' Company in 1564–5. It was often reprinted and is alluded to in Fletcher's *Bonduca* (1614), II, i. A number of different ballads were set to the air; probably the earliest surviving version is in *The Shirburn Ballads*. See Chappell, i, 370–3, and Simpson, pp. 587–90. The following version is Simpson's, which differs slightly from Chappell's:

MUSICAL SETTINGS OF PATRICK CARY'S POEMS

Original is in the key of G.

But I fancy lovely Nancy &c.

The tune thus named appears under the title of 'Chestnut' or 'Doves Figary' in *The Dancing Master* (1651–90). A ballad registered in 1656 gives the words of 'The Batchelor's Choice' or 'A Young-Man's Resolution':

> To have his Love and Sweet-heart Nancy
> Whom he most heartily doth fancy,

set to the tune of 'Chess-nut'. The refrain gives Cary's wording:

> But I fancy lovely Nancy
> And she alone enjoyes my heart.

Cary's verses have the duple measure and falling rhythm of 'The Batchelor's Choice,' but, as they are dated five years earlier than this ballad, we cannot be sure that this is his source. However, the evidence seems strong enough to justify reproducing the melody, which I give from Simpson, pp. 95–6:

APPENDIX B

* Varied repeat in MS.

The Healths

This tune is found in *The Dancing Master* (1650–90); in the first editions it is called 'The Health'; later it appears as 'The Healths' or 'The Merry Wassail'. It is also found in *Musick's Delight on the Cithren* (1666). In spite of its jovial title, the air has a plaintive tinge appropriate enough for Cary's verses of farewell. Sir Walter Scott in *Woodstock* puts a courtly parody of Cary's first stanza on the lips of the disguised Charles II, sheltering in the house of Sir Henry Lee:

> Come, now that we're parting, and 'tis one to ten
> If the towers of sweet Woodstock I e'er see agen,
> Let us e'en have a frolic, and drink like tall men,
>   While the goblet goes merrily round.

Chappell points out (ii, 778) that Sir Walter, forgetful of his original, provides a last line which will not fit the melody. I give the tune from Chappell (i, 288–9), where a modernized version of Patrick Cary's words is shown:

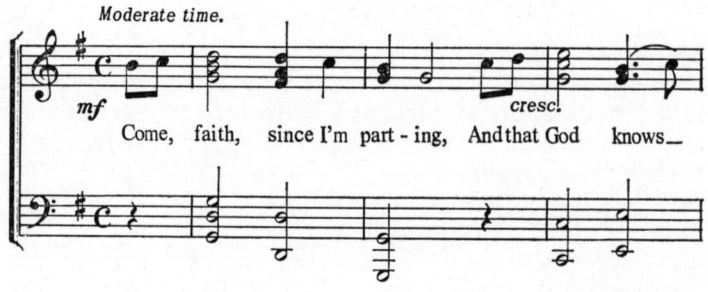

MUSICAL SETTINGS OF PATRICK CARY'S POEMS 121

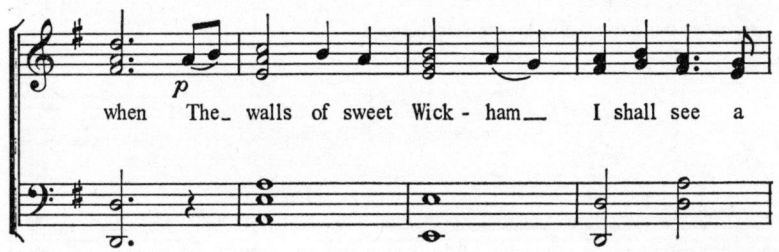

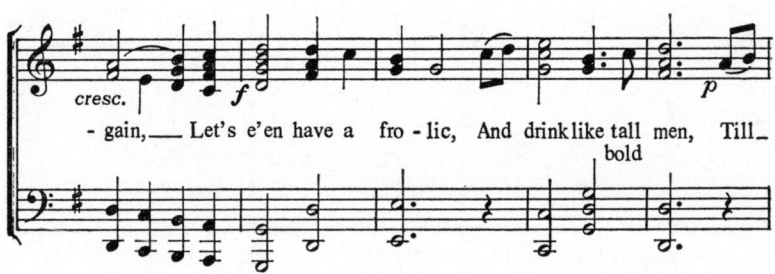

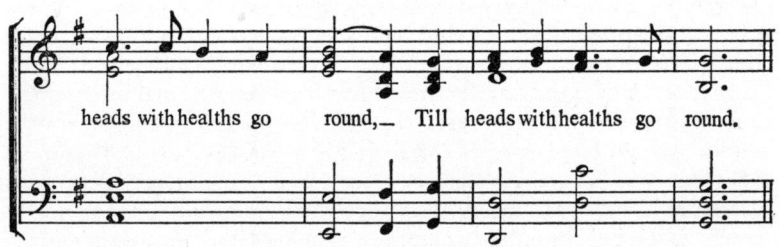

I'le tell thee Dicke that I have beene &c.

The tune is named from the opening line of a ballad written by Suckling on the marriage of Roger Boyle, first Earl of Orrery, in 1640. This was first published in *Fragmenta Aurea* (1646) and frequently reprinted. The music is first found in *180 Loyal Songs* (1685). Although Suckling's poem does not seem to have been printed as a broadside, a number of ballads were written in imitation and sung to the same tune, some of them parodies, including lampoons on Suckling's own reverses in the Civil War. It is not unlikely that Patrick Cary would remember Suckling whom he, an intelligent lad of ten or eleven, could have met in his brother's witty circle at Great Tew. For the tune see Chappell, i, 358–60; and Simpson, pp. 347–50. I give the latter version:

That we may row with my P. over the Ferry

I have been unable to trace this tune. If 'P.' stands for 'Prince' the words suggest a possible Caroline context. The refrain, with its 'derry derry downe' recalls a mention, in Bodleian MS. Eng. misc. b. 48, f. 2, of words beginning 'Oh England attend while thy fate I deplore', *c.* 1742, 'To the old Tune of Derry-down'. A well-known tune of that name is given by Chappell, i, 348–53, and Simpson, pp. 172–6. There is a general similarity about the first line (Cary has 'Good People of England! come heare mee relate'); and Cary's verses fit well enough the main part of the tune 'Derry down'. However, the refrains do not coincide. Cary's heading would be clumsy as a title, and if it is a first line its rhythm is different from his own. I suspect it may be a last line, rhyming with 'derry', as Cary's own 'merry' and 'sherry' do; but it does not perfectly match his last line, or indeed anything else in his verses. As his ear and his sense of rhythm are normally good, I can only suggest he has recalled his source incorrectly.

Will and Tom &c.

I could find no tune of this name, but Cary's model is almost certainly a song called 'Tom and Will were shepherds swains'. The words are based on a poem first printed anonymously in *Sportive Wit* (1656), later attributed to Sidney Godolphin (d. 1643), a close friend of Cary's brother, Lucius. The poem was reprinted in various collections, including the first volume of *Pills to Purge Melancholy* (1699). The tune associated with the ballad in *Pills* is first found in *Apollo's Banquet* (5th edition 1687) as 'A Scotch Tune in fashion'. In *Youth's Delight on the Flagelet* (9th edition *c.* 1690) it is called 'Billy was so blith a lad'. In Alexander Stuart's *Musick for Allan Ramsay's Collection of Scots Songs* (*c.* 1725) it appears as 'Peggie I must love thee', under which name it is discussed by Simpson, pp. 573–5. I give Simpson's version of the air:

And will you now to Peace encline &c.

In the collection known as *Rump Songs* (1662), i, 9, are some verses by Sir John Denham entitled 'Mr Hampdens Speech against Peace at the close Committee'. Their first line is 'But will you now to Peace incline', and they are set to the tune 'I went from England'. This must be the tune Patrick Cary has in mind: its full title is 'I went from England into France'. The music is found in John Gamble's MS. Commonplace Book (1659) together with a number of stanzas of the poem whose opening line gives the tune its title. The verses appear, without any musical indications, in Richard Corbet's *Certain Elegant Poems* (1646) and are often attributed to him, although it is believed they were written by Thomas Goodwyn. See Simpson, pp. 350–1, and 351, n., from which I have taken the melody:

Folias

The best-known tune that goes by this name was originally that of an ancient Portuguese dance, noisy and wild, performed by men dressed as women and acting as if insane—hence the name 'Folia'. The fundamental musical pattern has been used as a basis for variations by a great many composers, including Corelli, Vivaldi, and Bach. A number of melodies with this name are preserved in manuscripts in the Escurial and elsewhere; and as it is uncertain which was used by Cary I have not reproduced any. The fullest treatment is to be found in *Die Musik in Geschichte und Gegenwart*, edited by Friedrich Blume (1955), iv, 479–83. See also *Grove's Dictionary of Music and Musicians*, edited by Eric Blom (1878–89; 5th edition 1954), iii, 182; Macmillan's *Encyclopaedia of Music and Musicians*, edited by A. L. Wier (1938), p. 597; Percy Scholes, *Oxford Companion to Music* (1938; 9th edition 1955), pp. 365, 628.

Girometta

This is an old Piedmontese air, which has appeared in several later versions, e.g. Leone Sinigaglia, *24 vecchie canzoni popolari del Piemonte*, 2 serie (postuma); revisione di Luigi Rognoni, Milano; (G. Ricordi, 1956). The first line is 'Girometta de la montagna turna al to pais'. A French version also exists: 'Gioromette de la montagne, rentre à ton pays'. A more recent example of a song based on this melody is Gabriele Sibella, *La Girometta*, Chappell, 1939. As the air would need some adaptation to suit Cary's words, I have not reproduced a version. See *Songs in Collections, An Index*, edited by Desiree de Charms and Paul F. Breed (1966), pp. xxxi, 202.

MUSICAL SETTINGS OF PATRICK CARY'S POEMS

To Parliament the Queene is gonne &c.

I cannot find a tune by this name, but a similar rhythm and parallel phrasing occur in a title given in a Bodleian manuscript (MSS. Ashmole 36, 37, f. 259), 'To Oxenford our King is gone', c. 1605. No tune is given in the manuscript, but there is a song called 'The King is gone to Oxen Town' in *Pills to Purge Melancholy* (1706). However, the evidence is too flimsy to justify reproduction of the tune.

I'le have my Love, or I'le have none

For this tune I can get no closer than conjecture. There is a reference in a Bodleian manuscript (MS. Rawl. poet. 37, p. 44) to a tune 'I'll love my own true love or none', to which a hymn beginning 'In sonnets and in roundelays' is said to go. This sounds very like Cary's title. Another possibility is a broadside ballad, issued by Philip Brookesby, who was publishing ballads 1670–95, entitled 'The countrymans care in choosing a wife' to the tune of 'I'le have one I love &c', or 'The Yellow Hair'd Laddy'. See Simpson, pp. 803–5. I am not convinced that either of these tunes is Patrick Cary's source, and I shall not attempt to give a melody here.

Phillida flouts mee

The very popular ballad which gives the tune its name goes back to about 1600, being found in the Shirburn MS. and *The Roxburghe Ballads*. It is mentioned by the milkmaid in *The Compleat Angler* (1653). The tune appears in several slightly different forms in early seventeenth-century keyboard arrangements and in various eighteenth-century texts. See Chappell, i, 182–3; and Simpson, pp. 576–8. From the latter I give an eighteenth-century version of the melody as best suited for use with Cary's words:

APPENDIX B

Transposed from key of D.

Francklin is fled away

This title takes its origin from the eighth line of 'A mournful Caral' beginning 'Franklin my loyal friend O hone O hone', found in the Douce, Pepys, and Roxburghe Collections, and reprinted in *The Roxburghe Ballads*, vii, 418. The tune is in *Apollo's Banquet for the Treble Violin* (1669), in *180 Loyal Songs*, and in *Pills* (1707). A variety of songs and ballads have been sung to the tune, which is one of the many from which 'God save the King' has been said to be derived. See Chappell, i, 369–70; and Simpson, pp. 232–5, from which I give the melody:

Original a fifth higher.

Index of First Lines

	page
A Day full of Horrour, must	65
A greev'd Countesse, that e're long	29
Alasse! long since I knew	39
And can You thincke that this Translation	15
And now a Figge for th' lower House	22
Are These the Things I sighed for soe, before	45
By Ambition raysed high	44
Cease t'exaggerate your Anguish	32
Come (fayth) since I'me parting, & that God knowes when	13
Fayre Beautyes! if I doe confesse	9
Fayre-One! if thus kind You bee	5
Fondlings! keepe to th'Citty	23
For God's sake marcke that *Fly*	57
Good People of England! come heare mee relate	18
Great God! I had beene *Nothing* but for Thee	62
I blush, but must obay. You'l have itt soe	5
I n'ere yett saw a lovely Creature	8
Jacke! nay prithee come away	19
Looke, how Hee shakes for cold	52
Lowdly the Winds doe blow	49
Ned! She that likes thee now	37
O, permitt that my Sadnesse	33
Open thy selfe, and then looke in	60
Poore Heart, retire	30
Some prayse the Browne, and some the Fayre	36
Speake of somewhat else I pray	28
Surely now I'me out of danger	10
The Ermine is without all spott	6
The Parliament (t'is sayd) resolv'd	26
There's noe Woeman, but I'me caught	7

This Aprile last a gentle Swayne	34
'Tis a strange Thing this World	55
'Tis true. I am fetter'd	31
What use has Hee made of his Soule	58
Whilst I beheld the necke o'th'*Dove*	46
Who, without Horrour, can that HOVSE *behold*	64
Worldly Designes, Feares, Hopes, farwell	43

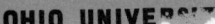